REVELATIONS
The Wisdom of the Ages

ABOUT THE AUTHOR

Paul Roland is a freelance journalist and author and has been a
regular contributor to various national publications in Britain,
Europe, the United States and Japan for over 12 years. His own
mystic experiences began while he was still a child and led him to
study various aspects of the esoteric, including practical magic, yoga,
meditation, Buddhism and the Kabbalah, the last mentioned with
one of the foremost Masters of our time.

DEDICATION

To my beloved father,
who opened my eyes to the light.

Published by Ulysses Press
P. O. Box 3440
Berkeley, CA 94703-3440

Text and Design copyright © 1995 Carlton Books Limited

10 9 8 7 6 5 4 3 2 1

Library of Congress Catalog Number
95 – 61354

ISBN 1-56975-047-5

Project editor: Tessa Rose
Copy editor: Nigel Matheson
Art editor: Fiona Knowles
Design: Steve Wilson
Picture research: Emily Hedges
Production: Sarah Schuman

Printed and bound in Spain

REVELATIONS
Wisdom of the Ages

PROPHETIC
VISIONS
AND SECRET
KNOWLEDGE

*to guide us
into the*

MILLENNIUM

Paul Roland

Ulysses Press

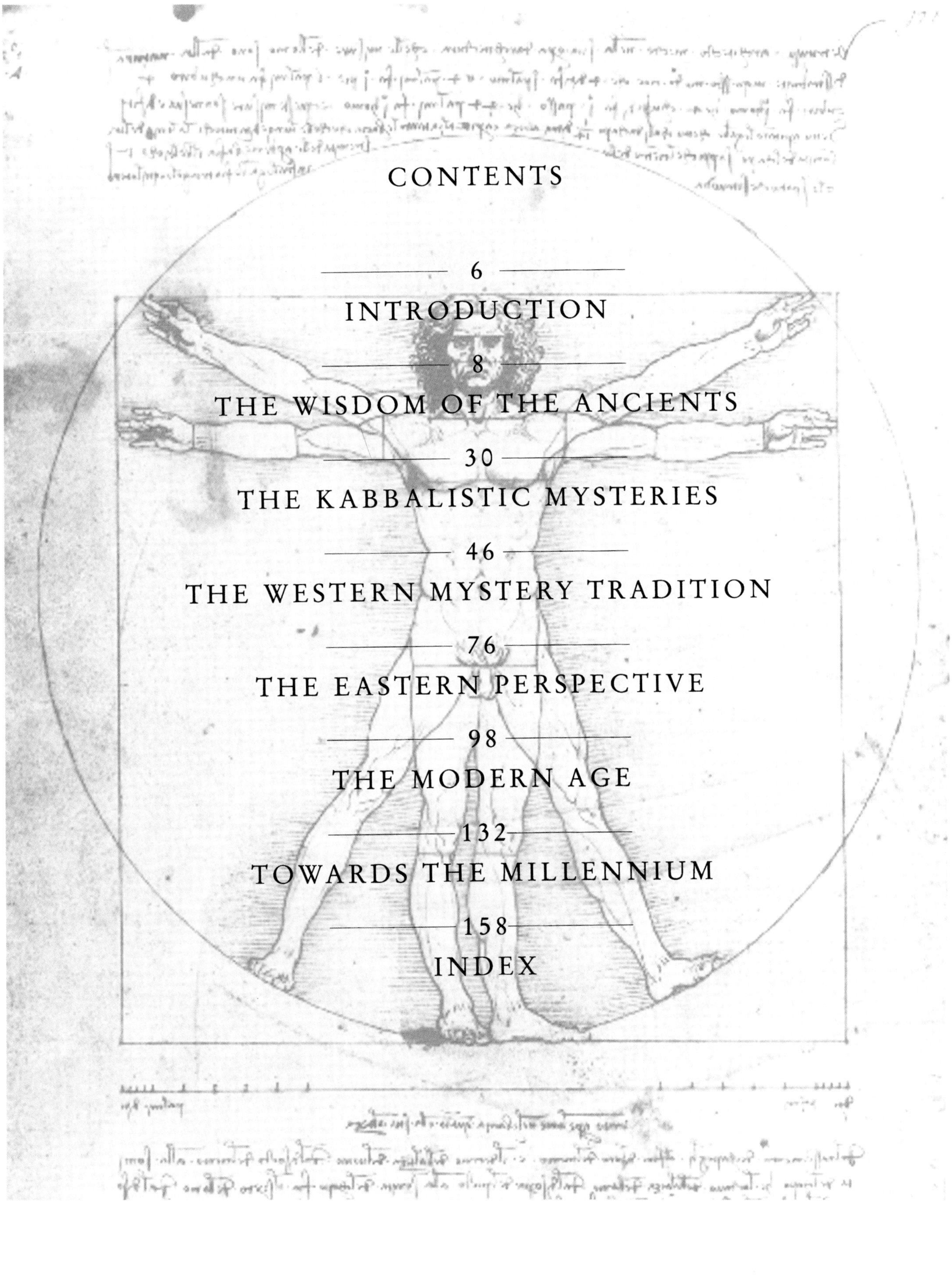

CONTENTS

6

INTRODUCTION

8

THE WISDOM OF THE ANCIENTS

30

THE KABBALISTIC MYSTERIES

46

THE WESTERN MYSTERY TRADITION

76

THE EASTERN PERSPECTIVE

98

THE MODERN AGE

132

TOWARDS THE MILLENNIUM

158

INDEX

INTRODUCTION

"Unless a man takes himself sometimes out of the world by retirement and self-reflection,

he will be in danger of losing himself in the world."

(BENJAMIN WHICHCOTE, 1609-83)

Most of humanity passes its time in idle pursuits, wrapped up in its own affairs. Will we awaken when the crisis comes?

Much of what is contained in this book has been kept secret for centuries.

The reason for this is that many of those to whom these secrets were originally entrusted considered that mankind was not yet spiritually mature, and so they presented their knowledge in parables, enshrined it in their sacred monuments and preserved it in the esoteric teachings of what became the major religions of revelation.

Over the centuries, these teachings, intended for the enlightenment of all mankind, became obscured by doctrine and dogma, or were deliberately misinterpreted.

This is not, however, a time for secrets, but for revelations – revelations concerning the true nature of Man and the Universe in which we exist. At three separate points in recorded history there have been unexplained leaps in the progress of human civilization and perception which cannot be accounted for by the purely scientific theories of evolution.

The first of these occurred around 3000 BCE when the peoples of Egypt, Mesopotamia and the Indus Valley in Southern Asia all began, as if spontaneously, to build the first cities of civilization. The second happened in the late 6th century BCE with the blossoming of philosophy, art and science in Greece and Ionia, which was matched by a spiritual awakening throughout India. The last took place in the 15th century, when an infusion of intense intellectual energy found expression in the Renaissance, a period when man accepted that he alone was responsible for his own destiny.

According to many of the masters and mystics, prophets and philosophers whose teachings are re-examined in this volume, we are now living on the threshold of another such stage of evolution, a New Age which could decide the destiny of humanity for future millennia.

It is a moment of crisis, but also of unprecedented opportunity. Whether we grasp that opportunity or turn our backs on it will depend upon whether or not we can free ourselves from our false sense of the separateness of all life as well as misconceptions about our own mortality.

In the last decade, we have witnessed the collapse of communism, the prospect of peace in the Middle East and Northern Ireland, the end of apartheid in South Africa and the development of cures for diseases and disabilities which had previously been considered incurable.

As if to balance these achievements, new conflicts have erupted. A world-wide economic recession has brought crippling unemployment, rising crime, a widening rift between rich and poor and a loss of dignity, self-worth and sense of purpose for those discarded in its wake.

The spectre of an, as yet, incurable new disease, AIDS, reminds us of our own mortality, while the destructive power of nature continues to rage unabated, often unpredictable and certainly out of our control. On the eve of the new millennium, it appears that we have mastered neither our surroundings nor ourselves.

Although we have both the technology and the resources to combat drought, famine and disease, we seem to lack the will or vision to do so. The concept of "One World" appears to be as remote as ever.

How are we to make sense of all this apparent chaos and confusion? Science cannot offer any answers – the world's greatest brains are still coming up with new questions. Technology has

Mysticism is the sower of true science.

expanded our horizons, but we seem reluctant to expand our minds to take it all in. The basic mysteries of Life remain a mystery, while the paradoxes posed by the actions of the smallest particles in the Universe continue to defy the laws of science and baffle the scientists.

Albert Einstein once remarked that, "Religion without science is blind and science without religion is lame ... The most beautiful and most profound emotion we can experience is the sensation of the mystical. It is the sower of all true science. He to whom this emotion is a stranger, who can no longer wonder and stand rapt in awe, is as good as dead. To know that what is impenetrable to us really exists, manifesting itself as the highest wisdom and the most radiant beauty which our dull faculties can comprehend only in their primitive forms - this knowledge, this feeling is at the centre of true religiousness."

Organized religion appears to have lost this simple spirituality. Consequently, religious observance seems increasingly irrelevant. Faith alone is no longer enough. The more we know, the less we believe. Now that most of the "civilized world" no longer believes in a Devil, whom we can blame for our own failings, we are going through a crisis of conscience.

Throughout history, there have been individuals who have sought and attained insight into simple Cosmic Truths which changed their lives and shaped the course of entire civilizations. These basic truths, which explain the origins of existence and our purpose in the Universe, have been known by many names. The philosophers of ancient China knew it as Tao, "The Way", mystics and occultists in the West have called it the "Ageless Wisdom" or the Perennial Philosophy. The philosopher Leibniz called it the "Perennial Wisdom" and concluded that all religions have an element of the truth, a strand of the Golden Thread, but no single tradition had all the answers. This book aims to unravel the entangled strands of the Golden Thread in the hope that it will be a guide along the path which leads to the Divine Destiny of mankind.

"If a man will begin with certainties, he will end in doubts; but if he will be content to begin with doubts, he will end in certainties." (Sir Francis Bacon)

THE WISDOM OF
THE ANCIENTS

The people of the Ancient World are often credited with being custodians of all the secrets of the cosmos. The question is: were they privileged to wisdom which we have lost, or is it just wishful thinking on our part that by probing the past we will rediscover archaic secrets which will help us to solve the problems of the present?

The civilizations of the Ancient World raised remarkable monuments to their gods, but they knelt in the shadow of superstition until men such as the Persian prophet Zoroaster, the Egyptian pharaoh Akhenaten and the Greek philosopher Pythagoras illumined the darkness of ignorance with the light of reason.

Ancient life was characterized by sacrificial cults and the worship of a pantheon of gods. Many of these creeds were founded on fear rather than devotion; fear of the unpredictable forces of nature; fear that the sun and moon, if not appeased, might leave man in darkness; and fear of capricious and malevolent gods.

The first step in the spiritual and mental evolution of mankind was therefore the rejection of these "religions" and the establishment of an essentially monotheistic faith in which man was perceived as a spark of the divine.

The teachings of Zoroaster introduced the concepts of resurrection, duality and final judgement. Meanwhile, in Greece, during the last centuries before the birth of Christianity, the first men to call themselves philosophers ("lovers of wisdom") taught that men, and not the gods, would determine their own destiny.

With the conquest of the Near East by Alexander the Great in the 4th century BCE, Greek as well as Assyrian, Babylonian, Anatolian, Persian and Judaic beliefs were channelled through Egypt and out into the world. In this way, the wisdom teachings embodied in such books as the *Corpus Hermeticum* of Hermes Trismegistos became the foundation of the Western Mystery tradition.

THE WISDOM OF ANCIENT EGYPT

"Art thou not aware, O Asclepios, that Egypt is the image of heaven, or rather, that it is the projection below of the order of things above? If the truth must be told, this land is indeed the temple of the world."

(HERMES TRISMEGISTOS, THE KORE KOSMO)

Winston Churchill's description of Russia as "a riddle wrapped in a mystery inside an enigma" could just as easily be applied to ancient Egypt, whose reputation as the fountainhead of secret wisdom is perpetuated in the mystique still surrounding its monuments and artefacts.

The grandeur and antiquity of Egypt's tombs, temples and pyramids, its exotic animal-headed gods, its legendary reputation for arcane knowledge and magic rites, as well as its cult of the dead, have all exercised a strange fascination over students of the Mysteries down the centuries. Many still believe that the archetypes and symbols of this ancient civilization are charged with magical properties and that their presence will aid them in their own psychic quest – or at least lend them an aura of credibility.

But did the Egyptians guard a profound wisdom, or was theirs a civilization mummified in its own mythology? Contrary to popular belief, the wisdom of ancient Egypt was neither secreted in mouldering papyri nor was it entrusted exclusively to the High Priests of the temple: it was, and remains, in plain sight – if only one knows how to look for and interpret it.

It is a mistake to search for hidden knowledge in Egypt. The wisdom of the ancient Egyptians is embodied in all that they constructed. Because they believed in the power of the written word, it was their custom to inscribe sacred texts in their holy places. By enshrining their knowledge in their monuments, they believed they were ensuring its perpetual fulfilment. The reason the modern mind finds this idea difficult to take in is that we tend to search for wisdom with the intellect rather than in what we see around us.

As with Solomon's Temple at Jerusalem, the temples of ancient Egypt were intended to act as the physical expression of a secret wisdom, guarded by a clandestine society within the priesthood. Temples were not only places of worship, they were also a manifestation of the Mysteries in architectural form. Even the material used for building them was symbolic, for symbolism was the key to the Mysteries. Brick

The enigmatic face of the Egyptian mysteries: The Sphinx at Gizeh.

The Weighing of the Heart in the Hall of Judges, presided over by Osiris.

symbolized water; sandstone, earth; limestone, air; with the indigenous minerals – basalt, diorite, syenite and granite – representing fire.

A radical theory, developed by Egyptologist R A Schwaller de Lubicz, compares the structural layout of the temple at Luxor to the interior of the human body with its nerve centres, and vital organs. He suggests that the sacred monuments of other dynasties were similarly intended to mirror the human anatomy with the temple as macrocosm and the human body as the microcosm.

In common with the Jewish Kabbalah and other metaphysical systems, the Egyptians acknowledged a hierarchy of refinement in the human body which reflected that of the cosmos. They noted the existence of physical, mental and spiritual levels within each being. The body (*aufu*) contained the shadow (*khabit*) and the *sahu* (the body of gold). The mental level comprised the will (*sekhem*), *ren* the name and *ab* the heart at the level of conscience. *Ka* was the spirit which animated the body, *ba* the soul and *khu* the Divine spark. The custom of placing sarcophagi of increasing refinement and decoration within one another symbolized this unity.

In spite of their apparent obsession with death, the Egyptians understood that the path to wisdom could only be travelled if the initiate was first grounded in reality – a principle shared by all serious schools of the Mysteries through the ages. If one cannot cope with the stress and responsibilities of life, how can one accept the discipline and sacrifice required on the spiritual path? For the Egyptians, the Mysteries did not provide escape from reality, but offered the secret of how to live life to the full.

THE EGYPTIAN BOOK OF THE DEAD

The Egyptian Book Of The Dead ("Chapters On Coming Forth By Day"), a collection of hymns, incantations and magic formulae, was intended to be read aloud to the dying in the belief that it would guide them on their passage through the underworld.

It also includes a description of the judgement which every soul

Sacred monuments hide ancient secrets.

has to undergo. Led by the jackal-headed god Anubis, the deceased enters the hall of the 42 judges presided over by Osiris, potentate of the kingdom of the spirit. The dead man's heart is placed on a scale and balanced against a feather, while he intones the Negative Confession exonerating himself from a catalogue of sins. If he has studied The Book Of The Dead and can claim to know the names of the judges, he then has power over them. Otherwise, the dead man risks having his heart devoured by a mythical beast and his body condemned to torment.

"The man who knows this book on earth, or has it written on his tomb, can emerge into the light in whatever way he wishes and take up his place without meeting any opposition ... he will flourish as he did on earth, doing as he wills like the gods."

(THE EGYPTIAN BOOK OF THE DEAD)

THOTH, GUARDIAN OF THE MYSTERIES

"I am Thoth, the skilled scribe whose hands are pure, a possessor of purity, who drives away evil, who writes what is true, who detests falsehood, whose pen defends the Lord of All; Master of Laws who interprets writings, whose words established the two Lands."

(THE EGYPTIAN BOOK OF THE DEAD, SPELL 182)

The worship of the Mysteries, personified by Thoth, was to be continued in the afterlife.

Thoth was the Lord of Wisdom, the guardian of the Mysteries, who, mythology tells us, was self-created, appearing on a lotus flower at the beginning of time. During the creation, it was Thoth who channelled the will of the Creative Power into words and thereby brought the universe into being. The idea that the universe was created by sound – by the vocalization of the will of a creator – occurs in the creation myths of many cultures, most notably in the Old Testament text: "In the beginning was the word." But for the ancient Egyptians, Thoth was more than "the tongue of Ra" (the sun god): he personified the act of creation and the expression of wisdom through language.

Thoth was most commonly depicted with the head of an Ibis and wearing a horned head-dress bearing symbols of the moon. In his hand, he would be seen carrying either a scribal palette or a palm branch on which he marked the passing of time.

Thoth was the custodian of secret wisdom, who entrusted his pupil Isis, the Light Giver, with knowledge, both human and divine, to pass on to those who sought the counsel of the gods. The authority of Thoth was invoked to legitimize the office of Pharaoh, but for ordinary Egyptians he was an ally in the underworld, providing the text of the confession each man had to make before Osiris and the 42 judges of the dead in the Hall of Judgement. Signifying the importance the Egyptians placed on the written word, Thoth was also called the "scribe of the gods", the "lord of writing", the "maker of the pallet and ink jar" and the "lord of divine words".

As a mythic figure in the story of Isis and Osiris, Thoth embodied the belief that knowledge, and not force, is true power – for it was the words of power which helped the gods to overcome their enemies. In his role as "lord of divine words", Thoth presided over the House of Life, an inner sanctum of the temple which served a similar function to a monastery library. Here were preserved The Books Of Thoth, the foundation of all knowledge. By the Thirtieth Dynasty, the House of Life had acquired the repu-

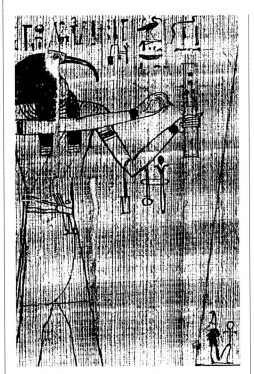

Thoth, the Scribe of the Gods.

tation as a house of secrets with the chief teaching priest of the period, Nakhtharab, referred to as the "leader of the masters of magic in the House of Life".

It is significant that the priests of Egypt were not merely theologians versed in dogma, nor simply guardians of archaic ritual, as their historical image suggests. All of them had, in fact, attained a high degree of knowledge in a practical field such as medicine or astronomy, for they understood that mystical insight should be channelled into some practical purpose.

The importance Egyptian priests placed on the study of natural laws was intended to provide insight into the relationship between man, nature and the cosmos, which in turn would promote a better understanding of the true essence and ultimate destiny of mankind. In addition to the religious texts, cosmology, astrology, mathematics, medicine and philosophy were considered worthy

subjects of study, although all knowledge was considered sacred and thus pursued with equal enthusiasm.

However, it was not only the priests who venerated wisdom. The Pharaoh Rameses IV is recorded as having attained an "excellent understanding like Thoth", after examining "the writings of the House of Life".

Despite his origin in legend, Thoth himself was credited with the invention of astronomy and mathematics, which were later equated with magic as "secret sciences". As Egypt's reputation for magic began to supersede its scientific achievements, Thoth's name too became associated with magic. As the supposed author of 42 volumes containing the wisdom of the world, he was venerated as a magician. This practice of attributing archaic texts to mythical figures led to Thoth's identification with the founder of Western magic, Hermes Trismegistos, resulting in the belief among scholars that an Egyptian scribe may have been the author of the *Hermetica*.

THE EGYPTIAN WISDOM TEXTS

... all the rivers – Assyrian, Babylonian, Anatolian, Persian, Jewish – met in Egypt as in a reservoir, and from Egypt flowed out to water the earth."

(HELLENISTIC CIVILISATION, TARN & GRIFFITH)

The Wisdom Texts are presented as advice given by a sagacious patriarch to wealthy young men eager to make their way in society. They consist of moral codes, maxims and treatises on tradition.

The "Instructions of Ptahhotep", which forms part of what has become known as the "Wisdom Literature", makes an important distinction between knowledge and wisdom. "Do not be arrogant because of your knowledge, and have no confidence in that you are a learned man, take counsel with the ignorant as with the wise, for the limits of excellence cannot be reached,

and no artist fully possesses this skill. A good discourse is more hidden than the precious green stone, and yet it is found with slave-girls over the millstone."

An exercise given to scribes was devised to remind them that knowledge was not merely the accumulation of innumerable facts but was intended "to expand the mind, to teach the ignorant, to know everything that is; what Ptah created, what Thoth brought into being, the sky and the objects on the earth, and what is in it ... "

Not all learned men, however, were impressed by the sayings of the Egyptian sages. Apollonius of Tyana, a Pythagorean sage and master magician of the first century CE, was lured by the reputation of Egyptian scholars and travelled to Egypt, but was not convinced that they had a wisdom worthy of study, and so journeyed on to India where he studied instead with the Brahmin.

ISIS UNVEILED

"Now Isis was a woman who possessed words of power; her heart was wearied with the millions of men, therefore she chose the millions of the Gods, but she esteemed more highly the millions of the spirits. And she meditated in her heart, saying, 'Cannot I by means of the sacred name of God make myself mistress of the earth and become a goddess like unto Ra in heaven and upon earth'."

(MAGICAL PAPYRUS, ANONYMOUS)

In Egyptian mythology, Isis was the "Supreme Goddess", the goddess of wisdom and the initiator into the Mysteries. So numerous were her attributes that she was known as "Isis Of Ten Thousand Names". She was depicted crowned either with a horned head-dress surmounted by a solar disc, or with the double crown of Northern and Southern Egypt. Beneath the head-dress, she wore a vulture cap and in her hand she held the papyrus sceptre – signifying learning – and the ankh, the hooped cross, signifying life, the unity of spirit and matter.

Isis represented the feminine aspect in its ideal form, as embodied in the myth of her search for the remains of her husband Osiris. He had been murdered by his jealous brother, Seth, who dismembered him and scattered the parts across Egypt. Isis managed to recover all but the phallus, which she replaced with an artificial member and, in so doing,

instigated and ennobled the art of mummification. It is the earliest known myth of resurrection.

One modern theory suggests that, if the histories of the gods are matched against those of mankind, the Aquarian age can then be read as heralding the birth of Horus, a Messianic figure, who will usher in a new golden age and reconcile the opposing forces of Seth and Osiris. Consequently, the period of the myth known as "The Sorrows Of Isis" would then correspond to the time of crisis in the 20th century.

Osiris, divine judge of the dead, promised resurrection to the righteous.

*Isis, whose mythical trials, "the sorrows",
were intended as a gate to contemplation.*

STAIRWAYS TO THE STARS

The methods by which the pyramids were built, and the secret purpose which some scholars have ascribed to them, have been the subject of fierce debate. It is possible that their construction was regulated by alignment with the stars. The southern shaft in the Great Pyramid of Gizeh which extends from the King's chamber appears to have been aligned with Orion, the star associated with Osiris, while the shaft from the Queen's chamber appears to have been aligned with reference to Sirius, the star associated with Isis.

There have also been attempts to prove that the positions of the pyramids at Gizeh correspond to the trio of stars that form the belt in the constellation of Orion and that the siting of other pyramids matches other stars in that constellation.

At the temples of Edfu and Esna, a priest known as the "Watcher of the Hours" observed the movements of the stars and marked the passing of each hour. An inscription on the statue of Harkhebi, the astronomer priest, credits the "hour watcher" with being "knowledgeable in everything which is seen in the sky, for which he has waited, skilled with respect to their conjunction and their regular movement; who does not disclose anything at all concerning his report after judgement, discreet with all he had seen".

It is quite probable that the movements of the stars were mythologized in the stories of the gods, in order to preserve this knowledge in coded form for the exclusive use of the priesthood.

Modern occultists often equate Isis with the Earth Goddess, or the Passive Principle. Others consider that hers is simply the tale of all those who seek knowledge and deeper understanding and that contemplation of the "sorrows" was primarily intended to open the reader's heart – "the gate of revelation". However, in ancient Egypt, before the neophyte could know Isis in spirit, he had to contemplate her terrestrial aspect. In practical terms, this meant that he first had to understand how the attributes of the goddess manifested themselves in nature.

The Egyptians understood that knowledge of this world is as important as that of the next, and that insight into one would enhance the experience of the other.

In what were known as the Lesser Mysteries, the neophyte would meditate in silence centring the "Isis within". In the Greater Mysteries worshippers, each dressed as the god with whom they wished to identify, would participate in re-enactments of the myths. Through this process, they hoped to succumb to a mystic union with the deity they had chosen – manifesting the god's attributes and absorbing divine wisdom.

A lower form of meditation was practised periodically by the rest of the populace, who, after seeking the permission of the priests, would be allowed to sleep in a chamber of the temple in the hope that they would be visited in their dreams by the gods. The story of the Lady Mehitousklet is typical. She believed herself to be incapable of bearing a child, and so sought permission to sleep in a chamber at the temple of Imouthes The Healer. In her sleep, she dreamt she was visited by the god who instructed her to go to a fountain in her husband's garden and uproot a colocase plant she would find growing there. She was to brew a remedy from it and administer it to her husband. According to the story, she followed this advice and conceived shortly afterwards.

The modern mind might conclude that this was as good a way as any of contacting the subconscious or "higher self", which is supposed to have knowledge of the cause of all our problems and their required solutions.

MOSES – PROPHET OR PHARAOH?

"The modern world has yet to value this man who, in an era so remote and under conditions so adverse, became the world's first internationalist, the most remarkable figure in the ancient world."

(CAMBRIDGE HISTORY, VOLUME II)

The Old Testament attaches prophetic significance to the moment when the child Moses, the prophet and founding father of the Jewish nation, took the crown from Pharaoh and placed it on his own head. That episode may, however, have been a veiled reference to the fact that Moses (born circa 1394 BCE) was not an adopted slave child but Akhenaten, son of the Pharaoh Amenhotep III.

It was Akhenaten who attempted to impose a monotheistic religion in Egypt during the 18th Dynasty, but he was deposed and exiled to Sinai around 1361 BCE. On his return 25 years later, he attempted to seize power from Rameses I, but after failing to do so it is believed that he persuaded the Hebrew slaves to follow him into Sinai with the idea of establishing his new religion in the desert.

There are certainly striking similarities between the teachings of Moses and the monotheistic religion which Akhenaten attempted to introduce, not the least of which is the duplication of moral

The light of Aten, the one god, presides over the Royal family.

precepts from the Negative Confession in The Egyptian Book of the Dead within the Ten Commandments. It may also be significant that Akhenaten's god, Aten, was the only Egyptian deity not to be represented by a mythical, animal-headed image but as a sun disc radiating light on the Royal family.

The theory that Akhenaten and Moses may have been one and the same person was first put forward by Freud in the 1930s and has been gathering credibility ever since. Freud argued that the Hebrew word *adonai* meaning "My Lord" was the equivalent to the Egyptian "Aten", the god of Akhenaten. Freud also cast doubt on the origin of the name "Moses".

The Bible states that the baby Moses was placed in a basket and cast adrift on the waters of the Nile by his mother, after Pharaoh had ordered all male Hebrew babies to be killed. It had been predicted that a Hebrew child would grow up to depose him. This uncanny variation on the Christ story continues with Moses being given a virgin mother, the daughter of Pharaoh, who we are told miraculously draws him from the water, assumes correctly that the child is of Hebrew origin, but adopts him nevertheless. More incredibly, the Bible implies that she gives Moses what has always been thought to be a Hebrew name.

At a time when the Hebrews were despised by the Egyptians, it defies credulity that an unmarried Egyptian princess would knowingly adopt a Hebrew child and that her maternal instinct would further extend to giving him a Hebrew name in defiance of her own people.

It was Freud's contention that the name Moses was not of Hebrew but Egyptian origin, the final "es" having been added in Greek translation to *mos*, which is the Egyptian word for child. In a second article, Freud raised the question of why Akhenaten/Moses should have risked his sovereignty to establish a monotheistic faith in direct opposition to the priesthood and their pantheon of Egyptian gods. The answer might be that Akhenaten was of Jewish descent and was

The Ten Commandments are uncannily similar to the Egyptians' Negative Confession.

MOSES' MAGIC

The Bible makes much of the "magic" performed by Moses to demonstrate that his God's power was greater than that of the Egyptian priests. And yet, even with the fate of his enslaved people resting on the outcome, the use of magic by Moses would have gone against the tenets of the Israelites who condemned magic as contrary to the will of God.

The descriptions of the acts performed by Moses are remarkably similar to those of the hand and rod ritual performed by Egyptian kings during the sed festivals, to confirm their authority. Furthermore, the rod Moses is said to have carried – "shaped and engraved in the image of a sceptre" – is uncannily close to that of the sceptre carried by the Pharaohs. Was Moses simply establishing his credentials before Pharaoh? He would then have been in a position to bargain with Pharaoh for the freedom of the slaves.

The description of this scene in the Koran is more detailed than that in the Old Testament, which may have been deliberately censored to excise any mention of Moses' Egyptian origins.

intent on introducing his god into Egypt.

Egyptologist Ahmed Osman claims to have identified Yuya, vizier to Thutmosis IV and Amenhotep III, as Joseph of the coloured coat. Yuya's daughter, Tiye, later married Amenhotep III and gave birth to Akhenaten. This would mean that Queen Tiye, and not the Pharaoh's daughter, would have been the mother of Moses. A sculpted head and statuette of Queen Tiye were discovered in a Semitic cave temple at Sarabit el Hadim in Sinai, where both Akhenaten and Moses are said to have spent their exile. A further discovery, in 1989, of the tomb of Aper-el, Akhenaten's vizier, appears to confirm that his highest official also worshipped the Hebrew God. This suggests that Akhenaten may have been deposed because the Egyptian priesthood feared the growing Hebrew influence. Whatever the true identity of Moses may be, the story of the exodus marks a significant historical turning point, when the ancient world switched from magic to monotheism.

HERMES TRISMEGISTOS

"Whatever is below is like that which is above, and whatever is above is like that which is below ..."

(THE EMERALD TABLET OF HERMES TRISMEGISTOS)

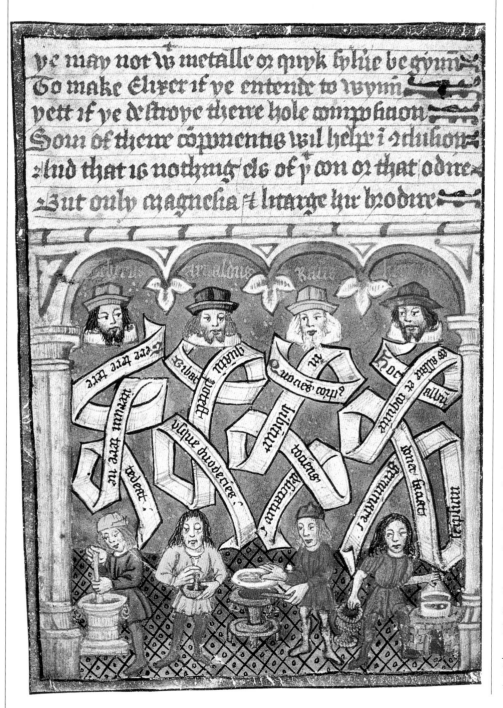

There are many colourful legends surrounding the discovery of The Emerald Tablet Of Hermes Trismegistos, which is generally regarded as one of the most remarkable artefacts of the ancient world and indeed one of the few secular texts to have had a profound and lasting influence on the Western mystic tradition.

The sage and magician Apollonius of Tyana is reputed to have discovered the corpse of Hermes in a cave and to have wrested the tablet from the dead man's hands. Another legend credits Alexander the Great with recovering the tablet from the tomb and taking it to Alexandria, from where its wisdom spread throughout the world. Sadly, neither of these tales is likely to be true.

Though once believed to have been an Egyptian sage, Hermes is now regarded as a mythical figure (the Greeks identified him with the Egyptian god Thoth), whose name was appropriated by a number of anonymous authors in the first and second centuries BCE to lend their work credibility. The name Trismegistos ("Thrice Greatest") may have been devised as a cryptic allusion to the fact that three successive scribes revised and edited earlier texts, including the Emerald Tablet, which were then incorporated into an eclectic body of work known as the *Corpus Hermeticum*. This would explain why the *Hermeticum* consists of Egyptian, Greek and Hebrew teachings enriched with elements of Gnosticism and Neoplatonism.

The seven Greek tracts which form the main bulk of the *Hermeticum* consist largely of traditional dialogues between teacher and pupil. The first,

The teachings of Hermes form the basis of Western mysticism, alchemy and chemistry.

"Poimandres", describes the creation of the universe as it was revealed to one of the pupils in a vision. In this state, the pupil "witnessed" the convergence of light and darkness out of which is heard "a holy Word". This, he thinks, "was the voice of the Light". In reply, Poimandres interprets the vision saying: "That light ... is I, even Mind, the first God ... and the Word which came forth from the Light is the son of God." The meaning here is that God is Mind, or consciousness and that all creation resulted from God willing the universe into existence. Contemporary practitioners of the Hermetic tradition would say that we are each a part of that Universal Mind and yet are separated from it by the false concept of "self". This is a notion shared by Buddhists.

Poimandres concludes, " ... in you too, the word is son, and the mind is father of the word. They are not separate one from the other; for life is the union of word and mind."

This assertion that unity is the funda-mental principle of all things is at the core of the *Hermeticum*, and of the Hermetic tradition which evolved from it. All creation, it states, manifests from a single point and is animated by the same life force. Man and nature are therefore interdependent, their relationship governed by the law of Antipathy and Sympathy. From this realization was to develop the concept of correspondences, which guided the course of alchemy and eventually led to the science of chemical medicine. It can also be seen as one of the earliest warnings against plundering and polluting the world's resources without thought for the future.

The wisdom contained in the *Hermeticum* is not the exclusive preserve of any one scholar or faith. It lies within the reach of everyone, but each person must seek it out for himself.

"Hermes saw the totality of things. Having seen, he understood, he had the power to reveal and show. And indeed, what he knew, he wrote down. What he wrote, he mostly hid

The Ancient Greeks identified Hermes with Mercury, messenger of Zeus.

away, keeping silence, rather than speaking out, so that every genera-tion on coming into the world had to seek out these things."

THE TEACHINGS OF HERMES

"If then you do not make yourself equal to God, you cannot appre-hend God; for like is known by like. Leap clear of all that is corpo-real, and make yourself grow to a like expanse with that greatness which is beyond all measure; rise up above all time, and become eternal; then you will apprehend God. Think that for you too nothing is impossible; deem that you too are immortal, and that you are able to grasp all things in your

thought, to know every craft and every science; find yourself home in the haunts of every living crea-ture ... but if you shut up your soul in your body, and abase yourself, and say, 'I know nothing, I can do nothing, I am afraid of earth and sea, I cannot mount to Heaven; I do not know what I was, nor what I shall be'; then, what have you to do with God? Your thought can grasp nothing beautiful and good, if you cleave to the body, and are

evil. For it is the height of evil not to know God; but to be capable of knowing God, and to wish and hope to know him, is the road which leads straight to the good; and it is an easy road to travel."

" ... for there is nothing that is not God. And do you say 'God is invisible?' Speak not so. Who is more manifest than God."

(CORPUS HERMETICUM; XI.2)

THE WISDOM OF

SOLOMON

"The beginning of wisdom is the most sincere desire for instruction, and concern for instruction is wisdom ... For she is a reflection of eternal light, a spotless mirror of the working of God, and an image of his goodness."

(THE WISDOM OF SOLOMON 6, 17)

According to Judaic tradition, King Solomon (who died in 928 BCE), the second son of King David, derived his celebrated wisdom directly from God (*Yahweh*). "The Book of Kings" describes how, after travelling to the sanctuary of Gibeon to make a sacrifice in gratitude for gaining the throne over his rivals, Solomon was visited in a dream by God, who told him:

"Because you have asked for the wisdom to rule justly, instead of long life for yourself or riches or the death of your enemies, I will do what you have asked. I will give you more wisdom and understanding than anyone has ever had before or will ever have again. I will also give you what you have not asked for; all your life you will have wealth and honour, more than that of any other king."

(1. KINGS 3:11–13)

According to the words of the Bible, Solomon's celebrated wisdom and wealth were granted to him by God.

However, legend attributes Solomon's knowledge to his command over, and communion with, dark forces led by the demon Asmodeus. The stories regarding the king's mastery of the magic arts, which circulated in the Middle Ages and which persist to this day, were partly the result of anti-Semitism, partly an irrational fear of anything to do with magic and were compounded by attempts to lend authenticity to the magical text books bearing his name.

The true source of Solomon's wisdom and power is more likely, however, to have derived from his study of the Kabbalah, the mystical aspect of Judaism. Solomon is credited with having written 3000 proverbs, many of which form the basis of "The Book of Proverbs", which enshrined his reputation as the personification of wisdom. Its influence can be seen in certain Muslim movements and Gnostic sects. The more worldly wisdom collected in "Ecclesiastes" in the Old Testament, with its warning against clinging to material possessions and indulging in earthly pleasures, appears to have been falsely attributed to him. Likewise, the "Book of Wisdom" appears to have acquired Solomon's name in an attempt to bring authority to the arguments presented within.

Solomon's reign was regarded as a golden age for the Jews. Historically, he

was the greatest of all Jewish kings. He instituted a centralized monarchy, installed a governor in each region of his kingdom to ensure stability and built great fleets to trade with other nations throughout the Mediterranean.

He also forged close links with Egypt, culminating in his marriage to a Pharaoh's daughter, while his friendship with Hiram, King of Tyre, led to his commissioning the King's architect, Hiram Abiff, to build the first temple at Jerusalem, the magnificence of which reflected his great wealth and power. This structure was designed to house the Ark of the Covenant, but the plans suggest that Canaanite, Mesopotamian and even Egyptian rituals took place within its walls. It is believed that Solomon consented to the worship of other Gods to appease his foreign wives, an act of tolerance which tainted his integrity and undermined his authority.

The story of Solomon's fall can be read as a warning against the complacency that comes with wealth, power and vanity of

Solomon dedicates his temple to the Lord. It symbolized the four worlds of existence.

the intellect. His oft-cited conclusion that "all is vanity" has long been interpreted as meaning that even the grandeur of kings must ultimately crumble to dust, yet close study of his commentaries on the Kabbalah suggests that his true meaning was that "all is illusion".

Three thousand years on, Solomon remains a symbol of ultimate wisdom. On the kabbalistic Tree of Life, there is an axis known as the "seat of Solomon" with access to the worlds above and below. It is the symbol of the Inner Teacher.

"And Solomon's wisdom excelled the wisdom of all the children of the east country, and all the wisdom of Egypt ... and his fame was in all nations round about."

(1. KINGS 4:20-31)

THE TEMPLE OF SOLOMON

The temple Solomon built in collaboration with Hiram the architect was constructed to represent the concept of the Four Worlds – the ground plan represented the physical, psychological and spiritual planes with the outer structure itself symbolizing Divine Unity. The two pillars which stood at the entrance represented the left- and right-hand columns on the kabbalistic Tree of Life (severity and mercy). They remain a feature in all the Lodges of the Mysteries to this day, where the candidate for

initiation, standing between them, represents the middle pillar of equilibrium. The temple took just seven years to build – the speed with which it was constructed led to rumours that it had been erected by magic.

There is speculation too that Hiram possessed secret knowledge of building similar to that of the architects who built the pyramids in Egypt. As the trustee of such secrets, Hiram was mythologized by the Freemasons who invented his "murder" for the purpose of a

ritual in which man liberates himself through art. For the ritual, Hiram is killed because he refuses to reveal the secrets of the Temple.

The real temple was destroyed by the Babylonians in 587 BCE and the site remained derelict until 70 years later, when a more modest building was erected by permission of the Persian king. Jesus is known to have taught in its Outer Court before its destruction by the Romans in 70 CE. Jewish tradition has it that a third temple will be built on the site in the age of the Messiah.

ZOROASTER – REVELATION AND REFORM

" ... there is in him a mind which is more capacious than the whole world, and more exalted than every worldly possession, with an understanding whose strength is perfectly selected, an intellect of all conquering power, and a sagacity of all-deciding ability."

(PAHLAVI DINKARD, BOOK VII)

Although little is known of the life of Zoroaster (c. 1700-1400 BCE), aside from the legends preserved in the Pahlavi literature of "Middle Persia", it is almost certain that he was the first prophet in history and certainly the first to preach a monotheistic belief.

The son of a pagan priest, Zoroaster was born on the borders of Afghanistan, in what is now Eastern Iran, with all the miraculous portents traditionally attendant upon the birth of a prophet, saint or Messiah. The scriptures state that he was conceived of a virgin by Ahura Mazda, the Creator, that he evaded numerous

Under Zoroaster, ritual sacrifice was replaced by fire worship.

assassination attempts instigated by jealous magi priests, calmed wild beasts and, while still a child, exhibited a wisdom beyond his years. After observing a period of silence from the age of seven, he took up the priesthood and was held in high esteem for his ability to memorize hymns and incantations, but, even as he learnt them, he began to question the purpose of all rites and rituals.

While still a young man, Zoroaster retreated into the mountains and lived the life of an ascetic, sleeping in a cave and sustaining himself on a diet of curd and milk. During a prolonged period of contemplation, he concluded that the cyclical nature of time, the seasons and the course of the planets indicated the presence of a universal architect – a creator.

Soon after, this spirit, whom he named Ahura Mazda, revealed himself to Zoroaster, who perceived that there was no reason for fear because his love was to be sought not by sacrifice, but by sublimation. In the ancient world, where the spilling of blood was encouraged to appease the gods, this was a revolutionary concept.

Unlike other prophets in the Abrahamic religions, Zoroaster did not physically experience the presence of God, but was divinely inspired from within. He was told of the importance of treating all living creatures as equal to man, and of regarding the earth and everything in it as the work of the Divine. "Who fosters not our Mother Earth behaves far worse than any of the bad." (Gathas; Yasna 51-6)

For the following 10 years, Zoroaster wandered alone, some say as far as China, preaching that there was but one God, who had created twin spirits, one malign (Angra Mainyu), the other the

Zoroaster, possibly the first religious leader to proclaim the existence of one god.

Holy Spirit (Spenter Mainya): who fought each other for control of the world.

Zoroaster's vision of dualistic forces, of Heaven and Hell, and the Final Judgement of mankind later had a profound, though rarely acknowledged, influence upon Jewish, Christian and Muslim thought. The religion he eventually founded, Gathic Mandaism, became the religion of three successive Iranian empires until Iran was finally overrun by the forces of Islam.

"Inform the people of the world, that they may see things both hidden and revealed. Whatever is bright and full of light, let them know that that is the brightness of my glory ... Wherever you may be in the two worlds you will find no place void of my light." (Zartusht-Namah)

THE GATHAS

The teachings of Zoroaster survive in the form of 17 hymns known as Gathas which comprise part of the Avesta, the Zoroastrian holy book. These Persian scriptures state that Ahura Mazda did not create Good and Evil, for these are human concepts, but Reality and Unreality. Reality is everything the Supreme Being created and Unreality is everything man has created – in his own mind.

The Gathas make mention of "the End of Time", which is not to be interpreted as the end of existence, but the beginning of eternity. It is the end of the first stage of man's evolution, for there is no end to creation, only a continuing

process towards perfection.

In keeping with the belief in Good and Evil, the scriptures maintain that, after death, the soul is judged by three spirits with the righteous permitted to enter Heaven and the evil condemned to Hell.

However, neither state is permanent, for the Final Judgement is reserved for the day of resurrection, Frashokereti ("Making Wonderful"). The suffering of the individual soul after death is the result of alienation from God, a punishment meted out by the individual himself and not by God.

The Gathas are believed to be the first sacred writings to refer to an afterlife in any detail.

GREECE – THE FIRST PHILOSOPHERS

"The true essence of things is hidden from man. He only knows the things of this world, where the finite is combined with the infinite. How can he then know essence?"

(PHILOLAUS)

Pythagoras believed that the Universe expressed a divine mathematical harmony.

Pythagoras (c. 592-510 BCE) was born in the same century as Lao Tzu, Buddha and Zoroaster, but few would consider him to be as significant a figure. And yet, he was much more than just the author of the geometrical theorem which bears his name. As well as mathematician, he was a mystic and is believed to have been the first man to call himself a philosopher ("a lover of wisdom").

Pythagoras' philosophy was founded on the Orphic Mysteries, which were the basis of an esoteric religious movement offering mystical insights. In the mythical figure of Orpheus, the healer and harpist, was embodied the idea that human beings must transcend their baser instincts if they are to realize their true potential. Devotees refused to take part in the sacrificial rites of the official Dionysian cult and instead dedicated themselves to overcoming the evil they associated with the body, which they called the "tomb of the soul". In return, they were promised immortality in the next world.

Pythagoras incorporated the Orphic concept of reincarnation, purification and food taboos into his own teachings. But it was in expressing the basic principle of the cosmos through numbers that he was to prove a profound influence on philosophers and mystics over the following centuries. Pythagoras believed that reality is founded on numbers, that everything on Earth and in the heavens shares the same principles of unity and proportion and that it is through numbers that man will gain knowledge of the invisible world.

The Seven Liberal Arts as depicted by Raffael. ('The School of Athens', fresco c. 16th century).

Initiation into his inner circle, the *mathematicoi*, was dependent on the passing of an exam and a three-year study period followed by five years of austerity and silence. Having proved themselves worthy, initiates were then entrusted with the sect's most closely guarded secret – the secret of the spheres. Pythagoras' theory was an encapsulation of the idea that the universe works to a harmony which man, being incarnate, cannot perceive. If man is to attain completeness, he must rediscover this divine vibration within himself – after which, he can work in harmony with the unseen forces in the universe.

To promote his ideas, Pythagoras attempted to establish a religious and political community at Crotona, a Greek colony in Southern Italy, but it was disrupted by the democrats who viewed the group as elitist.

Aged about 80, Pythagoras died in a fire which consumed the building he shared with his pupils. After his death, philosophy turned from mysticism to metaphysics and became a science of ideas. Pythagoras' mantle was taken over by Socrates (469-395 BCE), whom the Oracle at Delphi had declared to be the wisest and most knowledgeable man of his time. Socrates claimed to possess an inner guide, which he called his "daimon" and which urged him to go in to the market place and open men's minds. This he did by a structured argument which forced his opponents to question their principles and, more significantly, their pretensions. The essence of Socrates' philosophy was that ignorance is the curse of humanity and that learning can help people to think for themselves and find out who they really were.

The 20-year-old Plato became one of Socrates' youngest pupils and was with his master when he was condemned to death for "corrupting youth with his philosophy".

Such was the impact that Socrates had on Plato that the young man burnt his books of poetry and devoted the rest of his life to philosophy. After the death of his mentor, Plato fled to Maegara where he studied under the mathematician Euclid, before journeying on to Egypt to acquire the wisdom of the High Priests. On returning to Athens, Plato opened the first academy of philosophy, where he intended to train politicians and encourage them to adopt ethical principles in public life. He adapted Pythagoras' ideas on proportion and harmony to illustrate an ideal social order. Having inspired and fostered the first philosophers, the Greek mystery religions were destroyed by them, when the new philosophy concluded that the intellect no longer required religion.

Epicuros, whose name has been erroneously associated with the pursuit of pleasure.

THE FORGOTTEN PHILOSOPHER

Once much maligned, Epicuros (341-270 BCE), who gave his name to the art of sensuous indulgence, is now regarded as one of the greatest intellects of ancient Greece. He was the author of approximately 300 learned volumes of which only fragments now survive. In these, he discoursed on such diverse topics as astronomy, meteorology, physics, ethics and the harmony of atoms: this was an attempt to reawaken interest in wisdom at a time when Greeks were preoccupied with a series of political and moral crises.

"One cannot have a happy life without wisdom, honesty and justice," he wrote, "but these three are inseparable from pleasure."

Epicuros' enemies successfully sought to undermine his influence by criticizing his endorsement of pleasure. This was a distortion of the frugal philosopher's message, since his definition of pleasure was that which came with peace of mind and fullness of being, not the indulgence of the senses. Epicuros believed that man's potential is eroded by fear, particularly the fear of death, and that all people, regardless of their station in life, should educate themselves to overcome fear and enjoy the pleasure that comes with inner peace.

ATLANTIS

"The myth of Atlantis has caused so much ink to flow (on freaks and fantasies, if not worse) that every rational person setting out to speak of Atlantis must first of all remind the reader that it is a myth ..."

(SIR FRANCIS BACON, THE NEW ATLANTIS)

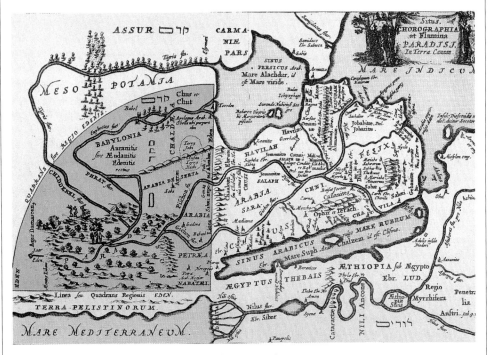

The location of the Garden of Eden according to Herbinius (1678).

Atlantis, the lost continent described by Plato as being "larger than Libya and Asia put together", continues to fascinate the modern mind because it satisfies our need to believe in a source of perennial wisdom and conforms to an ideal image of civilization.

Plato did not invent Atlantis, but in his dialogue, "Critias", he was the first to describe in detail its lush sub-tropical vegetation, glittering capital and magnificent scientific achievements. There were heated public baths, artificial fountains and even a racecourse, all made possible by the discovery of a local ore, Orichalcum, which 'was more precious than anything but gold'. Plato was eager to promote his theory that a state founded on the principles of "harmony" and "proportion" would be a superior system to that of an empire. He thus regarded the myth of Atlantis as the perfect setting in which to present his political philosophy.

Plato's inspiration and much of his source material came from the writings of the Greek politician Solon, who in 590 BCE recorded a tale told to him by an Egyptian priest. The priest, who was keen to prove that the historical records of Egypt were older than those of Greece, had regaled Solon with the story of an island-continent in the Atlantic beyond the straits of Gibraltar, which 9000 years earlier had been the centre of a highly advanced civilization as well as the seat of a formidable military empire. The empire succeeded in conquering Egypt, but was beaten back by the Greeks and soon afterwards was subject to a sequence of terrifying natural disasters which sent it to the bottom of the ocean.

The tale became a staple of Greek storytellers and was certainly familiar to the young Plato who, in adapting it, sketched in such convincing detail that innumerable scholars have since set out to verify its existence. They have cited Solon's manuscript as "evidence" that Plato's story was based on a real lost continent, despite the fact that Plato had described a Bronze Age civilization at a time when none could have existed.

The stated dimensions of the Atlantean capital and its concentric harbours are also wildly impractical. Plato's figures would mean that the Royal City of Atlantis would have been 300 times larger than modern London and its concentric canals would have run to a total length of 1,135 miles (1,816 kilometres). The only plausible explanation for this over-estimate is that the scribe, who translated Solon's original manuscript, might have confused the Egyptian symbol for 100 with that for 1,000. This would not only reduce the dimensions to more realistic proportions but would make the given date tally with the destruction of Crete – an event from which Plato probably drew his inspiration. The Greeks themselves did not take the story as anything more than the moral fable Plato intended it to be. Even his most devoted pupil, Aristotle, believed his mentor had invented it all.

Nevertheless, the modern myth of Atlantis began in earnest in 1882 with the publication of *Atlantis: The Antediluvian World* by ex-American congressman Ignatius Donnelly. Originally, he was inspired after reading documents held in the Library of Congress, but his fanciful account was his own invention. Donnelly concluded that Atlantis was the location of the Garden of Eden and he credited its people with the invention of alphabetical writing and scientific medicine.

Subsequent writers claim to have found firm evidence of the migration of the citizens of Atlantis in the customs and religious rites of both the South American Indians and the Egyptians. Donnelly had pointed out that both civilizations had built pyramids and

mummified their dead. One of the earliest theories linking Atlantis with Egypt was put forward by the 19th century archaeologist, Augustus le Plongeon, who suggested that the goddess Isis may have been a former Queen of Atlantis. Subsequently, the search for the lost continent's secrets has centred on Egypt.

Among those who claimed paranormal insight into the mystery was the celebrated 20th century psychic, Edgar Cayce, who believed that the Sphinx at Gizeh was the site of an Atlantean Hall of Records. Here was stored the wisdom of the antediluvian world awaiting redis-

covery. Another psychic researcher, H C Randall Stevens, suggested that there might be an underground Masonic temple of Atlantean origin behind the Sphinx with passageways connecting it to the three pyramids on the same site. Stevens went further still, predicting that Atlantis will resurface in the year 2014.

The fact that Atlantis continues to fire the imagination says much about our need to believe that we have the potential to create such a paradise here on earth. Atlantis may have been a myth, but bringing such ideas into being will be the aim of the new Millennium.

THE GOLDEN AGE

There are few cultures which do not preserve the myth of a Golden Age and the wisdom which has been lost with its passing.

The Greek poets wrote of an age predating that of their gods and goddesses when a "golden race" lived an idyllic life in harmony with nature. The Judaeo-Christian tradition, too, preserves the idea of an earthly paradise, the Garden of Eden, from which man was exiled and to which he strives to return.

The Babylonians told stories of the Seven Sages, who built magnificent cities ruled by a dynasty of immortal kings but, when their wisdom failed them, their greatness diminished and their lives were shortened to a mortal span.

Hinduism has a similar saga in the **Krita Yuga***, which also says that seven sages (the* **Seven Rishis***) "connected with the origin of*

humanity and knowledge" established an age of Enlightenment under Krishna and that all beings were then wise and virtuous by nature. This age, too, declined and the "eternal yoga" taught by Krishna faded from men's minds. Both Buddhism and Hinduism describe this golden age as part of a four-age cycle, each one of great length and marking a further decline in morals and piety.

While Buddhism speaks of nirvana as a state of the spirit, Lamaistic Buddhists speak of the city of Shambhala as a place of "quietude" and Ancient Wisdom which is to be found in an unspecified location in the north of the world. It was later seized upon by theosophists, Madame Blavatsky and Alice Bailey, as "proof" that Atlanteans had built an "etheric" city in the Gobi desert!

Plato's political parable gave birth to a myth.

NEOPLATONISM – THE PHILOSOPHY OF ORIGINS

"The soul of each single one of us is sent that the universe may be complete."

(PLOTINUS; ENNEDS, IV, 8, 1)

Between the 3rd and 6th centuries BCE, the Neoplatonists fused the philosophy of Plato with Eastern mysticism to form a school of philosophy which exercised considerable influence over the scholars and magicians of the Middle Ages.

Neoplatonism's most ardent exponents, Plotinus, Proclus, Iamblichus and Porphyry, held that all things, whether material or spiritual, emanated from a single transcendent Godhead, a view which has led to Neoplatonism becoming known as the philosophy of origins.

Its founder, Plotinus (205-270 CE), though not a Christian himself, was to have a profound impact on the Christian mystics. Saint Augustine called him "the wisest philosopher", possibly because he was the first to define the idea of an Absolute.

Plotinus argued that a true philosopher is one who is not distracted by the world of the senses, but who seeks "a liberation from all earthly bonds, a life that takes no pleasure in earthly things, a flight of the alone, to the alone".

After studying the dialogues of Plato and the metaphysics of Aristotle, Plotinus sought inspiration from the East among the oriental philosophers of Alexandria. From them he adopted the idea that the mystic must contemplate the Divine within himself rather than worship an external God. Plotinus saw all creation in terms of harmony: chaos and conflict were the symptoms of disharmony resulting from our turning our back on the "choir master" of the Universe. He envisaged creation as a series of descending steps away from the One (God). Evil was therefore simply a descent into ignorance as one moved away from divine influence.

In his metaphysical manifesto, The Enneads, Plotinus described his own experiences of contact with the indefinable. "Many times it has happened: lifted out of the body into myself; becoming external to all other things and self-encentred; beholding a marvellous beauty ... it was scarcely vision, unless of a mode unknown; it was a going forth from the self."

It is ironic that the pagans embraced Plotinus' theories as an endorsement of their resistance to Christianity, while the Christians interpreted them as confirmation of their own beliefs.

Porphyry (234-310 CE), a prolific writer and pupil of Plotinus, attempted to define the nature of God as represented by the "cosmic Man of Light", the macrocosmic man "who has heaven for head, aether for body, earth for feet and for the water round (him) the ocean's depths". He identified the same concept in a number of traditions, most notably the Anthropos of the Hermetic school and the cosmic man, Adam Kadmon, of the Kabbalah.

A highly excitable type, Porphyry was often racked with severe nervous tension and driven to thoughts of suicide. At such times, he became

Iamblichus practised philosophy alongside dream divination and magic.

ensnared in his own intellect. "The One, who is above substance and Being, is neither being nor non-being, but rather acts, and in himself is pure action in that he is the Being, the Being who is before Being and like the idea of Being."

In his more lucid moments, he argued the case for philosophy as the true cult of the Absolute, while religions involved the worship of lesser gods. He considered the teachings of Jesus to have given a distorted view of God and set out his case in a tract untactfully entitled "Against Christians", which nearly cost him more than just his popularity. Nevertheless, his writings remained an influence on esoteric Christianity.

In his eagerness to reinvigorate paganism, Iamblichus (c. 250-330 CE) a pupil of Porphyry, criticized his mentor's works, contributing to the erosion of the school's ideals, which he further under-

mined by espousing the merits of dream divination and theurgy (a method of communicating with the divine through the animation of statues).

It was left to Proclus (412-485 CE), a wealthy young Greek who abandoned his ambitions of becoming a lawyer to restore the image of philosophy which was then looked down on as an intellectual indulgence. In his "Elements Of Theology", one of the last significant works of pre-Christian philosophy, Proclus envisaged creation as having evolved from a number of emanations from the Godhead. These could be explored in the imagination, a concept similar to that described in the Kabbalah. By endorsing the practice of ritualized mysticism, the work of Proclus effectively marked the final transmutation of Plotinus' ideals from mysticism into magic.

Porphyry attempted to define the nature of God and questioned the teachings of Jesus, which nearly cost him his life.

THE LETTER OF PLOTINUS

The Neoplatonist philosophy, which attempted to reconcile rationalism and mysticism, can best be elucidated from a letter Plotinus wrote to his fellow philosopher Flaccus in 260 CE.

"I am weary already of this prison-home, the body, and calmly await the day when the divine nature within me shall be set free from matter ... Purify your soul from all undue hope and fear about earthly things, mortify the body, deny self-affections as well as appetites, and the inner eye will begin to exercise its clear and solemn vision. You ask me to tell

you how I know, and what is our criterion of certainty ... External objects present us only with appearances. Concerning them, therefore, we may be said to possess opinion rather than knowledge ... our question lies within the ideal reality which exists behind appearance ... It follows, therefore, that this region of truth is not to be investigated as a thing external to us, and so only imperfectly known. It is within us ... Knowledge has three degrees – opinion, science, illumination. The means or instrument of the first is sense; of the second, dialectic; of the third, intu-

ition. To the last I subordinate reason. You can only apprehend the Infinite by a faculty superior to reason, by entering into a state in which you are your finite self no longer, in which the Divine Essence is communicated to you. This is Ecstasy. It is the liberation of your mind from its finite consciousness. Like can only apprehend like; when you thus cease to be finite, you become one with the Infinite ... I myself have realized it but three time as yet and Porphyry hitherto not once. All that tends to purify and elevate the mind will assist you in this attainment ... "

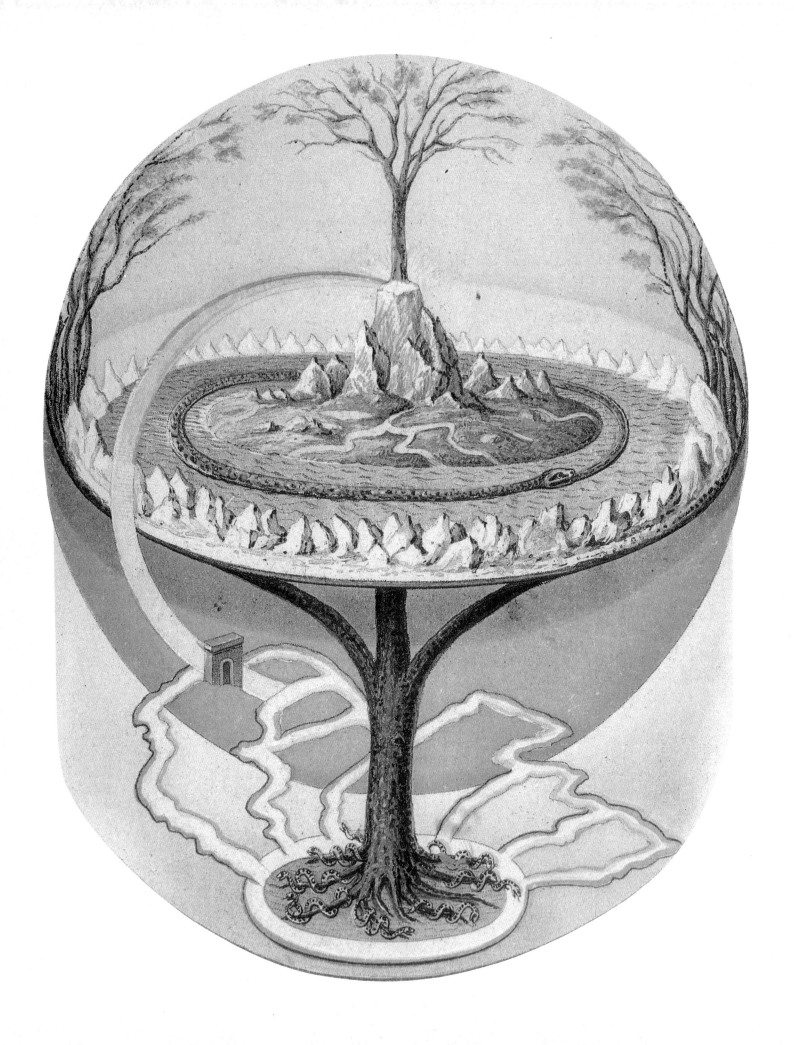

THE KABBALISTIC
MYSTERIES

The Kabbalah, the mystical aspect of Judaism, forms the foundation of the Western esoteric tradition. Its central symbol is the Tree of Life (the Otz Chiim), which has been assimilated and adapted by the three religions of revelation (and later by occultists) as a practical system for perceiving the attributes of God, mankind and the universe.

The structure of the Tree Of Life theoretically mirrors that of both the universe (macrocosm) and man (microcosm). Mastery of it enables the initiate to enter the upper and interior worlds, to realize oneself as Adam Kadmon (the Divine Man) and ultimately achieve Divine Union.

Initially the Kabbalah was a metaphysical teaching, a discussion of the essential truths behind the sacred texts of the Torah (Book of Instruction) imparted orally from rabbi to pupil. A living tradition, it has been reinterpreted for successive generations, the Tree being a diagram that can be applied to explain the attributes of every aspect of creation.

For the kabbalist, God is not the severe law-giver of the Old Testament but the Absolute who drew back so that the four worlds of Emanation, Creation, Formation and Action could come into existence, so that He might perceive Himself.

According to kabbalistic teaching, in withdrawing to create a void the Absolute caused light to stream forth at 10 different levels known as sefirot. These emanations represent the 10 attributes of the Divine and are governed by three pillars which maintain a balance between them. They are the guiding principle for those who wish to realize their true self and manifest the Divine on Earth.

KABBALAH – THE TREE OF LIFE

"Ten sefirot out of Nothing. Ten not nine. Ten not eleven. Understand this in Wisdom and in Wisdom understand. Enquire and ponder through their meaning, so as to return the Creator to His Throne."

(THE SEFER YETZIRAH, 6TH CENTURY CE).

In the Kabbalah, there is no absolute truth, only the truth of the Absolute. The nature of God is beyond our comprehension, but by studying the Kabbalah we can appreciate and ultimately experience its Attributes in every aspect of existence.

The most commonly used symbolic diagram in the Kabbalah is the Tree of Life, which is depicted as having 10 spheres, or sefirot, each representing an Attribute of the Divine. The sefirot have been described as being like multi-faceted sapphires through which are reflected the qualities of God. They are traditionally depicted ranged upon three Pillars which represent the unmanifest Divine Principles which govern them.

The three sefirot on the right-hand Pillar of Mercy correspond to the male aspects of active Force, the three sefirot on the left-hand Pillar of Severity represent the female aspects of passive Form, with the remainder on the central Pillar of Equilibrium, balancing and harmonizing the whole. The Tree is therefore a diagram by which we can visualize the various aspects of our own personalities and how they are manifested in the world.

The key to the Kabbalah is "balance" of what are in essence complementary Attributes. Imbalance in the individual can express itself in abnormal behavioural traits or in physical illness: on a wider scale, it can manifest in social disorder and even conflict between nations. Recognizing the causes of imbalance in oneself is one aspect of the work of the Kabbalist.

The configuration of the sefirot on the Tree represents a descent from the Divine, a model of the spiritual and physical structure of everything in existence, from the four interpenetrating worlds in which we exist to the principles of the machines that we have made.

Keter (the Crown) corresponds to the point of Emanation, the Godhead, to which all must ultimately return. It is traditionally expressed in the Divine name "Ehyeh Asher Ehyeh" ("I Am That I Am"). Hokmah (Wisdom) corresponds to the male creative Force which is balanced by Binah (Understanding), the passive female aspect manifesting as Form. Together, they form the first triad of the Tree, at the level of Azilut, or Emanation.

In the Kabbalah the fable of Moses and the burning bush symbolizes Enlightenment.

THE TREE OF LIFE

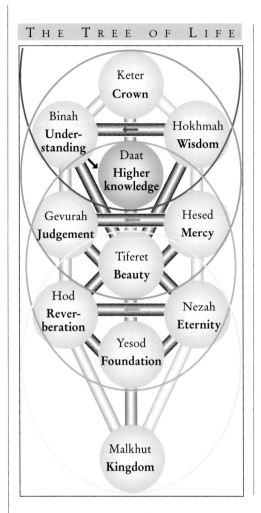

← *Intellect*   ▮▮ *Pillar of Equilibrium*
← *Emotion*   ▮▮ *Pillar of Severity*
← *Action*   ▮▮ *Pillar of Mercy*

○ **Azilut**   *World of Emanation*
○ **Beriah**   *World of Creation*
○ **Yetzirah** *World of Formation*
○ **Asiyah**   *World of Action*

This is the realm of the Divine Will or Intellect from which the lower aspects were brought forth. From Azilut emanated the sefirot of Gevurah (Judgement) and Hesed (Mercy) which together with Tiferet (Beauty), forms the second triad at the level of Beriah, or Creation. This is the realm where the Divine intention to create was defined but the universe and its inhabitants were unformed. The third triad at the level of Yetzirah, or Formation, is comprised of the sefirah Netzah (Eternity), Hod (Reverberation) and Yesod (Foundation).

Netzah represents the instinctive processes such as growth and renewal, while Hod represents the intuitive actions which control them. Yesod is a reflection of Tiferet and, as such, will produce either a clear image or a distorted reflection depending on the quality of the "mirror". In human terms, it is the place of the ego which can either be refined to mirror the Divine self or be warped by the Will to reflect our undeveloped natures.

In terms of the Divine descent into matter, this is the realm of archetypes where the model of every species took detailed form prior to its manifestation in the physical world. It is the realm referred to in the myth of the Garden of Eden, where the model for Man was separated into male and female components.

Although ten sefirot are marked, another, Daat (Knowledge), the place of the Holy Spirit, is represented as a broken circle to indicate that it is unmanifest and through it the Divine can enter existence.

THE HIDDEN TEACHINGS OF THE OLD TESTAMENT

Kabbalists believe that the fables recorded in the Old Testament veil the hidden teachings of the Hebrew prophets and the patriarchs. If read in the light of Kabbalistic knowledge, the familiar biblical stories can be shown to contain the mysteries of existence as well as the stages in Man's ascent back to the Divine.

Joseph's enslavement in Egypt can be interpreted as the soul's descent into incarnation; his multicoloured coat being a reference to the "etheric" body from which he

is separated. Significantly, the Hebrew name for Egypt is "confined". The Exodus from Egypt would therefore be an allegory for the journey out of the bondage of the physical world, through the desert of initiation, to the promised land of spirit. The slaying of the Egyptian by Moses can be understood to mean that he subdued his lower nature and freed his Higher Self. His retrieval of the sapphire rod from the ground is an obvious reference to an initiatory test which is echoed

in myths around the world from the Norse sagas to King Arthur.

The final stage of Moses' spiritual awakening is symbolized by his vision of the burning bush, a divine revelation through which he perceived the totality of the universe. This event marked the point at which Moses surrendered to Divine Will which required him to return to Egypt and free his fellow "slaves" by leading them across the Red Sea, the symbol of commitment to the spiritual path – the point of no return.

THE FOUR WORLDS

"When the Holy One who created the Universe wished to reveal its hidden aspect, the light within darkness, He showed how things were intermingled. Thus out of darkness comes light and from the concealed comes the revealed. In the same manner does good emerge from evil and Mercy from Justice, since they too are intertwined."

(THE ZOHAR, 13TH CENTURY CE)

The Kabbalah envisages four levels of existence – the Divine World of Emanation (Azilut), the World of Creation (Beriah), the World of Formation (Yetzirah) and the World of Action (Asiyyah).

The first world, Azilut, is a dimension beyond time and space, the unchanging realm of Eternity, where the laws and dynamics of creation are in place waiting upon the Divine Will. This is the realm of perfection, the closest to the Divine (Azilut translates as "proximity"), but there can be no fulfilment of such potential until it has manifested in existence.

The kabbalistic theory is that God manifested in the Divine Attributes of the sefirot in order to perceive Himself. Azilut is therefore the realm of Will or

Jacob was spiritually "asleep" when granted a vision of the higher worlds.

Intention and corresponds to the same level of consciousness in Man – in the Kabbalah, everything in the macrocosmos is mirrored in miniature in the microcosmos.

As one of the innumerable worlds within worlds which characterize this seemingly complex, but ultimately simple, metaphysical system, Azilut contains the interior levels of Calling, Creating, Forming and Making.

Calling could be interpreted as the Will to bring something into being, Creating as the planning work of the Intellect, Forming as the emotional aspect which engages the Intellect and Making as the final physical act.

The Kabbalah presents a logical system of ever unfolding creation, of inter-penetrating worlds, each containing the essence of those from which it has descended. Each stage can be likened to the growth of a tree, in which all the genetic information is stored in its seed and is self-perpetuating. The importance of establishing this "map" of existence is so that we can see our part in the process and work upon the aspects mirrored in our own personalities to achieve a balance. The allusion to the seven Days of Creation in the First Chapter of Genesis is understood by the Kabbalist to be a reference to the creation not of the Earth, but of the second World, the World of Creation (Beriah).

The first "Day" was therefore the time

when the chaos of Form and Force were brought into balance, forming the supernal triad of the Tree of Creation. Each subsequent "Day" corresponds to another level of existence unfolding within each of the lower worlds.

It is no oversight on the part of the biblical scribes that the whole process is repeated in the second chapter of Genesis, since this was intended to signify the unfolding of another world, the World of Formation (Yezirah), mythologized as the Garden of Eden.

This is the world of flux and phenomena, where the spirit "models" for particular species are refined before manifesting in their infinite variety in the World of Action. This fourth world, the physical world, the only one of

which most of us are conscious, is the river referred to in Genesis which flowed out of the Garden of Eden.

Here Form and Force are manifest as matter and energy, male and female. Here too, the four levels of Calling, Creating, Forming and Making can be perceived in the four elements of fire, (symbol of pure Will), air (Intellect), water (Emotion) and earth (Action). Everything in the physical world is a crude reflection of that which exists in a purer, less defined form in the worlds above. The hermetic law stating: "As above, so below," is a perfect summary of the kabbalistic concept of existence.

Ezekiel's vision was symbolic of the four worlds.

EZEKIEL'S VISION

The Kabbalah grew out of the Jewish mystical tradition known as the Work of the Chariot, so-called because it was based on the vision of the prophet Ezekiel, to whom the structure of existence was revealed in the form of a fiery chariot.

Ezekiel described the chariot as emerging from an amber cloud being drawn by four winged creatures each with four faces: those of a man, a lion, an ox and an eagle. He likened the chariot to a firmament (in Hebrew raki'a), a blazing platform, which turned upon "wheels within wheels".

"And above the firmament that was over their heads was the likeness of a throne, as the appearance of a sapphire stone; and upon the likeness of the throne was a likeness as the appearance of a man upon it above." (Verse 26).

In his description, Ezekiel repeatedly uses the Hebrew word demut which means "likeness", suggesting that what he describes is not to be taken literally but as an interpretation or impression.

For the Kabbalist, the vision is taken to be symbolic of the Four Worlds. The human form is understood to be that of Adam Kadmon,

the Divine Man – and not God as is commonly believed; his throne symbolizes the World of Creation; the chariot symbolizes the World of Formation; while Ezekiel himself represents Man in the World of Action.

Likewise, the four faces of the winged creatures symbolize the four realms within each world; the man is Primordial Man in the World of Emanation; the eagle represents the World of Creation, the realm of air; the lion the World of Formation, the realm of water, the emotions and the heart; and the bull the earthly World of Action.

MAN: THE MICROCOSM

"One man is equivalent to all Creation.

One man is a World in miniature."

(ABOT DE RABBI NATHAN, 2ND CENTURY CE)

The Bible says that God created Man in His own image, by which it is generally understood that God takes the same form as Man. This is clearly unsatisfactory, for God must have both male and female aspects and exist beyond the limitations of form.

The Kabbalist envisages that from the transcendent Absolute Nothing (Ayin), which is beyond existence, was brought forth the immanent Absolute All (Ayin Sof), which is without end – the infinite.

Unmanifest Attributes manifested into existence from the World of Emanation through Divine Will, unfolding in the configuration of the sefirot which, according to tradition, took the form of Primordial Man, the perfect being, Adam Kadmon. We are each Adam Kadmon in finite form and it is our purpose in life to realize this potential so that God can perceive God.

"Man contains all that is above in heaven and below upon earth... No World could exist before Adam came into being for the human figure contains all things, and all that is exists by virtue of it." (The Zohar, 13th century CE).

In applying the model of the Four Worlds, the soul could be said to exist in the World of Emanation; the astral, or "etheric", body in the World of Creation; the psyche in the World of Formation; and the physical body in the World of Action.

Daat, the unmanifest sefirot is the veil of Higher Knowledge, at the level of Transpersonal Consciousness through which, artists, mystics and scientists attain inspiration and insight.

In the Kabbalah the Soul of Man is the mirror of God, not the body.

THE FOUR WORLDS

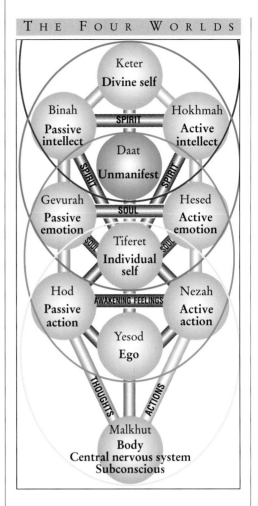

▌▌ *Pillar of Consciousness*
▌▌ *Pillar of Structure*
▌▌ *Pillar of Dynamic*

○ *Divine World*
○ *Spiritual World*
○ *Psychological World*
○ *Physical World*

The exterior Pillars on the tree of the psyche are re-named Structure and Dynamic, being the equivalent of Form and Force. On the Pillar of Structure Binah (Understanding) is concerned with contemplation and reflection, balanced on the Pillar of Dynamic by Hokmah (Wisdom), the Active Intellect representing revelation rather than reasoning.

At the level of the emotions is Gevurah (Judgement), the Super Ego, which can be expressed in terms of Discipline and Decision, while Hesed (Mercy), the Ego Ideal, is often expressed as Forgiveness and Love.

The practical aspect of the Kabbalah is best exemplified in the relationship between these two sefirot: Both in ourselves and in society, Judgement should always be tempered with Mercy. An imbalance in favour of Mercy would result in indecision in the individual, while, in the wider context of society, it might lead to social disorder and injustice. A severe swing towards Judgement would manifest in the individual as crippling self-criticism, and in society as a draconian judicial system, general intolerance and a lack of compassion. At a mundane level, the two aspects find balance in the quality of discernment. An imbalance would result in either fastidiousness or slovenliness, the opposite extreme.

Hod (Reverberation) corresponds to Passive Action and the Mortido, the death instinct; Nezah (Eternity) with Active Action and the Libido.

In psychological terms, the upper portion of the Tree is the realm of the Collective Unconscious, the central portion overlapping at Daat is the realm of the Individual Unconscious with the lower portion overlapping at Tiferet representing aspects of Personal Consciousness.

When superimposed on the human body, the sefirot correspond roughly to the position of the "subtle" energy centres which the Buddhists and Indian Yogis call the *chakras*. The practical Kabbalist works to harmonize all of these aspects with the aim of realizing the mirror image of Adam Kadmon.

PHYSICAL MAN

The validity of the sefirotic Tree as a structural model applicable to all aspects of existence can be appreciated if we take the model of Man one stage further from the level of the psyche to the physical, from the World of Formation to the denser World of Action. The sefirotic laws operate in our bodies in the same way as they work in the psyche and soul, but this time expressed in finite terms.

Just as we exist within the four worlds simultaneously on four different levels of consciousness, so the four Worlds exist within each of us as Will, Intellect, Emotion and the capacity for Action. At the physical level, these principles govern the mechanical, chemical, electronic and thought processes (see diagram opposite).

The Pillars of Force and Form are here expressed as energy and matter governed by the central Pillar of Consciousness. The central nervous system corresponds to Tiferet with Yesod as the autonomic. Malkhut is the region of the senses, our point of contact with the physical World. Binah and Hokmah correspond to the voluntary and involuntary psycho-biological processes; Gevurah and Hesed to the anabolic and catabolic processes which concern the assimilation and release of energy; while Hod and Nezah correspond to the monitoring and motor systems.

ZOHAR – THE BOOK OF SPLENDOUR

"Rabbi Simeon sat and wept, and he said, woe if I reveal these secrets and woe if I do not reveal them. The companions (initiates) who were there remained silent until Rabbi Abba stood and said to him, 'If our master wishes to reveal these matters, is it not written, 'The secret of the Lord belongs to those who fear Him,' and do not these companions tremble before the Holy One blessed be He?''"

("THE GREATER HOLY ASSEMBLY" FROM THE ZOHAR)

King Solomon's knowledge of the Kabbalah is concealed in the Torah.

The Sefer ha Zohar ("The Book Of Splendour") and the Sefer ha Yetzirah ("The Book Of Creation") are the cornerstones of kabbalistic literature. Together with the Sefer ha Torah – the core text of the Old Testament – they can be studied not only as books of wisdom but also as books of instruction, promising the adept direct experience of the higher worlds.

Occultists would add the Tarot cards to the list of Kabbalistic texts, for they consider the 22 cards of the Greater Arcana to be pictorial representations of the 22 paths connecting the sefirot on the Tree of Life.

Jewish Kabbalists would disagree, however, arguing that the secrets of the Kabbalah are concealed not in symbolism but in the allegorical fables of the Torah. Torah is traditionally translated as "The Book Of The Law", but is more accurately translated as "The Book Of Instruction" from the Hebrew Yarah to instruct. This is confirmed by the Zohar which states, " ... ignorant people consider only the clothes that are the story; they see nothing more than that and do not realize what the clothes conceal. Those who know a little better see not only the clothes but the body beneath them. The Wise ... consider only the soul, which is the essence of the real Torah."

By the Middle Ages, speculations as to the esoteric meanings of the Torah had been enriched with the records of rabbinical debate and were set down in the Sefer ha Zohar compiled by Rabbi Moses ben Shemtov of Leon in the 13th century. As was the custom, and in order to lend the text greater authority, he attributed the work to a legendary figure, Rabbi Simon bar Yokhai, who lived in the 2nd century CE and died it was said in an ecstatic vision of the higher worlds.

Rabbi Yokhai is the central figure of the Zohar, "the Master of the Secret", whose conversations with his son Rabbi Eleazar and their followers on the mysteries of existence comprise the greater part of the work. Through their exchanges, we learn about the origins and laws of the universe, the transmigration of souls and the ways of spiritual transformation.

The predominant theme of the Zohar is the spiritual make-up of Man and his purpose in the world. At one point, Rabbi Eleazar asks his father why God sends men's souls to Earth knowing that they have to die. The answer he receives is that Man's purpose is to know the glory of God (i.e. to understand the nature of the Divinity from which he has descended) and to manifest the Divine in the dense world of matter to bring about its transformation.

"The Holy One, blessed be He, made Man by printing the image of the kingdom of heaven within him, which is the image of the All. It is this image which the Holy One, blessed be He, beheld when he made the world and all the creatures of the world. This image is the synthesis of all creatures above and all creatures below, with no separation; it is the synthesis of all the sefirot, all their names, all their epithets and all their denominations."

The Zohar repeatedly underlines the unity of the sefirotic system which might appear to the uninitiated as fragmentary.

Occultists consider the Tarot cards to contain Kabbalistic secrets.

" ... in creating this world below, the world above lost nothing. It is the same for each sefirah: if one is illuminated, the next loses none of its brilliance."

In the ensuing centuries, the Kabbalah became synonymous with magic, with the 22 paths being envisaged as passageways to be travelled by the mystic or magician in the astral body. Its reputation as a magical system forced its initiates to guard their secrets well for fear of giving their persecutors another excuse for a pogrom.

"For every hand's breadth [of the mysteries] I reveal, I will hide a mile," wrote the 16th century kabbalist Isaac Luria. "With great difficulty I will open the gates of holiness, making an opening like the eye of a needle, and let him who is worthy pass through it to enter the innermost chamber."

It was to be another 400 years before such secrets could be revealed for the enlightenment of the world.

THE BOOK OF CREATION

The discovery of the Sefer ha Yetzirah between the 2nd and 4th centuries CE marked the break between the ancient mystical tradition known as the Work of the Chariot (Merkava) and the birth of the scholarly approach which characterizes the classical Kabbalah.

The principles represented by the sefirotic system were first set down in this anonymous work, which described the 10 spheres as being linked by 22 paths, each one corresponding to a letter in the Hebrew alphabet.

From this point on, the mystical significance of numbers and letters was held to be the key to the Mysteries. The 13th century Kabbalist Abraham Abulafia (1240-92) held that any man who could decipher the key would no longer need to believe in a Messiah because he could become his own Saviour.

"Everyone knows that the letters of our alphabet can be classified as individuals, species and genera ... Every letter is affected by accidents arising from either matter or form."

The secondary theme of the Sefer ha Yetzirah concerns the theory that speech is more than a means of communication; it was, and remains, a medium of creation.

"Every creature and every word comes from a single name," it states. That name is the secret name of God, the utterance of which set into motion the unfolding of existence and which is at the heart of the belief that to know the secret name of something is to exert influence over it.

THE CHRISTIAN

KABBALISTS

"He who shall know the mystery of the gates of Understanding in the Kabbalah shall know also the mystery of the Great Jubilee (the completion of the spiritual cycle)."

(PICO DELLA MIRANDOLA, 15TH CENTURY)

Mirandola, the father of Christian Kabbalah.

During the Renaissance, Christian mystics and scholars attempted to purge the Kabbalah of what they considered to be its "pagan elements". In so doing, they gutted it of its rich spiritual heritage, adopting only its glyph, the Tree of Life, and its cosmology.

By manipulating the numbers and letters which were at the heart of its magical system, they attempted to prove three things: that the Old Testament was essentially Christian in character; that it had predicted the coming of Christ; and finally that it "proved" Christianity to

Trithemius predicted the end of the world.

be the logical culmination of Judaism.

Even after these theories had been discredited, the Kabbalah continued to hold a fascination for humanists, mystics and occult philosophers who found in it verification of their own beliefs in the underlying unity of existence and the principles of universal laws. It is this secular version which has since become central to the Western Mysteries.

While Orthodox Christianity holds to the belief that Man is estranged from God through Sin, those who adopted the Kabbalah understood that Man is only estranged through his ignorance.

In common with other orthodox religions, Christianity teaches that faith, love, good deeds and rigorous adherence to doctrine are all that is required for Man to fulfil his obligations on Earth. The Kabbalist, however, maintains that knowledge is the ladder to self-salvation.

The father of the Christian Kabbalah was the Italian philosopher Giovanni Pico della Mirandola (1463-94 CE), who had been introduced to the basic principles by a converted Jew.

In 1486, Mirandola published his version of the Kabbalah under the title

Conclusiones Philosophicae, Cabalisticae Et Theologicae, in which he attempted to prove that the Kabbalah was the key to the Christian mysteries and also that it was the common thread linking Christianity to Greek philosophy.

The Church promptly declared him a heretic and condemned him for advocating the use of magic, but this only seemed to spur him on. "Magic," he argued, "is the highest and holiest form of philosophy."

In the cosmology of the Kabbalah, Mirandola found an explanation of how the word of God manifested on Earth in the form of Man, and how the myth of a Messiah is crucial to humanity – even to those who deny him.

The reinterpretation of the Kabbalah, which Johann Reuchlin (1455-1522 CE) drew up for a mainly Christian readership, had been accumulated from authentic Hebrew manuscripts, but this did not prevent its author from arriving at a number of erroneous conclusions. The manuscripts had been given to him as a gift by the grateful rabbis of

Pforzheim, on whose behalf he had interceded after the Emperor Maximillian I had ordered all Hebrew books to be burnt.

Reuchlin a former embassy attaché. diplomatically dedicated his book, *De Arte Cabalistica* (known as "The Bible Of The Christian Cabala"), to Pope Leo X, and was thereby spared the unwelcome attentions of the Inquisition.

Reuchlin knew that the Pope was interested in pythagorism, so he presented his theories in the form of a dialogue between a Pythagorean philosopher, a Muslim and a Jewish Kabbalist. The Jewish scholar explains that, "the cabala must never be sought through the crude contact of the senses, nor by logic".

In Reuchlin's view, the Kabbalah is "a symbolic theology, in which letters and names are not only the signs for things, but also their very essence." Although he maintained that the Kabbalah held the meaning of Jesus' mission, he helped promote the idea that all religions express the same ultimate truth.

The early Christian Kabbalists were educated aristocrats, but in their eagerness to prove the divinty of Christ they lost the spiritual core of the Kabbalah.

TRITHEMIUS AND THE SEVEN ANGELS

The most unlikely Kabbalist was John Trithemius (1462-1516), a German monk turned magician, whose library of 2000 volumes of occult lore drew students from all over Europe, including Johann Reuchlin.

Like Reuchlin, Trithemius fell foul of Emperor Maximillian I, who personally interrogated the monk after a letter had been intercepted, in which Trithemius described a book he was working on. "This book, in which I teach many little-known secrets and mysteries, will seem to all, especially the ignorant, full of superhuman, amazing, incredible things. Nobody else has ever spoken of them before me."

Despite his boast, these 'secrets' had been known for centuries, One theory, for which he can take full credit, was that of the seven angels which, he claimed, govern the seven planets from Creation to the end of the world. Each apparently reigns for 354 years and four months, a cycle which is repeated three times in total, meaning that the world is due to end in 2235!

However, Trithemius can not readily be dismissed as a crackpot, since he correctly predicted both the Great Fire of London and Luther's break with the Catholic church!

THE KABBALISTIC MYSTERIES

NOSTRADAMUS

" ... illustrious Michael Nostradamus, whose near divine pen was alone, in the judgement of all mortals, worthy to record under the inspiration of the stars, the future events of the whole world."

(MEMORIAL INSCRIPTION)

The prophecies of the French astrologer and physician Michael Nostradamus (1503-66), which the seer published in the form of 1000 cryptic quatrains (four-line verses), have given rise to much scholarly interpretation as well as spurious speculation over the past 400 years.

Although it is commonly believed that the Seer of Salon, as he was known, obtained his prophetic visions from studying the stars, astrological techniques alone (which are based on birth charts) could not account for the vast majority of his predictions which concerned people yet to be born.

As a young man, Nostradamus was taught Hebrew, Greek, Latin, astrology and medicine by his Jewish grandfathers, both of whom had been physicians and astrologers to "Good King René" of Anjou, Provence.

From them, the young Nostradamus would certainly have learnt the principles and practices of the Kabbalah with which he could have cultivated a natural talent for prophecy (although the Kabbalah itself is not a system of divination).

From clues encoded in the opening quatrains of his first book of verses,

Centuries (1555), it would appear that Nostradamus procured his uncannily accurate prophecies by use of a magical method once practised by the priestesses of the Greek Oracle at Didyma.

The Oracle's method of divination was recorded by the neoplatonist philosopher Iamblichus, who wrote: "The prophetess of Branchus either sits upon a pillar, or holds in her hand a rod bestowed by some deity, or moistens her feet or the hem of her garment with water ... and by these means ... she prophesies."

The description is strikingly like the system alluded to by Nostradamus in his opening quatrains.

"Sitting alone at night in secret study, Rested on a brazen tripod, An exigous flame comes from the solitude, Making successful that worthy of belief. The handheld wand is placed in the midst of the BRANCHES, He moistens with water his foot and garment's hem, Fear and a Voice make him quake in his sleeves, Divine splendour, the divine sits nigh."

The importance leant to the word "BRANCHES" by the use of capital letters suggests an allusion to the Greek god of prophecy, Branchus, from whom the prophetesses at Didyma received their visions. Nostradamus' own prophecies began in middle age with

Nostradamus published his prophecies in 1000 cryptic verses.

Nostradamus procured his prophecies by the same method as the Greek oracles.

involuntary flashes of precognition, or second sight. The earliest recorded occurrence was in Italy when he fell on his knees before a young monk, hailing him as "Your Holiness". It was only after Nostradamus' death that the monk, Felix Peretti, became Pope Sixtus V.

On another occasion, Nostradamus' talents were tested by a sceptical gentleman, a Seigneur de Florinville, with whom he was lodging. Florinville teased Nostradamus that he could not predict which of two pigs they would dine on that evening, whereupon Nostradamus calmly predicted that a wolf would eat the white pig leaving them to eat the black one.

His host immediately ordered the cook to kill the white pig, but after the animal had been slaughtered it was eaten by a young wolf cub which was kept in the household as a pet. The cook had no choice but to cook the black pig and the host was forced to eat the creature along with his words.

Demonstrations such as these ensured

Nostradamus' growing reputation as a seer and encouraged him to begin the series of prophecies which were to occupy him until the end of his life.

It may be significant that his predictions relating to events after the French Revolution have proved less reliable than those closer to his own time.

It would appear to show that the future is continually being revised by the increasing number of choices which we are daily forced to make, as individuals and collectively as nations. While we appear to be susceptible to astrological influences and guided by our own natures, our futures are largely determined by the one unpredictable element of human nature – free will.

NOSTRADAMUS AND THE NAZIS

To avoid being accused of practising black magic, Nostradamus couched many of his predictions within obscure symbolism and linguistic codes. Unfortunately, this deliberate ambiguity makes it relatively easy to draw a number of different conclusions from a single verse.

For example, the quatrains which are commonly believed to refer to the rise of Nazi Germany have been given a less dramatic, but no less plausible explanation by the English writer Robert Graves.

"Hunger-maddened beasts will make the streams tremble; Most of the land will be under Hister; in a cage of iron the great one will be dragged, When the child of Germany observes nothing." (II, 24)

Although it appears to be a clear reference to Hitler and the Nazis, it is Graves' contention that the verse refers to the decline of Venice. For Graves, Hister meant the Ister (the classical name for the river Danube), which seems more likely given the repetition of the name in another verse.

"In a place not far from Venus

the two greatest ones of Asia and Africa, of the Rhine and Hister will be said to come; cries and tears at Malta and on the coast of Liguria."

On the other hand, those who side with the "Hitler" interpretation read into this verse a reference to the Tripartite pact between Japan, Italy and Germany.

The third and final stanza is equally ambiguous.

"Liberty will not be recovered; it will be occupied by one who is black, proud, low-born and iniquitous; when the matter of the bridge is open, of Hister, Venice is greatly annoyed at the republic."

This would appear to be a reference to the concordat, the treaty signed between the Vatican and Mussolini in 1928 with the pope, Pontifex Maximus, likened to a bridge between the Vatican and the fascists (pontifex is Latin for "bridge-maker"). Graves however, argues that it is speaking of the disquiet aroused in Venice when Charles V of Austria sought to interfere in the politics of Italy and Malta after he became Charles I of Spain.

THE ESSENES

"The Law was planted in the garden of the brotherhood to enlighten the heart of Man ... all the hidden things of truth and secrets of inner knowledge."

(THE BOOK OF HYMNS OF THE DEAD SEA SCROLLS)

Until the discovery of the Dead Sea scrolls in 1947, little was known about the Essenes, a puritanical Jewish brotherhood referred to in the writings of Philo of Alexandria, Plinius and Josephus Flavius.

With the discovery of the 500 manuscripts, all that survived of the Essenes' library, in the caves near Qumran, northwestern Jordan, the significance of the sect has become the subject of heated debate and unresolved controversy. It is not the authenticity of the manuscripts which is in dispute, but the nature of the sect itself and, in particular, the identity of their anonymous leader, "The True Teacher" or "Teacher of Righteousness" who may, or may not, have been Jesus.

The Essenes synthesized a profound and ageless wisdom, which once permeated the religions of Egypt, India, Persia, Greece, China, Tibet and Palestine, into a spiritual philosophy which has influenced all the major religious movements founded in its wake.

Although their origins are lost in the mists of prehistory, it is likely that the Essenes were the elect to whom Moses imparted the esoteric communions he received on Mount Sinai; whereas the mass of Israelites were given the exoteric teachings – the Ten Commandments.

The Essene Book Of Moses differs in small but significant details from the version in the Old Testament. In place of the commandment to obey one's own mother and father, for example, there is the reference to harmonizing the forces of heaven and earth.

"Honour thy Earthly Mother, that thy days may be long upon the land, and honour thy Heavenly Father, that eternal life be thine in the heavens, for the earth and the heavens are given unto thee by the Law which is thy God."

However, the concept of an Earthly Mother and Heavenly Father are alien to traditional Judaism, which has prompted the theory that they may have been

Were John the Baptist and Jesus the Messianic leaders anticipated by the Essenes?

followers of Enoch from whom they took the concept of an "angelic" world .

They appreciated the fact that the quality of thought can affect the body and they tried to work with both the conscious and subconscious mind. They can also be said to have practised early forms of yoga, sensitizing the subtle energy centres of the body to receive earthly and cosmic forces.

The Essenes lived at a time of crisis known as "the Last Times", 200 BCE-100 CE, when predictions of imminent apocalypse and final Divine Judgement were rife. However, the brotherhood believed that crises were all part of the ebb and flow of evolution and that each one helped to precipitate progress. In their spiritual outpost in the desert, they composed

The caves of Qumran where the Dead Sea Scrolls were discovered.

themselves in readiness for the coming of the Messiah.

It is said that the Essenes were anticipating the coming of not one but two Messiahs: the first in the form of a priest who would redeem his followers through suffering and the other in the likeness of a king who would be wise and

regal. Many believed that John the Baptist fulfilled the former role and Jesus the latter.

If it is ever proved beyond doubt that Jesus was the "Teacher of Righteousness" referred to in the Dead Sea scrolls, the Jews may have to acknowledge that they failed to recognize their own Messiah and have dismissed his teachings.

If, however, as seems likely from the evidence, the "Teacher" was someone else – possibly Asaph ben Berechiah, a master of the occult and a confidant of King Solomon who lived 200 years earlier – it is the Christian faith which may have to reappraise its origins and acknowledge its debt to an initiate of the Essenes: a healer and Kabbalist, born Joshua ben Miriam, a man who was later known as Jesus.

EARTHLY AND COSMIC FORCES

The Essenes identified seven earthly forces which they referred to as the Angels of the Earthly Mother (comprising the Angels of the Sun, Water, Air, Earth, Life, Joy and the Earthly Mother) and seven cosmic forces, or Angels of the Heavenly Father (the Angels of Power, Love, Wisdom, Eternal Life, Work, Peace and the Eternal Father). They believed that these forces surround and permeate everything in the universe, that they work in harmony with the

Law (God) and that man must tune in to them if he is to achieve fulfilment and joy, which are his Divine right.

But the Essenes also accepted that man is not perfect and that his thoughts, emotions and actions frequently cause him to deviate from the Law and come into conflict with these forces, creating problems.

As a brotherhood, the Essenes aimed to live in harmony with these forces and the Law through daily communes in the morning

and evening, when they would meditate on the qualities and purpose of each "angel". To assist this meditation, they utilized a symbol they called the Tree of Life. This was similar to the sacred Bodhai tree of Buddhism, with seven branches stretching upwards to represent the heavenly forces and seven roots representing the earthly forces. Man was set at the foot of the trunk at the point of equilibrium between the upper and lower levels.

THE WESTERN
MYSTERY
TRADITION

The Western Mystery Tradition is not a clearly defined stream leading off from the source of all wisdom. It is a deceptively deep pool filled from diverse sources – pagan mythology, Celtic nature magic, Greek philosophy, the Judaic Kabbalah, Christian scholarship and Eastern mysticism.

On the surface, this Tradition reflects the light of Christianity but the early Christians were themselves an ill-defined and divided movement, a Judaic-Hellenistic sect with each group differing in their interpretation of the teachings of Jesus.

A faction known as the Gnostics advocated direct knowledge of the Mysteries as experienced by the Kabbalist Saul of Tarsus (Saint Paul) who had ascended through the 10 heavens "in the spirit". But the dominant faction, which eventually evolved into the orthodox Church, suppressed these teachings and thereby their own spiritual heritage. They edited and revised the gospels and renounced the possibility of reincarnation, a concept which recently discovered gospels appear to have endorsed. Whole communities of early Christian sects such as the Gnostics and the Cathars were tortured in the name of a Master who had preached only peace. Consequently, the Western Mystery Tradition has always run a troubled course with many of its greatest thinkers condemned as heretics and sorcerers, which has led to our enduring obsession with secrecy and secret societies.

As late as 1122, the French Christian scholar Peter Abelard was striving to overturn the dogma of blind faith which declared: "I must believe in order that I may understand." Instead, he stated, "I must understand in order that I may believe," adding, "By doubting we come to questioning and by questioning we come to perceive the truth."

JESUS – THE MAN AND

THE MYTH

"That which you do not know, I myself will teach you...

In Me, know the Word of Wisdom"

The enduring image of Jesus as the martyred messiah was an invention of the early Church.

Orthodox Christianity was founded on the belief that Jesus was the Christ, the one and only Son of God, the Messiah that the Jews had prophesied but not accepted.

No thought appears to have been given to the possibility that he may have been one of many divinely inspired teachers, or what the Hindus call an avatar, the incarnation of an aspect of the Divine who appears at moments of supreme crisis to awaken mankind and take on its suffering, but not its "sins". (The idea of sin is, after all, a human concept.)

In the proto-Gnostic texts, which predate the "official" gospels, Jesus is never referred to as "Christ", "Saviour" or "the Son of God". These titles originated with the early Church which obviously thought a Messianic, apocalyptic prophet would provide more persuasive propaganda than a pacifist teacher who claimed that the Kingdom of God was already here.

To this end, the Church judiciously edited the later, narrative gospels, which were tailored to fit the required image of the martyred miracle worker and Messiah. These scriptures deified Jesus by according him a virgin birth, the traditional method of endorsing prophets since the time of Zoroaster. Even Pythagoras and the Chinese sage Lao Tzu were supposed to have been the products of immaculate conception.

Other features of the Christ myth were derived from pre-Christian and pagan cultures. The central figure in the Persian mystery cult of Mithras was said to have been born on December 25 after being watched over by shepherds and, later, presided over his own Last Supper before being crucified – only to rise from the dead three days later!

In her book *Jesus The Man*, Barbara Thiering, an Australian scholar, argues that the "miracles", which have been an integral part of the myth, may originally have been intended as allegories of the reforms which Jesus brought about. For example, the story of Jesus turning water into wine may actually have been a veiled reference to Jesus dissolving the two-tier system of communion by water and wine practised by the Essenes.

The Essene community at Qumran by the Dead Sea offered baptism in water for the lower orders, reserving baptism by wine for those who embraced the monastic life. Water was considered good enough for the "unclean" – lepers, gentiles, married men, disabled people and women. By allowing everybody to take communion with wine, Jesus could be said to have turned water into wine.

Thiering finds equally plausible explanations for many other miracles and events described in the New Testament. In driving the money-changers from the temple, Jesus might have been overturning the practice of selling membership to various religious sects, which King Herod had set up 70 years earlier as a method of keeping the population under control. In the gospels, the moneychangers are described as selling "oxen, sheep and doves", which Thiering argues is not only highly unlikely in a place of worship but, as she discovered, these particular animals were the insignia of various groups in the region. Labourers had oxen as their emblem, village Essenes had a sheep to show they were followers of David, the shepherd king, and yet another group wore the sign of a dove to indicate that they stood for Peace. By paying for "oxen, sheep and doves", the wealthy would have been appeasing the authorities and buying

absolution at the same time.

In trying to bring about reform, Jesus would certainly have aroused the antipathy of the priests, and so may well have become known as the "Wicked Priest" rather than the "Teacher of Righteousness" mentioned in the Dead Sea Scrolls, although there is no conclusive proof that Jesus and the Essene leader thus referred to were contemporaries. The "Wicked Priest" was described as practising baptism and prophesying the rise of a new Jerusalem, but he was opposed to the harsh ascetic lifestyle demanded by his rival the "Teacher of Righteousness". According to the documents recovered from the caves near Qumran, the "Wicked Priest" was delivered to the gentiles and died as the "suffering servant" ("the Prince of the congregation, the Branch of David").

Few of the Christian myths were unique to Christianity and they only

Were the money-changers driven out of the temple for selling salvation?

served to separate the man from the message, a message which had been meant for all mankind. If we can first strip away the mythology, we may finally come closer to that message.

THE LAST TESTAMENT?

In 1927 in an extraordinary series of books entitled Life And Teaching Of The Masters Of The Far East, "spiritual explorer" Baird T Spalding described how he and his fellow travellers crossed the Gobi desert to seek the counsel of the "Hidden Masters".

Spalding claimed that during their expedition, he and his party were privileged to enjoy several psychic encounters with the spirit of Jesus, who spoke of himself as having been an incarnation of the Christ spirit.

"The history of the Christ did

not begin with my birth," he is reputed to have told them, "neither did it end with the crucifixion. The Christ was born when God created man in His own image and likeness. The Christ and that man are one; all men and that man are one ... That the Christ means more than the man Jesus goes without contradiction. Had I not perceived this I could not have brought forth the Christ ... When I said, 'I am the Christ, the only begotten of God', I did not declare this for myself alone, for had I done this I could not

have become the Christ ... in order to bring forth the Christ, I, as well as all others, must declare it; then must live the life, and the Christ must appear ... There are a great many of us joined together to help the whole world and this is our lifework. There have been times when it has taken our combined energies to ward off the evil thoughts, of doubt and disbelief and superstition that have nearly engulfed mankind. You may call them evil forces if you wish. We know that they are evil only as man makes them so."

THE GOSPEL OF THOMAS

"These are the hidden logia which the living Jesus spoke and

Didymos Judas Thomas wrote."

"And he said:

He who finds the inner meaning of these logia

Will not taste death"

So begins the Gospel of Thomas, the so-called "lost" gospel, which is believed to contain the wisdom teachings of Jesus as recorded by Thomas, his most beloved disciple.

The early Christian Church declared the gospel heretical because it did not conform to their image of Jesus as the Christ, the Messiah and the Son of God. Consequently, they ordered all copies to be destroyed.

For almost 2000 years, it was thought that not even a fragment had survived. Then, in 1945, a complete Coptic text translated from the Greek original was discovered among the Gnostic manuscripts at Nag Hammadi in Upper Egypt. Since then, the Gospel of Thomas has been at the centre of a controversy which promises to accelerate the disintegration of orthodox Christianity – unless the Church agrees to reappraise its origins and aims.

The disciples, who each went their separate ways after the crucifixion, are known to have differed over their inter-

Thomas, whose 'lost' gospel may contain the original teachings of Jesus.

pretation of Jesus' teachings: they also disagreed over his true nature and purpose. Consequently, each gospel presents its own version of Jesus' teachings according to the beliefs of its author.

It is worth noting too that, where the gospel of Thomas shares a parable with another gospel, it does not necessarily arrive at the same allegorical interpretation. This suggests that these interpretations may have been added at a later date to endorse the views of theologians. It also makes a strong case for the Gospel of Thomas as the source of the other gospels.

Thomas is said to have been especially close to Jesus to the extent that he is often affectionately referred to as his brother or "twin" – both "Didymos" and "Thomas" translate as "twin" – suggesting a strong spiritual affinity between the two. Thomas' gospel is unique in that, unlike the "authorized" gospels, it does not contain any narrative on the life of Jesus, nor any commentary on his teachings. In addition, no mention is made of the Virgin birth, the "miracles", the crucifixion or the resurrection. The text is composed entirely of Jesus' words (114 verses called "logion" from the Greek logos, meaning "the word"), leaving the interpretation to the reader.

It is in the interpretation that the wisdom of Jesus is revealed, shorn of all the Messianic mythology and dogma which was imposed upon it over ensuing centuries. In contrast to the other gospels, Thomas' Jesus does not prophesy an apocalypse with the coming of God's Kingdom on earth, but instead denounces all those who put their faith in such prophecies.

"His followers said to him, 'Twenty-four prophets have spoken in Israel, and they all spoke of you.'

He said to them, 'You have disregarded the living one who is in your presence and have spoken of the dead'."

References to "the dead" occur elsewhere and, in this context, imply that all those who are not awakened to the true reality of life are as the dead.

Asked when "the new world" will come, Jesus points out that it is already here, but until we are awakened we cannot see it. "What you look for has come, but you do not know it." And later, " ... the father's Kingdom is spread out upon the earth and people do not see it."

The verses repeatedly stress that "the Kingdom" is within us – and not, as the Church has insisted, in the heavens barred to the "sinner" by Saint Peter. One reason for the Church's vehement opposition to the Thomas gospel was the inclusion of Jesus' repeated warning to us not to entrust our spiritual development and well-being to others, be they priests, politicians or prophets. "Jesus said:

If those who guide your Being say to you: 'Behold the Kingdom is in the Heaven',
then the birds of the sky will precede you,
if they say to you: 'It is in the sea',
then the fish will precede you.
But the Kingdom is in your centre
And is about you.
When you know your Selves
then you will be known
and you will be aware that you are the sons of the Living Father.
But if you do not know yourselves
then you are in poverty, and you are the poverty."

The last line seems to be saying that not only would we be the poorer for ignoring our divine nature, but that by refusing to take responsibility for our progress, we will be perpetuating spiritual ignorance.

It may be significant that, after the death of his beloved teacher, Thomas journeyed to the East while all the other disciples travelled westwards.

Luke appears to have completed his gospel from a 'lost' text.

Matthew and the other disciples may have founded a rival sect to thwart Thomas.

THE GOSPEL ACCORDING TO "Q"

Even before the discovery of the Thomas manuscript, scholars had suspected that both Matthew and Luke had compiled their gospels from the same source, a lost "sayings gospel", which they named "Q" after the German word for "source" (Quelle).

In an effort to discover what it might have contained they compared the two "official" gospels, filtering out all the sayings that were shared by both works as original source material. After the discovery of the Thomas manuscript, the scholars compared the works and discovered that about a third of the material in "Q" was shared by Thomas leaving a large amount of material that appeared to have been taken from another source, a second "lost gospel".

It now seems likely that there were two opposing groups of early Christians, one of which adhered to the proto-Gnostic teachings recorded in "Thomas" and "Q" – these present Jesus as a simple holy man – while the other faction adapted and revised both "sayings gospels" to fit their need for an apocalyptic saviour.

A campaign is currently being waged by scholars to have the Gospels of Thomas and "Q" included in the Bible, but this is vehemently opposed by the Church which claims that the canon is the "property of the Church" and therefore not to be challenged.

GNOSTICISM – THE SEARCH FOR SECRET KNOWLEDGE

"Gnosticism is a quest for redeeming knowledge and a quest for one's self."

(M MIRABAIL, THE FIFTY KEY WORDS OF ESOTERICISM)

During the formative years of Christianity, a number of ascetic groups known as Gnostics (from the Greek "gnosis" meaning "knowledge") emerged to challenge the authority of the church and its interpretation of the teachings of Jesus. Although each sect differed in its doctrines and practices, some quite radically, they all shared the belief that man's salvation depended on his search for secret knowledge, knowledge they claimed lay hidden in the gospels.

The Gnostics placed the pursuit of knowledge above faith, a fact which brought them into conflict with the church, culminating in their violent repression and dispersal by the 4th century CE. Thousands of Gnostic texts were destroyed by the church.

According to Gnostic doctrine, it was not sufficient merely to have faith. Salvation only comes through self-knowledge. In the Gnostic texts, Jesus says: *"If you bring forth what is within you, what you bring forth will save you.*

If you do not bring forth what is within you, what you do not bring forth will destroy you."

The Gnostic view of Christ was that he brought salvation not from sin, but from ignorance. Ignorance was seen as the root-cause of all human suffering.

The Gnostics found the idea of Jesus' resurrection "in the flesh" abhorrent – the flesh was to be despised as the prison of the soul – and they considered Jesus to be beyond matter, a projection of the divine being, not a man of flesh and blood.

The destruction of the library at Alexandria – a symbol of "lost" knowledge.

The Gnostics further antagonized orthodox Christianity by claiming that the Church Fathers had only insisted that Jesus returned in the flesh after his crucifixion naming Peter as his successor, so that those who claimed to have witnessed his resurrection could not be denied. In this way, the church legitimized the succession of Peter as first Bishop of Rome and those of his successors. In fact, the Gnostics were not blaspheming God, as the church accused them of doing, but were against a church they accused of having set itself up as the intermediary between God and man.

The established church promised that, in return for a little patience and faith, the world would be miraculously healed by divine intervention, but the Gnostics encouraged men to change themselves. Valentinus, the most renowned of Gnostic teachers, stated that by attaining self-knowledge each individual would be contributing to the universal order, restoring the Universe to its primordial unity.

The Gnostic philospher Philo of Alexandria (c. 20 BCE-50 CE) is believed to have been the originator of the doctrine of the 'Logos', later adapted by the Christian scholars. In the original Greek text the Gospel of St John declared:

"In the beginning was the logos and the logos was with God and the logos was God."

Although the Gnostics professed to be seekers after secret knowledge and spirituality, in practice they appear to have been intolerant, often inhumane and elitist. Collectively, they constituted an anti-Semitic, ascetic sect with little love for the world or its inhabitants. One of the most disturbing aspects of the movement was its wholesale revisionist attitude to the Old Testament, whereby destructive characters such as Cain and Esau were regarded as misunderstood heroes. This may have been due to their rather confused cosmology which mixed the Greek belief in a transcendent God with the patriarchal creator of the Old Testament.

In Gnostic cosmology, the supreme God of Truth was transcendent, beyond good and evil, and did not interfere with the ways of the world. He was the Divine Being, the loving father, whom Jesus spoke of. Beneath him, a second, minor Creator (the demiurge) held dominion over the world and was the cruel and capricious God of the Old Testament. This God was unaware of his true origins and believed

himself to be the only God. The material world was considered evil, because it was ruled by this deluded deity, while the world of the spirit was held to be good. Life was to be endured not enjoyed, all striving, other than that towards knowledge of the Divine Being, was considered futile.

At a time when the world was in a state of confusion, Gnosticism appealed to many and it continues to hold some attraction for those who cannot comprehend a God who refuses to intervene in a world full of apparent evil and injustice.

Th Gnostics saw the many evils of the world as acts of a deluded God.

THE GNOSTIC MANUSCRIPTS

Almost all Gnostic texts were destroyed by the early Christian Church Fathers, though a number of manuscripts survived, hidden in tombs and caves throughout Egypt for nearly 2000 years.

In 1945, the most significant of these, the Nag Hammadi codices, were unearthed by an Arab peasant and his brothers digging in the mountain caves of Jabalmal-Tarif for fertilizer. Returning to their home with the bundles of papyri wrapped in leather, they deliberated over what to do next. By the time

they had decided to try and sell their find, their mother had burned most of it in the oven to warm herself! What remained they sold for a small sum, unaware that they had made a discovery as significant as that of the Dead Sea Scrolls.

The Nag Hammadi texts were written immediately before and after Christ's life, which implies that they are "truer to the word of Jesus" than the New Testament Gospels which were written up to several hundred years later. For this reason, they were regarded by

scholars as "spiritual dynamite" and their publication was delayed for over 45 years.

Among the 53 surviving texts are gospels which were not included in the New Testament. The First Apocalypse of James is said to contain the original, uncorrupted teachings of Jesus whom the author refers to as "Rabbi" and in which Jesus talks of his followers as "the sons of light" – a term used in the Dead Sea Scrolls by the Jewish sect of the Essenes, and not by the early Christians.

IN SEARCH OF THE

HOLY GRAIL

"Any object, intensely regarded, may be a gate of access to the aeon of the gods."

(JAMES JOYCE)

The Knights of the Round Table were renowned for their valour and skill at arms, but only the humblest of them succeeded in finding the Grail.

The Holy Grail of Arthurian legend is the cup from which Christ drank during the last supper, but the mythology is far older than Christianity and the Grail has become much more than a sacred artefact. For many, it is a symbol of lost wisdom. For mystically-minded Christians, the legend of King Arthur's quest for the Grail is an allegory for the spiritual journey to the Divine. It is also a fable of how simple faith, the faith of the lowliest knight, Sir Perceval, is shown to be all that is required to find the "treasure" of God.

For modern mystics and occultists, the imagery and archetypes of the Grail legend are used for an inner-journey of self-discovery known as Path Working and, in this form, the Grail itself is often visualized as the vessel of secret wisdom hidden in the depths of the psyche. Those who work with the Grail imagery in this way explore various states of consciousness equivalent to the paths on the kabbalistic Tree of Life. By identifying with Arthur, Lancelot or Merlin, modern mystics can explore aspects of their own psyches which correspond to the qualities embodied by these characters. It becomes almost irrelevant whether these figures really lived or not, or even whether the Grail itself ever existed.

The Grail is the spiritual centre for the knight on his quest – in seeking it, or the similar symbols of other traditions (the Sufis, Greeks, Tibetan Buddhists and pre-Christian Celts all had their "cups of knowledge"), the seeker attempts to find his true nature.

It is significant that the three knights who succeeded in finding the Grail personify those qualities deemed necessary for setting out on a spiritual quest. Sir Galahad is depicted as the pure knight whose way is the way of the Spirit; Sir Perceval, the simple knight, walks the way of the Heart; while Sir Bors, the contemplative, goes the way of the Mind. The characters of the Grail Quest represent the full range of human aspirations and experience. It may also be worth noting that the knights who found the Grail were all said to have consequently lost the power of speech. What they had learnt in their search was evidently not to be conveyed to those who had not made the same journey themselves.

The idea that the Grail is the key to an ageless secret knowledge and not just a Christian relic comes from the most unlikely of sources – the Bavarian knight Wolfram von Eschenbach, author of the most celebrated Grail romance, *Parzival*, on which Wagner's opera was based. In his introduction to the tale, von Eschenbach claims that his text is the only authoritative version because it was based on the writings of a Jewish alchemist named Flegetanis, which predated all other known versions of the story. Flegetanis' manuscript was given to von Eschenbach by a singer from Provence named Kyot, who is credited with translating it.

"Kyot," wrote the Bavarian nobleman, "the well-known master, found in Toledo, discarded, set down in heathen writing, the first source of this adventure. He first had to learn the abc's, but without the art of black magic ... A heathen, Flegetanis, had achieved high renown for his learning. This scholar of nature was descended from Solomon and born of a family which had long been Israelite until baptism became our shield against the fire of Hell. He wrote the adventure of the Grail ... The heathen Flegetanis could tell us how all the stars set and rise again ... To the circling course of the stars man's affairs and destiny are linked. Flegetanis the heathen saw with his own eyes in the constellations things he was shy to talk about, hidden mysteries. He had said there was a thing called the Grail, whose name he had read

The Knights' quest for the Grail was a metaphor for the inner journey.

clearly in the constellations. A host of angels left it on the earth." The reference to "heathen" in this context is to Hebrew, while the reference to learning "the abc's, but without the art of black magic" is most certainly a reference to the Hebrew alphabet and the Kabbalah. It may also prove significant that Kyot's home region of Provence in the south of France was a centre for Cathar and Sufi mystics.

The mystical meaning of the Grail Quest is that wisdom is not found in sacred relics or mouldering medieval *grimoires* – magical texts – but within ourselves. It awaits all who seek the Grail of spirit.

SECRETS OF THE GRAIL

The following exercise is just one example of how the archetypes and images of the Grail legend can be used to search for self-knowledge. The details will change each time you practise the exercise.

Make yourself comfortable in a chair. Close your eyes. Breathe deeply, concentrating on your breath, counting it in cycles of three until you feel relaxed. Then imagine entering a peaceful wooded glade. Take your time and note as much detail as you can. After a few moments, you notice a door at the far end of the glade partially hidden by vines. Brush

these aside and push the door gently open.

Step inside and, as your eyes adjust to the light, you find you are inside a secret chamber. Again, take your time to fill in the details. What kind of chamber is it? Highly decorated or hewn roughly from the earth? Before you, at the far end of the chamber, is an altar upon which you glimpse the outline of a chalice. This is the Grail for which you have searched for so long and endured so much. Take a few minutes and ask any question you desire, or simply ask what message the Grail has for you

at this moment in your life.

Then approach the Grail, pick it up and look into it. What is written inside the chalice? If you see nothing now, do not despair. The answer may come in a day or two.

Now replace the cup and, as soon as you feel ready to leave the hidden chamber, go back the way you came.

Return gently to normal consciousness by counting from 10 down to 1. Analyzing the imagery after each exercise should reveal much about your subconscious state, secret fears and aspirations.

THE CATHARS –

CUSTODIANS OF THE

CHRISTIAN SECRET?

"God is not all powerful. He is totally simple, he does not desire evil and cannot perpetuate it. "

(THE BOOK OF TWO PRINCIPLES)

The ruthlessness with which the Cathars were persecuted by the Catholic Church in the 13th century has lent weight to modern theories that the sect might have been custodians of a secret that, had it gained widespread acceptance, would have brought about the downfall of the papacy. This secret, enigmatically referred to as "the Cathar treasure", is said to have been smuggled out of the sect's besieged citadel at Montségur in southwest France in 1244, prior to their capitulation, and preserved in code in the trumps of tarot cards for the future illumination of humanity.

Any thought of a "treasure" consisting of precious artefacts can be ruled out, since all the Cathars' monetary wealth is known to have been spirited out of the citadel three months earlier.

The sect may well have guarded a profound secret importance, but their basic teachings appear to have been as dogmatic as any of those they so vehmently opposed. Catharism, like Gnosticism before it, thrived on the deprivation and uncertainty of an era, when only belief in an evil God seemed to explain the injustice and chaos of the world.

The movement, which began as a new form of Gnosticism, took root in the Balkans in the 10th century and, within

The Castle of Montségur.

the space of 200 years, had spread throughout Germany, Flanders, Spain and France, where it flourished in the independent principality of the Languedoc. Here the Cathar community enjoyed a certain security until 1208, when Pope Innocent III declared a merciless crusade to eradicate them. This campaign lasted 20 terrifying years and saw the wholesale slaughter of men, women and children. It was here too that the Inquisition began. Ironically, most of the teachings of the Cathars have survived in the records of the Inquisition, although these should be viewed with a certain amount of scepticism, considering the circumstances under which they were extracted.

The Cathars considered themselves to be part of a movement returning to the purity of the early Christians (hence the name "Cathar" from the Greek *katharos* meaning "clean"), though they referred to each other as "the Good Christians" or "the Goodmen". Like the Gnostics before them, they believed that the world is ruled by an evil force, the God of the Old Testament, often referred to as the Monster of Chaos, while the Supreme Being surveys creation with detachment and does not intervene.

Since the world was essentially evil and the human body a prison of the soul, Cathars forbade procreation because it would bring another soul into the world. Their ultimate aim was the extinction of mankind so that the souls of men could be free in the world of spirit. Until then, only Jesus could offer salvation from the world of matter.

According to the Cathars, Jesus' mission had been to warn mankind that they were worshipping an evil God, a belief which naturally aroused the wrath of the Church. The sect further upset orthodox Christian opinion by insisting that Jesus was a "phantom", an ethereal spirit, not a man of flesh and blood, and therefore could not have died on the cross. They believed that he continued to guide and inspire mankind from a higher plane of existence. His true teachings, they claimed, were to be found in the "sayings" gospels, rather than in the texts edited by the church to legitimize its own authority.

A speech made by Cathar Jacques Authie before the Inquisition in 1305 made this distinction quite clear. *"There are two 'letters', one of which is ours, and which the Son of God gave us when he came into this world, and this is true, reliable and good; but after the Son of God had given it, Satan created an imitation which is false, evil and unreliable, and it is this that the Church of Rome holds to. If those of the Church of Rome saw the*

The God of Light and the God of Illusion – the great symbol of Solomon.

original, few among them would recognize it, for they are blind; and although there may be some among them who would understand it, such is their attachment to the world that they would hide it from others and not wish to follow it."

The Cathars placed no value in faith for their salvation, they were in search of the "gnosis", the knowledge that comes only with direct experience.

So what was the "treasure" of the martyrs of Montségur? One popular theory is that it was the Holy Grail of Arthurian legend, the cup from which Jesus was said to have drunk during the Last Supper. The authors of the controversial book *The Holy Blood and The Holy Grail* believed that it might have been some form of proof that Jesus had survived the cross. Other scholars believe the "treasure" to have been a collection of manuscripts containing the sect's secret teachings, which originated in the Ancient World and which have since been zealously guarded by occult groups in Europe and America.

THE CATHAR TESTAMENT

A curious postscript to the history of the Cathars came to light in 1971 with the publication of a fascinating book, **The Cathars And Reincarnation** *by the late Dr Arthur Guirdham. Guirdham claimed to have uncovered convincing evidence that fate had conspired to reunite the souls of martyred Cathars in "soul groups", some of whom may now be initiates of secret societies dedicated to preserving their teachings. This discovery came after Guirdham*

had subjected a female patient, who was experiencing recurrent nightmares, to regression therapy.

Curiously, it transpired that both she and Dr Guirdham had experienced a similar nightmare about past lives. From her descriptions during hypnosis, it seems that they had both been connected with the Cathars, a sect which both claimed to have had no previous knowledge of.

Dr Guirdham had her recollections of the sect verified by two

eminent scholars in the field and concluded: "Without ever studying it she has a detailed knowledge of its ritual and practices. She acquired some of this knowledge from dreams, others from her recurrent nightmares and from what she calls visions, but most of it was provided by stories and notes she felt impelled to write as a schoolgirl in her early teens. It is utterly impossible that she could have had access to the detailed literature of Catharism at that age."

MAGIC – THE YOGA OF THE WEST?

"Natural magic or physical magic is nothing other than the deepest knowledge of the secrets of nature."

(DEL RIO, 16TH CENTURY)

There appear to be as many definitions of "Magic" as there are people who profess to know its secrets.

Magic is not a clearly defined art with a universal doctrine to which all adhere. It is all things to all men. For some it is an art, for others a science.

The notorious Aleister Crowley defined it as "the Science and Art of causing change to occur in conformity with Will", which left no doubt as to who was at the centre of his universe. Occultist Dion Fortune, however, took a rather more enlightened view, refining the definition to "the art of producing changes of consciousness in accordance with the Will".

For the magi of pre-Zoroastrian Persia (from whom the term "magic" is derived; magi meaning "wise"), it was the practical extension of their religious rites. Throughout the ancient world, the roles of priest and magician were often indistinguishable. As the pagan cults were superseded by monotheistic religions, so the term "magic" became synonymous with the primitive beliefs of the "old religions".

Until recently, orthodox Judaism regarded the Kabbalists as practising a dangerous, if not diabolical art. Now practical kabbalism is being reassessed as the "long lost" mystical aspect of Judaism which may well revitalize the religion.

The Kabbalah itself offers significant insight into the nature of magic and the mind of the magician. Kabbalists have theoretically proven that the forces involved in practical magic operate in the realm of Yesod (Foundation) on the Tree of Life. Yesod is the place of the lower Self, the ego, and with Netzah (Nature) and Hod (Intelligence and Imagination)

The seal of Solomon signifies the Unity of Man and his Universe.

makes up the triad of Yetzirah (Formation) at the lowest point on the Tree – see pages 32-37.

The magician can therefore be regarded as operating in the lowest realm of spiritual endeavour, where the latent forces of nature are acted upon by the imagination and driven by the desires of the ego.

The practice of ceremonial, or High

The practice of "magic" is condemned by orthodox religion as "primitive" and "pagan" because it preserves elements of the old religions.

magic, which developed in Europe during the Middle Ages appears to have originated in Ancient Egypt and Babylonia. Both civilizations had highly developed magical systems which, after their decline, were preserved by the scholars of Alexandria. From there, their ideas and manuscripts filtered through Byzantium and were later carried to Europe by the returning Crusaders and their followers. By the Middle Ages, these had been augmented by a hierarchy of angels and demons from Judaic and Christian cosmology.

The most infamous of medieval grimoires, *The Little Key Of Solomon*, emphasized that even that vilest of magicians, the necromancer (who sought "wisdom" by conferring with the dead), first had to align himself with the angels before dealing with demons.

"God wanted to perfect His works by making a creature which was half divine and half earthly: this is Man whose body is coarse and earthly, while his soul is spiritual and heavenly. He set the earth and all its creatures below man, and gave him the means of drawing close to the angels, who are there, some of them to control the movement of the stars, and others to live in the elements. You can therefore recognize many of them by their signs or their characters and make them familiar and compliant."

Through a combination of Will and aspiration, the medieval magicians of Europe sought to cultivate heightened perception with which they could perceive other levels of existence. They carried out their conjurations within a consecrated circle, sealed with sacred signs and symbols, which effectively

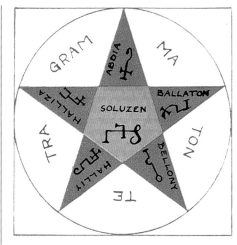

The Pentagram signifies the relation of the human soul to the Absolute.

defined their sphere of influence. It also ensured that having altered their level of consciousness, they still remained "grounded", so that they would not be unbalanced by the sights and sounds that would assail their senses.

SECRET SIGNS AND SYMBOLS

The signs and symbols used by magicians have become familiar to most of us through their use in horror movies and on the covers of occult fiction, but their meaning remains a secret of the adepts. The most common symbols are the geometrical designs representing the Mysteries of creation which were used in rites of conjuration and evocation. Of these, the most familiar are the Triangle and the four-, five- and six-pointed stars known as the Tetragram, the Pentagram and the Seal of Solomon.

The Triangle represented the pre-Christian concept of the trinity of the deity, of time and of creation. The position of the magician at its point or base indicated whether he was conjuring spirits from heaven or from hell. The Tetragram symbolized the four elements and was used in the conjuration of the elementary spirits – the sylphs of the air, the undines of the water, the fire salamanders and the gnomes of the earth.

In alchemy, the Tetragram represented the elements salt, sulphur, mercury and azoth; in occult philosophy, it represented the ideas of Spirit, Matter, Motion and Rest; and, in hieroglyphs, it represented the man, eagle, lion and bull. The

Pentagram was the sign of the Microcosm which could signify Evil if two points were in the ascendant, or Good if standing on two points with one at the top.

It is the Pentagram and not a heavenly star which is said to have led the magi to the birthplace of Jesus of Nazareth. This symbol has been used not only by magicians but also by the Rosicrucians, the Freemasons and modern occultists who utilize it to signify the relation of the human soul to the Absolute.

The Seal of Solomon is symbolic of Man the Microcosm. When enclosed within a circle, it signifies the Unity of all existence.

MAGIC – THE NATURAL PHILOSOPHY

"Man is superior to the stars if he lives in the power of superior wisdom. Such a person, being master over heaven and earth, by means of his will, is a magus and magic is not sorcery but supreme wisdom."

(PARACELSUS)

For Paracelsus, the Renaissance physician, magician and philosopher, magic was a method by which Man could gain insight into his true nature and that of the universe.

"The magical is a great hidden wisdom and reason is a great open folly ... No conjuration, no rites are needful; circle making and the scattering of incense are mere humbug and jugglery. The human spirit is so great a thing that no man can express it; eternal and unchangeable as God Himself is the mind of Man; and could we rightly comprehend the mind of Man, nothing would be impossible to us upon the earth."

The problem, Paracelsus concluded, was that Man undermines his potential by doubting both his divinity and ability to influence his environment. "Because Man did not perfectly believe and imagine, the result is that arts are uncertain when they might be wholly certain."

Practical magic is based on the concept of correspondences, the subtle fields of energy which are said to link minerals, plants and people. The 16th century philosopher and magician Agrippa Von Nettesheim viewed magic as the practical application of these natural laws of sympathy.

"If it is desired to bind and cast a spell by using the influence of the sun or any one of the planets, neither the sun, nor the planet which is invoked to help accomplish the work can hear the prayers addressed to them, but they are moved by a sort of natural link which ensures that all parts of the world communicate with one another and form one whole."

For the 17th century German nature mystic Jakob Boehme, the power source of magic was the life force in nature.

The Welsh alchemist and mystic Thomas Vaughan (who died in 1666) shared Boehme's opinion that magic was a means to Divine Union and claimed to have attained ecstatic states of a religious nature through the practice of magic and alchemy. However, he felt compelled to justify his activities, which he knew would be considered as the way of folly not wisdom.

"That I should profess magic ... and

For the great magician/philosophers Paracelsus and Aggrippa Von Nettesheim spells and conjurations were mere theatrics. The mind of man was the source of true magic.

justify the professors of it withal is impiety with many but religion with me ... Magic is nothing but the Wisdom of the Creator revealed and planted in the creature ... Magicians were the first attendants our saviour met withal in this world, and the only philosophers who acknowledged Him in the flesh before that He Himself discovered."

In *The Lemegeton Of King Solomon*, a notorious book of spells from the 17th century, the magician is viewed as a proto-scientist and philosopher. "Magic is the Highest, most Absolute, and most Divine Knowledge of Natural Philosophy," stated its anonymous author, "advanced in its works and wonderful operations by a right understanding of the inward and occult virtue of things; so that true Agents being applied to proper Patients, strange and admirable effects will thereby be produced. Whence magicians are profound and diligent searchers into Nature; they, because of their skill, know how to

Agrippa believed that the phantoms and phenomena of magic were in the mind.

anticipate an effect, the which to the vulgar shall seem to be a miracle."

By the 19th century, magic, mysticism and science had taken radically different directions. Magic was no longer regarded as a complementary branch of science but as a reaction against rationalism and reason. The religiously-inclined condemned the practice as blasphemous while mystics dismissed it as a dangerous indulgence, a diversion on the path to divine wisdom.

It would be wrong to regard magic as representing the first faltering steps of science. The magicians imagined the world to be inhabited by spirits which they sought to subdue through their Will, while the scientist strives to understand the nature of matter and energy and harness these in accordance with natural laws. And yet, magic acknowledges subtle Universal Laws and other levels of existence, which science, with its theories of parallel universes and sub-atomic particles, is only now beginning to consider.

It seems likely that, for Man to truly comprehend the nature of existence, magic, mysticism and science will ultimately have to be reconciled.

THE PRINCE OF MAGICIANS

Cornelius Agrippa Von Nettesheim, the 16th century occult philosopher dubbed "the Prince of Magicians", believed that the phenomena released through magical rites and invocations were phantoms of the magician's own mind. He therefore recommended that only those with a thorough knowledge of physics, mathematics and theology should consider practising magic.

"Sacred ceremonies and the rite surrounding them have such virtue that even if they are not understood or scrupulously observed, they are none the less effective and clothe us in divine power if they are carried out with faith. Initiation in the mysteries of religion indeed confers dignity and by this dignity you can bring all magic gifts to life."

In such works as his three-

volume encyclopaedia Occult Philosophy, *published in 1531, the recurring theme is that Unity is the fundamental law of the universe and that Man's destiny is to reconcile the forces and elements of the universe within himself. "Man ... hath in himself all that is contained in the greater world, so that there remaineth nothing which is not found even truly and really in Man himself."*

FRIAR BACON

"The end of all true philosophy is to arrive at a knowledge of the Creator through knowledge of the created world."

The English alchemist and visionary Roger Bacon (c. 1214-92) possessed one of the most remarkable minds of his time. Although not an inventor himself, he foresaw the technological revolution of later centuries and anticipated the invention of the laser, aeroplanes, motor cars, tanks, diving suits, poison gas and optical lenses.

Through his alchemical experiments he was one of the first Europeans to appreciate the potential of gunpowder, whilst his geographical writings inspired Columbus to embark on the voyages that were to lead to the discovery of the New World.

He was a free thinker in an age of scholasticism, when knowledge usually came from second-hand sources because scholars had little command of the original language and so were forced to read texts in translation. Bacon maintained that no scholar was worthy of the name unless he was versed in Greek, Arabic and Hebrew, which he considered to be the languages of philosophy and the natural sciences.

While his contemporaries were content with the theories of self-appointed authorities, Bacon did not accept anything until he had proved it for himself. "Authority may impel belief," he wrote, "but cannot enlighten the understanding."

After graduating from Oxford University, which he had entered at the age of 12, Bacon lectured for a time before entering the Franciscan Order in Paris in 1234. There, he studied the secular sciences claiming that his intention was to prove that the Bible contained all knowledge and that there was no substitute for spiritual illumination.

Nevertheless, Pope Clement IV kept him under guard. Bacon was strongly suspected of practising magic, despite his impassioned treatise against it!

"Concerning those secrets, which are revealed in Magicians' writings, although they contain some truth, yet in regard those very truths are enveloped with a number of deceits, as its not very easie to judge betwixt the truth and the falsehood, they ought all worthily to be rejected."

Yet, as a firm believer in the power of the word, Bacon was not prepared to dismiss incantations and conjurations as mere theatre. His conclusion was that practical magic produced a pale imitation of the phenomena which occur in science and nature. His scientific inventions were inspired by a close study of natural phenomena, but ironically his greatest visions were inspired by fear of the Antichrist.

Bacon shared his fellow monks' belief in the imminent arrival of the Antichrist who, he was certain, would use the wonders of science to confound humanity if we did not master the technology in time, " ... such as burning glasses which operate at any distance we can choose, so that anything hostile to the commonwealth may be burnt – a castle, or army or city or anything; and the flying machine, and a navigating machine by which one man may guide a ship full of armed men with incredible speed; and scythe-bearing cars which full of armed men race along with wondrous machinery without horses to draw them, and break down or cut through all obstacles."

Despite these alarming prophecies, it seems likely that Bacon was locked up because of his enthusiasm for alchemy, "the spiritual science", which he divided into its speculative and practical aspects. Speculative alchemy, he wrote, "describes the generation of things from elements or from anything which is inanimate ... This science is unknown by most

Bacon was imprisoned for describing alchemy as "spiritual science".

scholars. Alongside this speculative form of alchemy, there is another which teaches how to make noble metals, colours and many other things by Art, better or more abundantly than they are produced by nature. Such a science has the advantage over all those that went before, for its results are of great usefulness ... Its work confirms theoretical alchemy and, consequently, the natural philosophy of medicine."

When the Pope died in 1268, Bacon was released, returning to Oxford with the great works he had compiled during his solitude, the *Opus Majus*, the *Opus Minus* and the *Opus Tertium*. 10 years later, he was again imprisoned in Paris by the Church authorities because of the "novelties" in his writings, this time for 14 long years. On his release, he returned to Oxford and died shortly afterwards.

Bacon's writings inspired Columbus to embark on his voyages of discovery.

THE FAMOUS HISTORIE OF FRYER BACON

Three hundred years after Bacon's death a highly coloured biography entitled **The Famous Historie Of Fryer Bacon** *was published anonymously.*

Many of the exploits, experiments and adventures were obvious adaptations of medieval stories with our hero interceding on behalf of lovelorn ladies and impoverished gentlemen who have sold their souls to the devil. The final tale, however, appears to be cautionary, for it concludes with a penitent and contrite Friar Bacon renouncing his knowledge as inferior to the doctrines of the Church.

Bacon's fall is brought about by

two youths who pester him to let them look into his "magic mirror", an early camera obscura. When they see their fathers fighting a duel, the youths come to blows and finally kill each other. A remorseful Bacon breaks the glass and calls his students together to make his impassioned speech.

"My good friends and fellow students, it is not unknowne to you, how that through my art I have attained to that credit, that few men living ever had ... I have unlocked the secret of art and nature, and let the world see those things, that have layen hid since the death of Hermes, that rare and

profound philosopher ... yet all this knowledge of mine I esteeme so lightly, that I wish that I were ignorant, and knew nothing: for the knowledge of these things (as I have truly found) serveth not to better a man in goodnesse, but only to make him proud and thinke too well of himselfe. What hath all my knowledge of natures secrets gained me? Onely this, the losse of a better knowledge, the losse of divine studies which makes the immortall part of man blessed."

In despair, the fictional friar then burns his books: Bacon must have been turning in his grave.

ALCHEMY

"I wish with all my heart that he who seeks this secret of the wise men, having considered in his mind these ideas of the life and resurrection to come, should draw profit from them ... I would like him ... to open the eyes of his spirit completely ... these forms have been used to represent some great secrets "

(NICHOLAS FLAMEL, DIED 1417)

The alchemists and the Kabbalists shared a great secret – that all matter, from minerals to man himself, is imbued with a life force which cannot be destroyed but can only be transformed.

For the alchemists, this led to the search for the "Philosopher's Stone", the legendary substance thought to be capable of transmuting base metals into gold, curing all afflictions and bestowing eternal youth. This search was bound up with the hunt for the "prima materia", what today would be known as the DNA from which all life had been created.

The mysterious amalgam the alchemists sought was said to have originated in fire, been brought forth in water, carried down from the heavens by the wind and cultivated in the earth. It therefore combined the four elements which, once processed, would reveal the secret source of all life.

For some, the search culminated in discoveries which would lay the foundation for modern chemistry. For others, it ended in destitution,

The alchemists sought the secrets of life by transmuting base matter into the gold of spirit.

despair or death as punishment for dabbling in the magical arts. But those who looked beyond the symbolism found a parallel science – spiritual alchemy, the means by which man could transform his base elements into the pure gold of spirit. In refining the elements which make up humankind, they too hoped to discover the secret of all creation.

"The physical Philosopher's Stone and the mystical Philosopher's Stone are similar but not identical. To achieve the second, is to be able to achieve the first supremely. Having achieved the first, one knows which way may lead to the achievement of the second, but it does not necessarily mean that the journey has been made. The distinction is essential."

(Savoret, *What Is Alchemy?*)

Although its origins are obscure, the word "alchemy" is thought to derive from the Arabic al chem, meaning "the art of Egypt". Certainly the earliest known alchemical texts, dated around 200 BCE, are of Egyptian origin. In these, a system of correspondences was drawn up detailing how the various metals and minerals were subtly affected by the planets whose qualities they embodied. Saturn was said to be in sympathy with lead; Jupiter with tin; Mars with iron; Venus with copper; Mercury with mercury; the Moon with silver and the Sun with gold.

It was believed that if one could break the code in which the alchemists enciphered their secrets, the corresponding elements and qualities in man could then be tapped into.

After Arabia had conquered Egypt and the Eastern Mediterranean in the 7th century CE, Arab scholars translated and adapted the Greek and Egyptian alchemical texts. In the process, they incorporated their own advanced ideas on medicine, astronomy, astrology and mathematics, which in turn were translated into Latin by Christian scholars and thence transported to medieval Europe.

Despite attempts by eminent men such as Doctor Arnald of Villanova (who died in 1311) to have alchemy accepted as a spiritual process symbolizing the Resurrection, it was declared heretical and the alchemists were driven underground.

By the 17th century, the first serious studies of the occult sciences were beginning to influence the religious mystics of Europe. Jacob Boehme (1575-1624) wrote extensively on the subject,

The four elements of "prima materia".

although he couched everything in Christian terms, viewing the process as symbolizing the awakening of the Christ spirit within.

It was left to 20th century psychoanalyst Carl Gustav Jung (1875-1961) to finally drag alchemy out of the dark ages of magic and superstition. He interpreted it as an "individuation process", a forerunner of psychology rather than chemistry, involving the "transformation of the personality through the merging and blending together of the noble and base elements, the conscious and the unconscious". It would appear that from conception to final decay, we humans are each undergoing an alchemical process – the transformation of flesh, mind and spirit, with each element working upon the other. Whether it is through intellectual insight, mystical illumination or merely the inexorable process of evolution, we will all ultimately attain the "Great Work" of which the alchemists wrote – the perfection of spirit and union with our source.

THE ALCHEMIST'S PROPHECY

The search for the "Philosopher's Stone" did not die with the coming of science. In 1925, the fabled French alchemist Fulcanelli (aka Jean-Julien Champagne) published a book entitled The Mystery Of The Cathedrals, *in which he claimed that the secrets of alchemy were encoded in the carvings of the central porch of Notre Dame and in the cathedral at Amiens.*

"As a sanctuary of tradition, science and art, the cathedral is not to be seen purely as a work devoted to the glory of Christ; it is a vast collection of ideas, of popular faith, perfect for revealing

the thinking of our ancestors on any subject we choose."

Although it is believed that Fulcanelli died in 1932, several men claimed to have met him in mysterious circumstances over the next 20 years and each time the alchemist appeared younger than before! In 1937, seven years before the development of the atomic bomb, Jacques Bergier, research assistant to the French atomic physicist André Helbronner, was approached by a man he believed to be Fulcanelli in a Paris laboratory and warned of the dangers of the "liberation of atomic energy", which the

alchemist claimed to have known "for a very long time".

Fulcanelli (if indeed it was he) concluded by explaining the "secret" of alchemy. "There is a way of manipulating matter and energy so as to produce what modern scientists call a field of force. This field acts on the observer and puts him in a privileged position vis-à-vis the Universe. From this position, he has access to the realities which are ordinarily hidden from us by time and space, matter and energy. This is what we call the Great Work."

PARACELSUS

"Man is not body. The heart, the spirit, is man. And spirit is an entire star, out of which he is built. If therefore a man is perfect in his heart, nothing in the whole light of nature is hidden from him."

Paracelsus personified the spirit of the Renaissance – a genius in a world of fools.

Paracelsus was a larger than life figure, a man of unrivalled insight and imagination, who strove to reconcile the apparently contradictory worlds of magic and science, but who was finally brought down by his belief that he was a genius in a world of fools.

He was born Theophrastus Bombastus von Hohenheim in the village of Einsiedeln, near Zürich, Switzerland, in 1493. His father, a doctor, taught him alchemy and medicine and fired his imagination with talk of the Philosopher's Stone – which, according to legend, turned everything it touched into gold, cured all ills and invested its owner with eternal youth. From his later writings, however, it would seem that the young Paracelsus viewed the stone as a metaphor for the spiritual quest and not as the magic mineral many of his contemporaries were still seeking.

The invention of the printing press in the 15th century made available the texts of the classical philosophers, copies of the *Hermetica* and other influential works, to those who could afford them. Paracelsus studied these and discovered in them a profound and eternal wisdom filtered

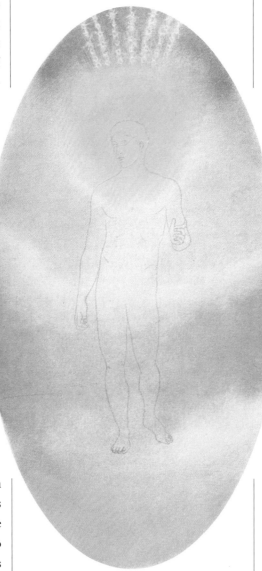

Paracelsus was one of the earliest physicians to acknowledge the existence of the aura.

through the philosophy of Plato and the Neoplatonists, Pythagoras, Hermes Trismegistus and Zoroaster. He came to the conclusion that, if man simply thought of himself as divine, then he would be so. Every man, he argued, is what he perceives himself to be.

Unfortunately, he took his own theory too literally and became an unbearable egotist, adopting the name Paracelsus meaning "greater than Celsus" – the renowned Roman physician of the first century CE. Having thus reinvented himself, Paracelsus set off through Europe in the guise of a wandering scholar, lecturing to packed halls of enthusiastic students and infuriating the medical establishment with his disdain for their irrational and outmoded thinking. While lecturing at Basle University, he ordered his students to burn the books of Galenus and Avicenna, whose archaic theories still dominated medical thinking at that time. In their place, he advocated research and experimentation.

But, by separating science from superstition, Paracelsus aroused the enmity of the medical fraternity. His behaviour often betrayed his contempt for them and was responsible for the word "bombastic", from his middle name, coming into common usage to describe forceful argument and overblown language. On one infamous occasion, he invited the most eminent physicians in the country to a lecture at which he promised to reveal his greatest secrets. With high expectations they awaited the appearance of the great man, who duly entered bearing a dish of steaming dung! As his audience made a bolt for the exit, Paracelsus berated them yelling: "If you will not learn the mysteries of putrefactive fermentation, you are unworthy of the name of physicians!" He was later forced to leave Basle after losing a court case which he would certainly have won, had he not made so many powerful enemies who were able to influence the verdict against him.

Intolerant, ill-tempered and intemperate though he may have been, his work persuaded many alchemists to turn from pursuit of the Philosopher's Stone to the development of chemical medicine. Similarly, he inspired others to revise their view of alchemy and adopt a metaphysical meaning to their search. Paracelsus has also been credited with the discovery of ether as an anaesthetic and laudanum as a tranquillizer.

In his later years he devoted himself to promoting his theory that man and nature were psychically connected – that one sublime energy pervaded all. In this he acknowledged the existence of the

Paracelsus is considered to be the father of homeopathy.

aura – a psychic energy field which radiates from the body of all living things, the colour and quality of which is believed to reflect the physical, spiritual and emotional state of the individual.

"The vital force," he wrote, "is not enclosed in man, but radiates round him like a luminous sphere ... In these semi-natural rays the imaginations of man may produce healthy or morbid effects." And, he concluded, "If the spirit suffers, the body suffers also."

THE FOUNDER OF HOMEOPATHY

Paracelsus set great store by the power of the imagination as a means of healing. "Resolute imagination is the beginning of all magical operations," he wrote. His definition of magic, however, was different from our own. "Magic" he asserted, "is a teacher of medicine preferable to all the written books." He saw magic in all natural phenomena, the study of which led to him laying the foundations for homeopathy.

It was Paracelsus who first promoted the idea that like acted on like, that minute doses of minerals set up a subtle but important reaction in the body – "the intersection of the organism and the universe" – to effect a cure.

"That which comes from the heart of the macrocosm comforts the heart of man – gold, emerald, coral; that which comes from the liver of the macrocosm comforts the liver of man."

ATHANASIUS KIRCHER –

THE EMBODIMENT OF

THE RENAISSANCE SPIRIT

"Nothing is more beautiful than to know the All."

(A. KIRCHER)

Athanasius Kircher (1602-80), the German Jesuit scholar, possessed an insatiable thirst for knowledge, a restless yearning to know all there was to know of man and the universe. On numerous occasions, his curiosity nearly cost him his life.

Kircher once insisted on being lowered into the crater of an active volcano immediately prior to eruption and, on another occasion, he narrowly avoided being crushed by the water-wheel he was intent on investigating.

In his volume on astronomy and optics, Ars Magna Lucis Et Umbrae, Kircher defined four levels of knowledge which man can attain: Sacred Authority which is given by the grace of God; Reason which is perceived through the inner eye and whose source is divine; Common Sense which comes from the sun; and Worldly Authority, which he depicted as a candle burning fitfully amidst the dark clouds of ignorance.

In an effort to trace the origins of all wisdom, religion and language back to a single source, Kircher immersed himself in a lifelong study of the major mystery traditions, while still professing belief in the absolute veracity of the Old Testament and the superiority of the Catholic faith over all living religions.

His "prisca theologia" stated that men are not the fallen descendants of Adam, rather they are of divine origin and their religions have all been divinely inspired too. According to Kircher, the gods of mythology and of pagan sects were merely a crude form of the fundamental forces at work in the universe, and their worship should not be dismissed merely as primitive idolatry.

All traditions, Kircher argued, share a belief in the same fundamental realities. "All peoples always have an idea of the principle of all things." In Christian terms, he saw these basic principles personified in the Father, Son and Holy Spirit. In Zoroastrianism, by Virtue, Wisdom and Intelligence. In the Egyptian mystery religion, they are depicted as Hemphta, Phtha and Amun among others.

Kircher identified these principles as operating at every level of existence, where each is embodied in an archetype. The "Father" in the world of the spirit corresponds to the Sun in the solar system, the heart in the human body, the lion in the animal kingdom and so on. Each archetype, according to Kircher, is not simply a symbol, but actually manifests the qualities and characteristics of

Kircher concluded that Noah was the father of all wisdom.

its equivalents at other levels. "A symbol is a notation signifying some arcane mystery ... it leads our soul by a certain similarity to the intelligence of something very different from the things of sense perception."

As a good Jesuit, Kircher was forbidden to condone the beliefs of the non-Christian peoples of the East, but there was little risk of censure if he credited the pre-Christian civilizations of Greece and Egypt with lost knowledge. This he did with such zeal that he was led to many erroneous conclusions, all of which detracted from his otherwise correct assumption that Egypt, and not Greece, had been the crucible of the arts and sciences.

In his eagerness to prove that ancient Egypt was the source of all wisdom, Kircher compiled a 3000-page treatise on the meanings of hieroglyphics, crediting them with preserving "the highest mysteries of divinity".

In 1822, after Jean François

Kircher attempted to master a new subject every few years, publishing 30 encyclopedic volumes by the age of 78.

Champollion had successfully cracked the hieroglyphic code with the aid of the Rosetta Stone, Kircher was shown to have been almost entirely inaccurate! In many other respects, however, his writings have proved to be an invaluable source of lost knowledge.

Throughout his life, Kircher drew no distinction between the objective world of logic and the subjective realm of mind, between science and art, or between matter and spirit. He viewed all knowledge as eternal and attempted to master a new subject every three or four years.

From his late twenties until his death at the age of 78, he published a remarkable catalogue of works totalling 30 encyclopaedic volumes. These weighty tomes covered such diverse subjects as Egyptology, acoustics, astronomy, astrology, "the true and false meanings of numbers", symbolism, logic, linguistics, philosophy, geology, the Far East, music, magnetism, the causes of plague and even sundials.

KIRCHER'S ARK

Although he believed in the literal truth of biblical events, Kircher recognized that every religion hides its esoteric teachings within its parables and mythology.

He became convinced that the dimensions of Noah's Ark were not arbitrary, but mirrored the proportions of the human body, as did the measurements of Solomon's Temple and the Altar of Moses. The story of the Ark, he asserted, though historical fact, was also a timeless allegory of the soul's turbulent journey through the storms of life.

Kircher's researches led him to name Noah as the father of all wisdom and his sons Shem, Ham and Japhet as the patriarchs of the post-diluvian world. According to Kircher, Shem became the first pharaoh of Egypt, "from whom like a Trojan Horse came all the antique philosophies of the eternity and plurality of worlds, the life and divinity of the stars, the absurd dogmata of metempsychosis and the transmigration of souls, opening the window to all impiety".

Kircher accounts for the disparity in names by declaring that the name of the first pharaoh, Cheops, was derived from Chemis, the Greek equivalent of Ham.

Originating from Egypt, the Mysteries spread out to Asia, India and the Americas, together with the teachings of Zoroaster, Pythagoras, Plato and the Kabbalah, all preserved in the writings of Hermes Trismegistos – another descendant of Ham!

THE ROSICRUCIANS

"An august fraternity whose doctrines, hinted at by the earliest philosophers, are still a mystery to the unworthy. I do not blame them for their discretion."

(LORD EDWARD BULWER-LYTTON, ROSICRUCIAN)

The Rosicrucians have been the subject of much speculation since pamphlets bearing their name were privately circulated throughout Europe during the 17th century.

These leaflets purported to be the manifestos of a secret society dedicated to the overthrow of the papacy and the promotion of occult philosophy. According to the first of these, the "Fama Fraternitatis", which circulated in Germany in 1614, the order was founded by Christian Rosenkreutz (1378-1484), a German monk who, at the age of 16, had travelled to the Middle East in search of secret wisdom. Apparently, he found what he sought at Damcar in Arabia where "the Wise Men received him not as a stranger, but as one whom they had long expected".

They imparted to him their knowledge of the Kabbalah, alchemy, mathematics and the arcane

The Rosicrucians flourished as a fraternal secret society.

sciences, then assisted him in translating a mysterious book known only as M, which was said to explain all the secrets of the Universe.

On his return to Germany, Rosenkreutz formed the Rosicrucian Order with three fellow monks for the purpose of bringing about "a universal, and general reformation of the whole wide world". The order adopted a seven-petalled rose and a cross as its symbol, the rose signifying evolution and the cross the triumph of the spirit over death.

When sufficient numbers had been recruited, Rosenkreutz sent them out into the world to spread their knowledge, but only after they had sworn an oath not to reveal the existence of the Order for the next 100 years. According to the literature of the Rosicrucians, Rosenkreutz died in 1484 at the remarkable age of 106 and was buried in a specially constructed vault whose dimensions had occult significance. The location of the tomb was known only to the inner circle, the secret going with them to the grave.

The authentic history of the Rosicrucians, however, began 130 years later with the circulation of the unsigned pamphlets. The first of these, the "Fama Fraternitatis", prophesied a new era of spiritual freedom in which hitherto hidden "secrets of nature" would become common knowledge, guiding humanity to a harmonious destiny in accord with universal laws.

The pamphlets aroused such interest that a slew of secondary literature appeared in which authors speculated as to the true identities of the Brotherhood, their location and even the practicalities of bringing about a new era.

As a result, a second pamphlet mysteriously appeared in 1615, the "Confessio Fraternitatis R C", detailing the aims of the organization. These included an end to sectarianism, political divisions and the authority of the papacy. The document ended by inviting applications for membership, but neglected to include an address.

This was not, it seems, a careless omission, but a vital clue to the mystery. While such genuinely creative individuals as Descartes, Leibniz and Goethe scoured

The Rose and the Cross symbolized the revival of Christian myticism.

Europe in vain for the lodges of the Rosicrucians, others, inspired by the ideals outlined in the pamphlets, established their own orders of the Rosy Cross. The anonymous author must have sat back and roared with laughter. The fact is that the

Rosicrucians were almost certainly the wishful creation of frustrated idealist, Johann Valentin von Andrea, a lecturer at the university of Tübingen.

It is likely that von Andrea, disillusioned by the attitudes of his time, came to the conclusion that a new era would not be bestowed on Humanity by a kindly creator, but could only be brought about by the will of idealistic individuals who believed in Humanity's innate potential. Von Andrea's part was to inspire mankind, to plant the seed of such a possibility in the imagination of like-minded men. As if to confirm this, he wrote in his will: "Though I now leave the Fraternity itself, I shall never leave the true Christian Fraternity which, beneath the cross, smells of the rose, it is quite apart from the filth of this century."

THE RESURRECTION OF CHRISTIAN ROSENKREUTZ

For modern Rosicrucians, the legend of Christian Rosenkreutz is of symbolic rather than historical value, the most significant element being the rediscovery of their founder's funeral vault. According to legend, the door to the vault was discovered accidentally. Inscribed over the entrance was the promise "POST CXX ANNOS PATEBO" - "after 120 years I will stand open". The prophecy was apparently fulfilled to the very day. Within the

vault, Rosenkreutz's followers found magic mirrors, manuscripts and, most significantly, the perfectly preserved corpse of their founder. "A fair and worthy body, whole and unconsumed."

In the 17th century, this story was taken as the portent of the new era promised in the pamphlets. "For like as our door was after so many years wonderfully discovered, also there shall be opened a door to Europe ... which already doth begin

to appear, and with great desire is expected of many."

In the 18th century, the legend was perceived as being an alchemical allegory by those seeking the transmutation of base matter into the gold of spirit. A century later, it was generally regarded as an allegory on the life of Jesus and an inspiration for a revival of Christian mysticism. In our age, it tends to be viewed in the light of Jungian psychology.

JAKOB BOEHME (1575-1624)

"The visible is a symbol of the invisible world."

In 1600, at the age of 25, Jakob Boehme, an uneducated German shoemaker, had the first of a series of dramatic mystical experiences that were to have a profound influence on the greatest philosophers of succeeding centuries. Transfixed by the glint of sunlight reflected in a burnished pewter dish, he fell into a hypnotic state in which he seemed to stare deep into the heart of nature, into the foundation of all things. In this heightened state of awareness, Boehme went for a walk in the countryside where he was overcome by a sense of the unity in nature, the overwhelming feeling that all living things are the expression of a vital force. "In the light, my spirit immediately saw through all things and recognized in all creatures, in plants and in grass, what God is, and what he is like, and what is His will ... a gate was opened unto me, so that in a quarter of an hour, I saw and learnt more than if I had studied many years in some university."

In understanding the origin and essence of all things, Boehme also gained an insight into the make-up of man. He discovered in himself what he called "the three worlds", namely the divine, the dark world ("as the original of nature to the fire") and the external visible world of the flesh. Expressing this experience, however, proved exasperating. "Interiorly I saw it all well enough, as in a great depth; for I looked through as into a chaos wherein all things lie; but the unravelling thereof proved impossible." It was not until 12 years later that he was able to publish what he had learnt in what was to be the first of more than 30 books.

As a devout Protestant, Boehme expressed everything in terms of an omnipotent and omnipresent God (*Urgrund*, or "original source") and was shocked when theologians put him on trial for trying to reconcile the Protestant and Catholic churches to the idea of a non-denominational creator. "When I plainly found out that good and evil are in all things, as well in the elements as in the creatures; and that in this world the God-fearing fare no better than the Godless, I fell into depression and sadness ... But as, in my awakened zeal and eagerness, I stormed violently against God and all the Gates of Hell ... my spirit at last broke through into the innermost Birth of the Divinity and was caught up in Love, as a bridegroom embraces his dear bride."

However the theologians did not share his joy and Boehme was thrown into prison from which he was released only after he had promised never to write again. It was not until the 19th century that his theories on the "meaning" of nature were popularized and expanded upon by such thinkers as Nietzsche, Hegel, Schopenhauer and the visionary artist William Blake.

Boehme regarded his wisdom as God-given, although on closer examination he appears to be suggesting that each man has a dormant higher self, which, when awakened, sees beyond our world of illusions to the world as it really

Blake's visionary pictures captured the "meaning" of nature.

is. This higher self is our true self and the source of supreme wisdom.

"It is not I who am myself, who knows these things, but God who knows them in me ... Since it is God who creates them, it is not me myself making them, but God in me; it is as if I were dead during this birth of sublime wisdom."

Boehme concluded that although man's spirit lives in God his conscious mind lives only in the material world. What we call "God" lives through us, existing through our being here and interacting with nature as well as with each other. Evil, therefore, is not a separate force but a lack of awareness or an absence of light: " ... darkness is not only the absence of light, but the fear caused by the brilliance of the light." To receive this wisdom, all we have to do is stop "thinking and willing", at which point the voice of wisdom will come through the stillness.

For Boehme, wisdom was not to be belittled with predictions or excessive preaching as to how man should live – although he did state that every element of creation is part of a "grand design" and that we should be content to leave this be. He compared the universe to a huge clock in which each element serves a small but significant function within the overall mechanism. Each part is dependent upon the others and, despite our impression that the world is chaos and contradiction, all is in fact as it is meant to be.

Boehme's writings, all but the first of which were published posthumously, are the more credible for the fact that he was a stable, rational and respectable family man, who, despite his intuitive wisdom, continued his occupation as a shoemaker until the end of his days.

Boehme's theories inspired the 19th century German philosopher, Georg Hegel.

For Boehme every element of creation was part of a "grand design".

NICHOLAS BERDIAEV (1874-1948)

Of the many Christian thinkers inspired by Boehme, the most interesting must surely be Nicholas Berdiaev (1874-1948). Like Boehme, Russian-born Berdiaev found himself in conflict with the orthodox church for attempting to reconcile mysticism with religion ... this was after he had already offended the authorities with his revolutionary sympathies. Branded as an ideological enemy of the people, he was deported from Russia in 1922, settling first in Germany and then France where he lived until his death in 1948.

Disillusioned with both the church and communism, Berdiaev turned to mysticism where he discovered that the only real possibility for lasting change in the world lay in first changing oneself. "I am only a seeker of truth and of life in God," he wrote, ' ... not a leader.'

*Through his books **A New Middle Age** (1924) and **Of The Destination Of Man** (1935), Berdiaev attempted to unite East and West through a spiritual rather than a social revolution. Mass culture, he argued, has robbed people of their individuality; mediocrity and injustice prevent the individual from realizing his true potential in the modern world: and the 20th century is but a prelude to a new era, when mysticism will alter the nature of humanity.*

THE FREEMASONS

"It is no exaggeration to say that today Perfection, the Absolute or the Principle to which one aspires – whether we call it God, Reason or the Great Architect of the Universe – comes about in one's progress towards Knowledge. Is this not the object of the Reintegration which the Tradition asks of the initiate?"

(PAUL NAUDON, LA FRANC MAÇONNERIE)

The popular image of Freemasonry is that of a philanthropic secret society composed mainly of professional men and establishment figures who indulge in rather theatrical rituals in an effort to lend their activities a certain mystique. No doubt many of the society's members would also view their activities in such a light, for throughout its 300-year history, Freemasonry has been run along the lines of a secular, fraternal brotherhood dedicated to the performance of charitable deeds. Their secret signs and handshakes are said to date from the Middle Ages when itinerant stonemasons needed a way of proving their degree of craftsmanship to one another.

Masonic theories and teachings, however, date back much further, possibly even to those zealously guarded by the architects of the ancient world, whose structures are said to embody the principle laws of the universe. Mastery of these

The secrets of the Freemasons are to be found in their signs and symbolism.

principles is believed to have enabled the Egyptians to construct their pyramids, temples and sacred monuments with an accuracy that continues to confound modern mathematicians.

It may well be that the medieval Masonic guilds preserved these age-old secrets in the great cathedrals of Europe, whose floor plans were modelled on the Temple of Solomon and whose very structures symbolize the Four Worlds of existence.

The first Masonic Lodges were formed in England at the beginning of the 17th century, attracting working masons who perceived the society as nothing more than another craft guild or early trade union, as well as what can be called "speculative" masons, educated men and mystics who wished to be initiated into the inner philosophical fraternity.

Those initiated into the inner Mysteries were told that the principles employed in the construction of buildings reflected the metaphysical laws upon which the universe had been constructed by the "Divine Architect". In the ritual known as the Second Degree, the initiate is reminded of the "regular progression of science from a point to a line, from a line to a *superficies* (plane), from a *superficies* to a solid". This teaches that every aspect of creation, including man himself, comes from a single source and carries within it the essence of all that has gone before. As the microcosm, man therefore conforms to the same fundamental principles as the universe, the macrocosm.

The Tracing Board of the First Degree is what would now be termed a "visual aid" for the initiate to be shown the principles of creation, the Four Worlds and his place within them. Such symbolism is intended not merely as an intellectual exercise but as a practical demonstration of the forces at work within mankind and the world.

In contemplating the various elements of the Tracing Board and their relationship to one another, the candidate is in effect examining his own psyche. By understanding himself better, he can then control his passions rather than be controlled by them.

After initiation, the new member is admitted to the Lodge as an Entered Apprentice where his position is again represented in appropriate symbolism, this time by a stone known as a Rough Ashlar, a block separated from the mass but not yet shaped by experience. In accepting this stone, the candidate shows he does not wish to be a part of the general mass of humanity, but desires to

Ritual is central to the masonic initiation into the Mysteries.

fashion himself into a foundation block for the "Temple of God".

Through the words of one of the characters in *War and Peace* Leo Tolstoy summarized the Masons' aims: "The first and chief object of our Order, the foundation on which it rests and which no human power can destroy, is the preservation and handing on to posterity of a certain important mystery, which has come down to us from the remotest ages, even from the first man – a mystery on which perhaps the fate of mankind depends. But since this mystery is of such a nature that nobody can know or use it unless he be prepared by long and diligent self-purification, not everyone can hope to attain it quickly. Hence we have a secondary aim: that of preparing our members as much as possible to reform their hearts, to purify and enlighten their minds, by means handed on to us by tradition … ". Their third and ultimate aim is the total transformation of mankind.

SECRETS OF THE TRACING BOARD

The Tracing Board is a Masonic teaching aid which illustrates the principles by which man and the Universe are said to operate.

There are three boards, one for each Degree, or level, in the Lodge. During the course of a candidate's initiation, the significance of the symbols is explained by an elder member after which the initiate is encouraged to contemplate the symbols in the hope that he will understand the

inner workings of his own psyche.

The Tracing Board of the First Degree depicts a chequered floor symbolizing the apparently opposing elements of the physical world which in reality are interdependent and make up an integrated whole. Corinthian and Doric columns represent the law of Duality on earth, just as the sun and moon shown in the top half of the picture illustrate the same law operating in the universe.

The staircase, or Jacob's Ladder, shown ascending to the Divine has three principal rungs representing the qualities of Faith, Hope and Charity required at each degree. Faith is required of the Apprentice, the new member, Hope of the Fellowcraft, the initiate who can glimpse the goal towards which he is striving, and Charity which is needed by the Master Masons, those who are to teach the new initiates.

THE EASTERN PERSPECTIVE

Western *thought has been strongly influenced by the Greek philosophers, who viewed the intellect as the means by which to reconcile the conflicting forces at work in man. The great teachers of the East simply accepted that these forces exist and looked inward for illumination.*

The Western wisdom tradition is based on the discussion and interpretation of doctrine, whereas the faiths and philosophies of the East maintain that wisdom comes through the intuitive understanding of basic truths culminating in the indescribable experience of Enlightenment.

These Truths have found sublime expression in Taoism, the perennial philosophy of China; in the *koans* of Japanese Zen Buddhism, the philosophy of paradox; in the poetry of the Sufi mystics; in the teachings of Buddha; in the Hindu Upanishads; and in the practice and philosophy of Yoga.

Although the concepts of *karma* and reincarnation are now widely accepted in the West, along with the practice of Yoga and meditation, there is still resistance to the wisdom of the East due to what might be called the cult of the individual. The Zen master, D T Suzuki, who helped to introduce Zen to America in the 1960s, acknowledged this distinction when he wrote: "Whenever I see a crucified figure of Christ, I cannot help thinking of the gap that lies deep between Christianity and Buddhism. This gap is symbolic of the psychological division separating the East from the West.

"The individual ego asserts itself strongly in the West. In the East, there is no ego. The ego is non-existent and, therefore, there is no ego to crucify."

HOLY SCRIPTURES –

THE UPANISHADS

"In the whole world, there is no study more profitable and more edifying than that of the Upanishads. They have been a comfort to me throughout my life, and they will comfort me at the hour of my death."

(SCHOPENHAUER)

Contemplation of the Upanishads is a key to ancient wisdom.

The Upanishads are the esoteric teachings of the Hindus and deal primarily with the nature of the individual soul (*atman*) and its relationship to the Universal Soul (*Brahman*). While the orally transmitted Upanishads date from between 1000-500 BCE, the majority were added in the 3rd and 4th centuries BCE, at the time when Hinduism was undergoing a transition caused by the advent of Buddhism and Jainism.

Almost all the texts are presented as dialogues between master and pupil (*upanishad* means "the lesson") and they are drawn from the teachings of various schools. These are in stark contrast to the practices of the more populist Vedic religion with its emphasis on rituals and the worship of external gods. For the Hindu mystic, the Upanishads reinforce the belief that wisdom and religion are incompatible. The ultimate aim of the Hindu is the union of the individual soul with the universal soul. However, according to the innumerable sages who contributed to the work over many centuries, man's soul has become fettered to the material world by illusions. To be free, we have only to discover our true nature. In his commentaries on the Upanishads, the 8th-century philosopher Sankara noted: *"The self must be known here, in this life ... if the self is known here, there is supreme knowledge, and the aim of life will have been reached ... if the self is not known, then life is useless ..."*

Knowledge of the self can only be attained through contemplation. It is not something that can be learnt – it must be experienced. It is not enough to accept that "all is Brahman"; true wisdom and freedom from the cycle of rebirth can only be achieved when we have experienced unity with the Universal Soul.

"Whoever in truth knows the ultimate Brahman, becomes Brahman himself. He surpasses affliction, frees himself of sin. Liberated of all ties, he becomes immortal."

The Upanishads suggest that, if man knew that his soul was immortal, he would not waste his life in pursuit of transient things nor mourn the loss of that which cannot die.

"The wise who knows the Self as bodiless within the bodies, as unchanging among changing things, as great and

omnipotent, does never grieve. What grief or attachment can there be for a realized soul – a man of wisdom – when all the animate and inanimate objects of the world have become his self, when he sees oneness everywhere?"

For the writers of the Upanishads, wisdom is an intuitive understanding that can only be attained by surrender to the Universal Soul. Clinging to the perception of ourselves as individuals, independent of and impervious to the feelings of others, will only bring unhappiness. *"As a man when in the embrace of a beloved wife knows nothing within or without, so this person when in the embrace of the intelligent soul knows nothing within or without. Truly, that is his (true) form ..."*

In stating that the individual soul is derived from the divine – that atman is Brahman in essence – the authors of the Upanishads make one of the earliest recorded references to the concept of microcosm (man) and macrocosm (the universe). And they do this in imagery which recalls the kabbalistic image of Adam Kadmon – cosmic man (see page 36). *"The universe is like a gigantic man and we may speak of his eye which is the sun, his breath which is the wind, of his limbs, his heart, and his thinking. Man is also the universe in miniature and we may speak of the sun which is his eye, the wind which is his breath."*

While the Greek and Chinese sages maintained that knowledge gives rise to virtue, the early Upanishads suggest that an enlightened person rises above right and wrong, which are, after all, man-made concepts. *"Truly, if there were no speech, neither right nor wrong would be known,* neither true nor false, neither good nor bad, neither pleasant nor unpleasant. Speech indeed makes all this known."

The Hindu mystics hid their knowledge of the hierarchy of existence in fanciful concepts of the Universe.

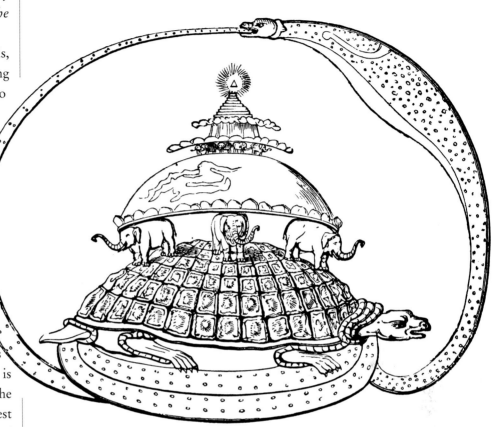

YOGA AND THE UPANISHADS

It is in describing the virtues of Yoga that the Upanishads distill the quintessence of Hindu wisdom.

In the Katha Upanishad, the story is told of a young man's confrontation with Yama, the god of the Dead. The young man, Naciketas, asks Yama, "Does man continue to live after death?", to which Yama replies that such secrets are not to be revealed to the "immature man of confused mind distracted by the folly of riches". But Naciketas persists in his ques-

tioning and eventually convinces Yama that he is sincere. Then the god answers that wisdom comes through Yoga, the system of subduing the senses and stilling the mind.

"When cease the five knowledges (NB senses), together with the mind, and the intellect stirs not – that, they say, is the highest course. This they consider as Yoga – the firm holding back of the senses. Then one becomes undistracted. Yoga, truly, is the origin and the end."

YOGA

"The yoga gives birth to knowledge, knowledge to yoga. One, who has both yoga and knowledge, has nothing left to obtain."

(THE ISHAVARAGITA)

With people in the West facing greater stress than ever before, increasing numbers have turned to Yoga as a natural alternative to tranquillizers and sleeping pills. But Yoga is not just a physical discipline to relax the mind and tone the body. It was developed in the East more than 4,000 years before Christ was born as a means of overcoming pain and transcending death. In the Upanishads Yoga is described as the only means by which the soul can escape being dragged into oblivion by the passions. In devising the various techniques which slow down the heartbeat and still the breath, the first yogis succeeded in attaining complete control over the physical body and, through meditation, realized that their real self was immortal.

The numerous postures (*asanas*) with which we are familiar today were only taught to initiates after they had proved themselves worthy through observance of the five restraints (*yama*) and the five disciplines (*niyama*).

"No one must teach this absolutely secret discipline to someone ... who is not a disciple, who has not pacified himself."

(THE MAITRI UPANISHAD)

The *yama* is a moral code which demands truthfulness, honesty, moderation, non-possessiveness and non-violence. The five *niyamas* encourage purity, contentment, study of the sacred texts, austerity and a constant awareness of the Divine. Together, they form part of the "Eight Limbs of Yoga" which lead ultimately to union with the Absolute. The other disciplines are *asana* (posture), *pranayama* (breath control), *pratyahara* (withdrawal of the senses), *dharana* (concentration), *dhayana* (meditation) and *samadhi* (super consciousness).

There are over 1,000 *asanas*. Each one is named after a particular animal, plant or object in the belief that, in contemplating these, the yogi will assimilate their qualities.

For practitioners of Raja Yoga (Royal Yoga), the postures are a preliminary to years of rigorous spiritual discipline in

Mastery of Yoga techniques can lead to supernormal powers.

which they can expect to attain paranormal powers known as *siddhis*. These powers, which are said to include clairvoyance and indifference to pain, are, however, not the ultimate aim of Yoga, merely the result of having attained a degree of control over mind and body. They mark the yogi's ascension to a higher state of consciousness indicating that he is on the right course, but they must be treated as distractions to be noted and then discarded. They are not supernatural but supernormal. We are all said to have these abilities, but, as long as our consciousness is grounded in the physical world, they remain dormant.

The higher forms of Yoga were designed to activate the *chakras* which are the energy centres in the "etheric" ("astral" or "subtle") body. These send the life force (*prana*) through a network of "etheric" energy channels to vitalize the whole being. *Prana* is present in all

The asanas, *or postures, were devised as a spiritual discipline.*

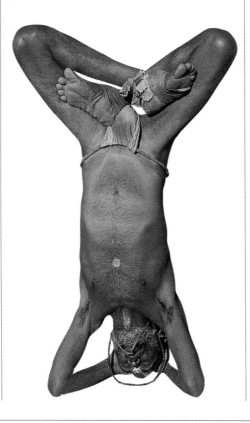

living things and also in air, food, water and sunlight. It is the animating force. Regular practice will unblock the energy channels in the "etheric" body, which can then absorb more life force for sustained vitality and health. It is in integrating exercises for both the physical and the "etheric" body that Yoga is such an effective vehicle for spiritual, mental and physical well-being.

Despite the European reluctance to embrace Yoga's more demanding forms, modern Indian masters feel it is their spiritual duty to bring this wisdom to the West. In 1957, the venerable Swami Sivananda sent his pupil Swami Vishnu Devananda to bring the message to America with the words:

"Many souls from the East are reincarnating now in the West. Go and reawaken the consciousness hidden in their memories and bring them back to the path of Yoga."

THE TEN PATHS OF YOGA

There are 10 paths of Yoga, each leading to the same destination, but varying in how they get there. Though often taught as the expressions of different traditions, these paths are complementary and can be taken together.

Bhakti Yoga is the yoga of love, devotion and faith and involves the chanting of praise to Brahman (God).

Dhyana Yoga is the yoga of contemplation and meditation.

Hatha Yoga is the form most widely practised in the West. Its original aim was to enable the

practitioner to attain control over the body so that it did not distract from sustained contemplation.

Juana Yoga is the yoga of wisdom in which individuals discover their true nature through the philosophy of The Vedata (the sacred Vedas of Hinduism).

Karma Yoga is the yoga of selfless actions, usually expressed in charitable deeds.

Kriya Yoga is the yoga of ritual and religious observance.

Kundalini Yoga is concerned with awakening the secret power of the "sleeping serpent" at the

base of the spine. This form is extremely dangerous unless practised under the guidance of an experienced teacher.

Laya Yoga centres on activation of the chakras, the psychic energy centres, through the repetition of mantras.

Mantra Yoga concentrates on chants and mantras to build a vibration that will harmonize with those of the "etheric" body.

Raja Yoga is the "royal road", which aims to channel mental and physical energy into a search for the spirit.

THE CHAKRAS

"Discover the serpent of illusion by the help of the serpent of wisdom and then will the sleeping serpent mount upwards to the place of meeting."

(THE TIBETAN)

*C*hakras are the energy centres in the "etheric" ("astral" or "subtle") body which, when activated, release the dormant life force (*prana*) ensuring health, vitality and, ultimately, enlightenment. But they can also store suppressed emotions which are dangerous to unleash without the guidance of a teacher.

Knowledge of the *chakras* – and the techniques used to awaken them – was kept secret for centuries. But now, with increasing interest in Eastern philosophy and alternative medicine, the idea that there might be hidden energy forces in the human body is rapidly gathering acceptance in the West.

There are seven main *chakras* which influence the physical and "subtle" bodies. Six are located along the *shushumna*, the "etheric" energy channel parallel to the spinal chord along which the life force flows. The seventh, the Crown *chakra*, is located above the brain. Interestingly, the *shushumna* corresponds to the major energy channel in Chinese acupuncture. When this, or any of the other energy channels, is blocked, ill-health results. But when each *chakra* is energized, it spins faster, improving the physical func-

tions with which it is associated. *Chakras* can be energized by meditative contemplation, through visualization or by the repetition of a *mantra*. This is a sound or phrase which, if intoned repeatedly, sets up a vibration that resonates in sympathy with a *chakra*, causing it to whirl faster, and so release its energy.

Balancing and energizing the chakras *leads to illumination, serenity and health.*

Although long thought of as exclusive to the religions of India, the concept of "etheric" energy centres is not entirely alien to the West. Medieval alchemists described a similar system of energy centres in the human body, which they believed corresponded to, and could be influenced by, the properties of specific metals and planets.

The Judaic mystics described a comparable set of energy centres, the sefirot, in terms of progressively refined spiritual centres on the kabbalistic Tree of Life, which can be matched against points on the human body. Sufism, Taoist Yoga, Buddhism and the Tantric tradition all integrate this concept. In practice, these traditions encourage gradual spiritual development in the belief that the *chakras* will open as the initiate matures. However, in Yoga and certain esoteric schools in the West, the energizing of the *chakras* is central to their disciplines. Although clairvoyants see the *chakras* as whirling vortices of energy, for meditative purposes they are usually visualized as lotus flowers. The Crown *chakra* is located at the top of the head and is usually visualized as a 1,000-petalled lotus flower. The number of petals is said to correspond to the number of "etheric" nerve channels meeting at this point. When fully opened, this *chakra* facilitates cosmic consciousness.

The Brow *chakra*, also known as the Third Eye, is located between the eyebrows where it influences the action of the pineal and pituitary glands producing increased psychic awareness. It is usually visualized as a snow-white lotus flower with two petals. Its *mantra* is "om", said to be the sound of creation.

The Throat *chakra* governs the power of speech. It is usually visualized as a sea-blue lotus flower with 16 petals. Its *mantra* is "ham", and its corresponding element is the ether.

The Heart *chakra* is found in the middle of the chest and this is the centre of spiritual awakening. The great guru Ramakrishna said of it: *"At this stage man has a spiritual vision of the divine light... His mind no longer runs after worldly pleasure."*

Those who have fully awoken the Heart *chakra* have enjoyed incredible experiences. The writer Gopi Krishna found himself writing poetry without conscious thought and in languages he had

never studied! This *chakra* is usually visualized as a smoke-coloured lotus flower of 12 petals. Its *mantra* is "yam" and its element is air.

The Solar Plexus *chakra* is located above the diaphragm and is concerned with the digestion and the emotions. It is the store-house of *prana* and is usually visualized as a red lotus flower with 10 petals. Its element is fire.

The Sacral *chakra* is found beneath the navel and governs reproduction. It is usually visualized as a white lotus flower with six petals. Its *mantra* is "ram" and its element is water.

The Root *chakra* is found at the perineum and is the domain of Kundalini. It is visualized as a yellow lotus with four petals. Its *mantra* is "lam" and its element is earth.

The Brow chakra *is traditionally depicted as the Third Eye.*

KUNDALINI – THE SLEEPING SERPENT

The serpent power of Kundalini was apparently unknown even to the wisest yogis in India until 1937, when an obscure Kashmir yogi, Gopi Krishna, unwittingly awakened it.

Gopi was meditating in a small room in his house near Jammu, when he experienced an intense, indefinable sensation at the base of his spine. It crept slowly upwards until "with a roar like that of a waterfall, I felt a stream of liquid light entering my brain through

the spinal cord."

Gopi had aroused the dormant power of Kundalini which, if released gradually, can energize the chakras, but otherwise can strike at the brain like earthed lightning. He came out of meditation depressed and unable to concentrate. In an effort to stabilize his emotions, he tried again, but triggered a second surge which proved even more traumatic than the first.

After his recovery. Gopi travelled the length and breadth of

India in search of a guru who could explain his experience, but in vain. After a prolonged period of experimentation and self-discovery, he published his own account of the phenomenon, Kundalini: The Evolutionary Energy In Man, in which he concluded that "the human organism is evolving in the direction indicated by mystics, prophets and men of genius, by the action of this wonderful mechanism located at the base of the spine."

BUDDHISM

"Of what I know, I have told you only a little ... And why have I not told you the rest? Because it would not help lead you to nirvana."

(SIDDHARTA GAUTAMA, THE BUDDHA, 556-486 BCE)

Buddhism is not so much a religion as a philosophy, which tries to help each individual to realize his true "Buddha nature", and so break free from the relentless cycle of death and rebirth. The title of Buddha ("Awakened One") does not refer exclusively to its founder, Siddharta Gautama, but to all those who have achieved and sustained an enlightened state of being. Siddharta was not the first "Buddha", but the first to distill his experience into a practical philosophy.

Born Prince Siddharta Gautama in what is now Southern Nepal, he was expected to enjoy the opulent lifestyle that was his by birthright. However, by the age of 29 he had become disillusioned with the futility of his life and sickened by the suffering he witnessed outside his palace walls.

Though happily married and lacking for nothing, Siddharta determined to search for some meaning in life. And so he forsook his princely gowns for the yellow robe of a pilgrim and set off on an arduous six-year spiritual quest along

Siddharta Gautama, an "Awakened One".

the Ganges plain of North East India. Here he sought out the most revered religious men of his day and entreated them to teach him all they could about meditation and philosophy.

But neither discussion nor contemplation brought him the answers he sought, and so he embarked on a life of extreme asceticism. Self-denial, however, served not only to bring him to the brink of starvation but also to the conclusion that, for him at least, this was not the path to Truth. Instead, he decided to follow a "middle way" between abstinence and indulgence. Having bathed, fed and rested, Siddharta then sat down to meditate beneath a fig tree at Bodh Gaya in the state of Bihar. After many hours of quiet contemplation, it is said that he attained Enlightenment, becoming a Buddha, an "Awakened One".

What is Enlightenment? A modern definition might be that it is an intuitive understanding of the completeness of all things resulting from an expansion of consciousness and detachment from the ego. Buddhists would say it is a state of Supreme Understanding which cannot be described, only experienced.

In attempting to communicate his experience to others and to guide them towards this awakening, Buddha taught what have become known as the "Four Noble Truths". These explain the cause of man's troubles and the means by which they can be overcome. The First Noble

The Great Temple at Bodh Gaya, in the state of Bihar, where Siddharta Gautama attained enlightenment.

Truth is that all life is "suffering" (the pain of separation from the source of a life founded on illusion), Buddha said.

The Second Noble Truth is that suffering is caused by desire, the desire for the ultimately valueless and transient things of this life and by estrangement from our true, Divine nature.

The Third Noble Truth is that desire can be overcome, and, when it is, suffering ceases.

The Fourth Noble Truth is that the path to nirvana (ie, freedom from *Karma* and the endless cycle of rebirth) is set out in the practical methods of the Noble Eightfold Path.

Buddhism is concerned with individual spiritual development in the belief that, when all are Enlightened, there will be an end to suffering. While the Christian, Islamic and Jewish traditions are based on the worship of an exterior God, Buddhism is based on contemplating the Divine within.

THE EIGHTFOLD PATH

"What we are today comes from our thoughts of yesterday, and our present thoughts build our life of tomorrow; our life is the creation of our mind."

The Eightfold Path was conceived by Buddha to free the individual from desire and suffering.

The First Step is described as "Right Understanding", which requires comprehension of the **Dharma** *(the teaching of the Buddha), because faith itself does not lead to spiritual growth or insight.*

The Second Step is "Right Thought", which expresses Buddha's wish that all who follow

the path should do so for the right reasons and not to gain spiritual superiority over others. These two aspects are considered to be the paths to wisdom.

The Third Step is "Right Speech", which requires not only rigid adherence to the truth but also acknowledgement that harsh or inappropriate words can be as destructive as deeds.

The Fourth Step is "Right Action", which can be interpreted as putting right behaviour into practice. This requires the observance of five precepts: Do not kill; Do not steal; Do not give way to promiscuity; Do not lie; and Do not take any form of intoxicant.

The Fifth Step, "Right Livelihood", urges the Buddhist to earn a living doing work which does not compromise the precepts of right behaviour and which does not enrich him at the expense of others. These last three steps constitute the morality of Buddhism.

The Sixth Step is "Right Effort", which finds expression in the commitment to still the mind and subdue the passions.

The practice and discipline of Meditation are encapsulated in the last two steps, "Right Mindfulness" and "Right Concentration", which ultimately lead to sublime realization.

BARDO THODOL –

THE TIBETAN BOOK

OF THE DEAD

"Our son, you are now going to test out three intermediate states, that of the hour of death, that of the truth within, and that of destiny."

(THE BARDO THÖDOL II)

Unlike its Egyptian equivalent, *The Tibetan Book Of The Dead* considers that the images perceived by the soul after death are not real but projections of the mind. The text itself takes the form of readings to be recited at the time of death and during the next 49 days – the time the soul is believed to hover in the *Bardo*, the intermediate state between death and rebirth. The purpose of the book is to allay the anxieties of the dying and to guide them through the various stages that determine whether they will attain *nirvana* or be reincarnated on earth.

Though written approximately 1,000 years ago, the accounts of the three stages of death are eerily reminiscent of recently reported near-death experiences described by innumerable people of varying faiths, cultures and backgrounds all over the world.

The first stage, which the Tibetans call *chikai bardo*, is the moment when the body has ceased to function but the

Bardo ("death") Mandala used in meditation (19th century).

person remains conscious, unaware that he is dead. In what might be described as his astral (or "etheric") body, the deceased finds himself floating free of his physical body, but unable or unwilling to leave the physical world behind.

"O nobly-born, at that time, at bridge-heads, in temples, by stupas [monuments containing ashes] ... thou wilt rest a little while, but thou wilt not be able to remain there very long, for thine intellect hath been separated from thy body. Because of this inability to loiter, thou oft-times wilt feel perturbed and vexed and panic-stricken ... Since thou canst not rest in any one place, and feel impelled to go on, think not of various things, but allow the intellect to abide in its own state."

Even then emotional attachments may cause the soul to linger, especially if it has a strong desire to communicate with family or friends.

"Even though thou feelest attachment for thy relations and connections, it will do thee no good. So be not attached, pray to the compassionate Lord; Thou shalt have nought of sorrow, or of terror, or of awe."

But eventually the soul must enter and be absorbed by the "clear, primordial light". The assumption is, that if a person has experienced the Light during life, he will not be afraid when drawn to it after death.

"Now thou art experiencing the clear light of pure reality. Recognize it ... Thine own consciousness, not formed into anything, in reality void, and the intellect, shining and blissful – these two – are inseparable. Their union is the

The six stages of death and rebirth.
(17th century wallpainting)

state of perfect enlightenment."

But for those who are unprepared or still bound by material concerns, this prospect is too terrifying and the soul retreats through a succession of dream-like states of its own making. This contradicts many recently recorded incidents of near-death experiences in which the "dying" person recollects an irresistible attraction to the light and a reluctance to return to their physical body.

The next stage is the judgement, a common feature of many otherwise differing religions, but here it is clearly intended to convey the idea that the deceased will be judged by his own conscience.

" ... *the Good Genius, who was born simultaneously with thee, will come now and count out thy good deeds [with] white pebbles, and the Evil Genius, who was born simultaneously with thee, will come now and count out thy evil deeds [with] black pebbles ... Then the Lord of*

REINCARNATION AND KARMA

"Just as a man casts off worn-out clothes and puts on new ones, so also the embodied self casts off worn-out bodies and enters others which are new."

(BHAGAVAD GITA)

The concept of reincarnation is not as alien to Western religion as it might appear. Although it is not accepted by the orthodox tradition, it has been a central principle of Jewish mysticism. It was also part of the Christian doctrine until 553 CE, when it was rejected by the church, although it is implicit in the teachings of Jesus, most notably in the precept, "whatsoever a man soweth, so also shall he reap".

Karma, however, is unique to the Indian religions. It is the "universal law" which states that past actions have an effect on the present life of an individual and that each thought and action creates an effect in the present or a

future life. Although the concept of karma as a spiritual law is characteristic of the Indian religions, each tradition has interpreted it in its own way.

The Jains adhere to the belief that the soul can change shape and size and that its progress or regression is determined by the deeds it performs while incarnate. On the other hand, the Brahmin conclude that the soul cannot change and that its progress is ruled by fate. The Brahmin doctrine asserts that an Indian who has lived a good life will be born to a Brahman woman, while those who have lived a bad life will be born to a woman of lower caste. This is not a doctrine universally accepted by Hindus, nor by Buddhists, who believe that each individual generates a "burden of karma" (both good and bad) carried from one life to the next until Enlightenment dispels whatever remains.

Death will say, 'I will consult the mirror of Karma'. So saying, he will look in the mirror, wherein every good and evil act is vividly reflected."

The "Lords of Death" are also seen as fearful imaginings, described in the book as "thine own hallucinations".

Having faced the consequences of his deeds, the deceased can then appeal to the compassion of the Buddha and Bodhisattva (a person who has attained Enlightenment, but out of compassion remains within the cycle of rebirth to

liberate others). If he cannot sway them, he must reincarnate. This is the most arduous stage, for after the ecstasy of liberation from the body, the soul must now enter a new housing of flesh and blood. For many souls, the fear of remaining in the limbo of *Bardo* is greater than that of reincarnating and the danger of making a hasty choice arises. The concluding prayers in the *Bardo Thödol* are intended to guide the soul to a favourable incarnation. For ultimately we are responsible for our own destiny.

ZEN BUDDHISM

"Preoccupation with the riddles of Zen may perhaps stiffen the spine of the faint-hearted European, or provide a pair of spectacles for his short-sightedness."

(C G JUNG)

Of the many forms of Buddhism which exist outside India the most enigmatic is surely Zen. Something of its character may be discerned from the apparently insignificant episode which led to the founding of the tradition in the 6th century BCE. According to legend, Siddharta Gautama, the Buddha, held up a golden flower in answer to a follower's question, but only one pupil, Mahakashyapa, understood its significance, which was that the communication of wisdom lies beyond the constraints of language.

In intuitively understanding this idea, Mahakashyapa attained enlightenment, going on to found the Dhyana school of Buddhism on which Ch'an (Zen) Buddhism is based. For the Zen Buddhist, illumination such as that experienced by Mahakashyapa is achieved by intuition rather than reason. Perhaps this is why Zen doctrines confound the Western approach to wisdom. Nevertheless, its increasing popularity in the West since the 1960s is proof that the gulf between the oriental and occidental is narrowing.

When Buddhism was first introduced into China in the 6th century, it assimilated certain Taoist features, ultimately evolving into two distinct schools, Soto and Rinzai. Both are founded on the principle that enlightenment comes only through prolonged meditation, but differ in other respects.

In Soto Zen, the phrase "Just sitting" aptly describes the meditation technique known as "Serene Reflection", during which the practitioner is encouraged to be "aware". In essence, it is a meditation on nothingness – an emptying of the mind. Soto can be roughly translated as meaning "gradual", but it is sometimes dismissed as "Farmer Zen" by Japanese practitioners of Rinzai whose methods might seem more extreme.

Rinzai, meaning "sudden", appealed more to the military, who readily embraced techniques which are intended to shock the mind into a state where values and perceptions are rendered meaningless so that a new reality can be perceived. It is not uncommon for a Rinzai master to answer his pupil's most profound question by hitting him with a stick!

A less painful method, and the one most commonly practised by followers of Rinzai in the West, is the use of *koans*, paradoxical statements or questions which apparently defy logic. One of the most famous examples is that posed by the 18th-century master Hakuin who clapped his hands and then asked, "What is the sound of one hand clapping?" Another is the famous exchange between the Indian sage Boddhidharma and one of his pupils. The pupil is said to have entreated his master to pacify his mind,

For the Zen Buddhist a pilgrimage is a form of meditation.

whereupon Boddhidharma replied: "Show me your mind." Not surprisingly, the pupil protested that he could not do so, to which the sage remarked: "There, I have pacified your mind."

Despite its apparent delight in paradox and obscurity as well as its strong emphasis on meditation, Zen is not a passive tradition. While most Buddhist traditions consider it unsuitable for monks to engage in agricultural work because they might inadvertently harm small animals or insects, the Zen schools actively encourage it.

In fact, Zen makes no distinction between religious and secular activity, but states that all activity must be undertaken as a form of meditation.

Zen meditation is a serene "emptying of the mind".

THE ZEN MASTER

The introduction of Zen to the West was largely the work of one man: the Japanese Zen master D T Suzuki (1870-1966). In the early 20th century, he was invited to lecture in North America along with two other scholars, each of whom helped to establish Zen groups in the United States. But it was not until the 1960s that Zen caught the imagination of American youth.

Suzuki maintained that true wisdom is beyond words: "Our language is the product of a world of numbers and individuals, of yesterdays and todays and tomorrows, and is most usefully applicable to this world. But our experiences have it that our world extends beyond that; there is another called by Buddhists a 'transcendental world' and when language is forced to be used for things of this [transcendental] world, it becomes warped ... Language itself is not to be blamed for it. It is we ourselves who, ignorant of its proper functions, try to apply it to that for which it was never intended. More than this, we make fools of ourselves by denying the reality of a transcendental world."

MEDITATION

"If there is no meditation, then you are like a blind man in a world of great beauty, light and colour."

(KRISHNAMURTI)

Meditation techniques have been used in the West by mystics and magicians for centuries, but only in the second half of the 20th century have they become a part of what might be called "New Age consciousness".

We in the West generally believe that knowledge can only be attained through study and that wisdom comes with experience. We pride ourselves on being practical and dismiss the idea that sitting in quiet contemplation can be anything more than rest and recuperation. And yet all of us inevitably meditate to some degree every day of our lives – and are the better for it. Whenever we lose ourselves in day-dreaming or an activity that requires concentration to the exclusion of everything else, we are actually engaging in a form of meditation. But the pleasure we get from these moments is fleeting and soon dispelled by the rush of conflicting thoughts, regrets and anxieties with which we absorb and indulge ourselves.

The great yogis and wisdom teachers of the world suggest that, if we can still

The secret of meditation is stillness, to allow the focusing of mental and spiritual energy.

our minds, even for 10 minutes each day, concentrating on something neutral such as a candle flame, we can obtain the peace of mind which normally eludes us,

causing much frustration and ill-health.

Unfortunately, we often confuse relaxation with recreation. While apparently passive pursuits such as watching television and reading might focus the attention, they do not still the mind.

In order to gain access to cosmic consciousness and the supreme wisdom which is locked deep in our subconscious, we must first learn to still our restless minds. The mind may be in perpetual motion but it rarely moves in one direction for very long. This wastes our greatest resource, mental energy, causing most of us to seek stimulation rather than stillness. Meditation focuses the scattered pinpoints of light that are our thoughts like a laser beam.

Focusing on a dot in the mind's eye, or on a candle flame, reduces mental activity and allows the practitioner of meditation to contact the higher self, which has all the answers we seek. But, like everything else, this process takes time, patience and practice. The mind must be re-tuned to a higher frequency if it is to receive true wisdom.

"Meditation does not come easily," wrote Swami Vishnu Devananda. *"A beautiful tree grows slowly. One must wait for the blossom, the ripening of the fruit and the ultimate taste. The blossom of meditation is an expressible peace that permeates the entire being. Its fruit ... is indescribable."*

There are many traditions of meditation, but only two basic forms.

Christian, Sufi and Yoga techniques are based on heightening concentration by focusing on a single object or subject, while the Buddhist approach can be summed up as the passive emptying of the mind. Yoga master Swami Vishnu Devananda explained the difference between concentration and meditation by saying: "During concentration, one keeps a tight rein on the mind; during meditation, the rein is no longer necessary, for the mind stays of its own accord on one single thought wave."

Through meditation, the ego which creates the illusion of separation is subdued, the meditator becomes one with the object of his meditation – sometimes just for an instant, ultimately for eternity.

In Yoga, there are two methods of meditation – *Saguna*, in which the mind is focused on a specific object, symbol or *mantra*; and *Nirguna*, in which the object is abstract. *Saguna* encourages detachment of the senses while *Nirguna* aims for absorption into the abstract, the Absolute.

But, as with the physical disciplines of Yoga, meditation in a diluted form can still achieve remarkable results. It can improve clarity of thought; it also helps concentration and health, as well as giving peace of mind, a calmer disposition and a generally more positive attitude.

Although the practice of meditation is very often solitary, extraordinary effects have been claimed for group meditations. In early 1994, an informal group of international meditators met in Washington for an experiment in mass meditation in the wake of the Los Angeles riots. After several weeks of regular meditation on the problems of violence and violent crime, police in some of the major cities recorded a fall in the crime rate of up to 30 per cent!

Buddhist monks at prayer in Thailand. In Buddhism prayer is the contemplation of the Divine within the self.

FIRST PRINCIPLES OF MEDITATION

1. Try to establish the habit of meditation. Condition yourself by meditating at the same time each day and it will gradually become easier to settle into it.

2. Choose a place where you will not be disturbed. Disconnect the phone.

3. Sit in a comfortable chair, or in the Lotus or Half-lotus position, with your back, neck and head in a straight line.

4. Do not let thoughts distract you. Count your breaths in cycles of three, if it helps to focus your attention. *If thoughts come into your mind, observe them with indifference.*

5. Focus on an object in front of you (such as a burning candle), or in your mind's eye – imagine a white dot, a simple shape or symbol, a number or colour. Later these can be developed into visualizations to create the habit of positive thoughts, to activate the chakras (energy centres) or even to heal your body. Don't try too hard. Above all: relax and don't worry – it gets easier with practice!

TAOISM – PHILOSOPHY

OF THE FIRST PRINCIPLE

"Abide at the centre of your being,

For the more you leave it, the less you learn."

To the Western mind, Chinese Taoism might appear to be a philosophy of paradox. It is founded on the belief that the universe is governed by the interplay between two forces, *Yin* and *Yang*, which emanated from a single energy source at the instant of creation. These two forces, which manifest as primal opposites (*Yin* – negative and passive; *Yang* – positive and active) are at the same time complementary. *Yang*, the masculine force, instigates change while *Yin*, the feminine passive, absorbs it giving birth to form. *Yin* and *Yang* are in constant flux, yet immutable and eternal.

All attempts by man to understand, analyze or control these self-sustaining forces are in vain and only lead to misconceptions.

"When the intellectuals appear, the great deceptions intervene. If we were to renounce wisdom and reject knowledge, the people would be a hundred times better off."

(THE TAO TE CHING)

According to the ancient Chinese philosophers, only by adhering to the *tao* ("the way") can we comprehend this duality and reconcile these forces within ourselves. Taoist philosophy, whose origins are older than recorded history, states that, no matter how hard we strive to assert our individuality, this momentum is drawing us back to the Supreme Unity from which we originally evolved. Consequently, there is no merit in individual action.

The wise man lives according to the movement of heaven ... he creates neither happiness nor misfortune, he merely reacts to the stimulus and only moves under pressure."

(THE CHUANG TZU)

It is in this respect that Taoism differs from other philosophies of the East which maintain that the destiny of mankind will be determined by the spiritual progress of the individual. While Buddhism states that we each have within us the spark of our own salvation, and that through compassion we help ourselves and others, the Taoist practises active non-involvement.

"Concentrate on doing nothing and everything will turn out well."

(THE TAO TE CHING)

It is almost a philosophy of futility and yet it has much in common with Zen Buddhism, on which it has had a

Legend has it that Lao Tzu copied out his teachings at a single sitting.

profound and lasting influence. Taoism and Zen share the belief that the only barrier to understanding the true nature of things comes from the misconceptions of our own minds: the way to illumination is through intuition and meditation on emptiness.

"Emptiness cannot be esteemed for itself. It is estimable for the peace to be found in it. Peace in the emptiness is a state which cannot be defined ... Alas, people now prefer to do good and be fair, which does not give the same result."

(THE LIEH TZU)

To the Western mind, these concepts appear to defy logic. But for the Chinese the only means of understanding it is to follow *tao*. Tao brings together three

The primal forces are represented by the symbol of Yin and Yang.

concepts – the universal energy which created and permeates all living things, the Ultimate Reality which lies beyond our imagination and universal "laws", with which we must live in harmony. Taoism is a doctrine of detachment, but its supreme principle, like that of its source, defies definition.

"When a superior man understands the Way
He follows it with zeal.
When an average man understands the Way
He adopts part of it, but leaves the rest.
When an inferior man understands the Way
He bursts out laughing.
If he did not laugh the Way would not be the Way."

(THE TAO TE CHING)

LAO TZU

Of all the Chinese sages, Lao Tzu, the founder of Taoism, is the most venerated of all. Even Confucius was moved to say of him, "of the bird I know that he can fly, of the fish I know that he can swim ... but the dragon, I can know nothing of him; he rises to the sky on the clouds and the wind. Today I have seen Lao Tzu, he is like the dragon."

While serving as Keeper of the Archives for the Chou dynasty,

Lao committed his thoughts to paper in the form of poetry, but left it all behind when he decided to leave China for the West following the dynasty's decline.

Legend has it that he arrived at the gateway to the western world riding on a water buffalo and was urged by the gatekeeper to write down his teachings before he departed. The old sage duly obliged, patiently writing out the 5,000 characters which comprise

The Tao Te Ching *(the "way" and the "virtue").*

It is unlikely that Lao would have approved of the populist religion which took his slim volume as its sacred text, justifying its rituals and formalized methods of expression as "natural extensions" of his philosophy.

"Rites are the external form of sincerity and faithfulness," he wrote, "but also the source of disorder."

THE TAOIST SAGES

"Stay at the centre of the circle and let all things take their course."

(LAO TZU)

Perhaps the most inexplicable aspect of Taoism is the fact that a tradition which advocates non-action has produced such a remarkable number of profound philosophical works.

Of these the most enduring and enigmatic are *The Tao Te Ching, The Chuang Tzu* and *The Lieh Tzu*. All three date from the last centuries before Christ, when China's ruling dynasties were decadent and in decline, and opposed to the very principle of change. This was a period of suffering and instability when the people were eager for something that would give them guidance and hope as well as make sense of the chaos. Many turned to the teachings of Confucius, who was attempting to reconcile traditional values with the new social order, while the more mystically inclined found comfort in the perennial philosophy offered by Lao Tzu, Chuang Tzu and Lieh Tzu.

Whether these venerated sages were actually the authors of the works accredited to them is questionable, but as we move towards the millennium the value of their teachings remains undiminished,

Taoist poets and philosophers sought to encapsulate the grandeur of nature.

suggesting that the cause of man's troubles has changed little in over 1,000 years.

Lao Tzu stressed the importance of contemplating the supreme transcendent reality, the *tao*, if we are to avoid distancing ourselves from the source of all happiness and wisdom.

Whereas his work, *The Tao Te Ching* (the "Way" and the "Virtue"), is made up of dicta and maxims, *The Chuang Tzu* is a collection of parables and anecdotes illustrating Taoist teachings and contrasting them with those of other schools. According to Chuang Tzu, some things, including the nature of a creator, are beyond our comprehension and we ought to accept this truth. *"If I say ' there is an instigator', I am only considering the tangible realities; if I say 'there is no creative force', it means I am considering only invisible emptiness ... We can talk about and reflect upon these problems, but the more we talk, the further we are from the mark."*

The Lieh Tzu (the "True Classic of

According to the Taoist sages, nature could only be appreciated through stillness.

Complete Emptiness") may also have been the work of Chuang Tzu, or his followers, for some of the tales appear in both books and no mention is made of the author by the most eminent historians of the period. *The Lieh Tzu* is a collection of parables and philosophical discussions between legendary characters, the central theme of which is: leave things be and everyone will receive what is rightfully theirs.

Though many of the tales are anecdotal, at one point Lieh Tzu questions our perception of life and death. Examining a skull, he comments: *"He and I both know that the distinction between life and death is merely imaginary; he knows by experience and I know through reasoning. He and I both know that clinging to life and fearing death is unreasonable; life and death simply being two phases, the one following inevitably on the other."*

In an effort to make sense of a world of apparent chaos and contradictions, we

Confucius taught that nobility was a virtue, not a birthright.

are constantly trying to categorize, justify and explain away everything under the sun. The Chinese sages found all of this quite useless. For them, it was enough just to be here. Common to all three of these renowned Taoist texts is the idea that we busy ourselves with things which ultimately do not matter.

We desire and value things which are transient and yet neglect to cultivate that which is eternal – our minds.

Together, these slim volumes appear to answer our need for permanent values in a world of change, for harmony amid apparent chaos and for a universal law beyond our world of injustice.

CONFUCIUS (K'UNG FU TZU 551-479 BCE)

Confucius' reputation as a source of ancient Chinese wisdom is largely unfounded. He was not a philosopher, but an intellectual and teacher who redefined the fundamental concepts of Chinese thought along humanistic if conservative lines.

For Confucius, nobility was a virtue not a birthright. He referred to anyone whom he considered modest and benevolent as a **Chun Tzu** *("Son of a Ruler") regardless of their status in life.*

At a time when China was struggling to free itself from the

feudal system, in order to become a nation, Confucius insisted that good government should carry with it moral responsibility.

After his death, his name was adopted by a Taoist sect which held that the nebulous **tao** *is not a supreme creative power but the spirit of etiquette, correct conduct and ceremonial. Confucianism denies the idea of an individual soul surviving death and instead stresses traditional worldly virtues such as respect for authority and the aged, loyalty and family values.*

Confucius' most celebrated sayings were collected in the **Analects** *("Selected Sayings"), many of which are as true today as they were then. When asked if there was one word which would serve as a rule for one's life, he answered: "Is not 'reciprocity' such a word? What you do not want done to yourself, do not do to others."*

But he was evidently not without humour: "The superior man understands what is right," he wrote, "The inferior man understands what will sell."

Sufism – The heart of Islam

"Be with this world as if you had never been, and with the other as if you were never to leave it again."

(AL-BASRI)

The knowledge the Sufis seek is not knowledge *about* Allah, but knowledge *of* Allah. Through praise, poetry, music and dance, they hope for an intimate experience of the Divine in which they can lose all sense of self. Referring to the type of ritual dancing exemplified by the sect popularly known as the "Whirling Dervishes", the Persian Hujwiri wrote, " ... this is not dancing, nor bodily indulgence, but a dissolution of the soul."

Legend has it that on hearing of the death of his teacher and mentor, Mevlana Jalaluddin Rumi (1207-73 CE), the celebrated Persian poet and spiritual father of the Dervishes, began spinning on the spot in a mixture of rapture and agony until his heart was pure again. It is this event which the Dervishes celebrate in their dancing.

Sufis believe that in selflessly seeking the love of Allah they will lose themselves and their audience in ecstasy, a state of surrender termed *fana*, or "passing away", which corresponds to the Buddhist concept of *nirvana*, or "extinction". The Sufi poets are particularly eloquent in expressing this exalted state of consciousness, contending that man is already at one with God but that he is simply not aware of it.

Sufis accept that evil exists but see it is a necessary aspect of God, a balancing force. Without evil, man would sink into complacency and never seek to discover his true nature. Fear and crises such as those the world is facing now are viewed as a symptom of imbalance rather than a tangible force to be feared.

For this reason, Sufi poets such as Rumi are being hailed by modern mystics as a source of spiritual insight of a kind which can melt hearts that have hardened to the pain of the world.

The first Islamic mystics appeared around the 7th century CE, 100 years after the death of the prophet Mohammed. But it was not until 150 years later that they identified themselves as Sufis, a term deriving from the Arabic word for wool – a reference to those who wore woollen shirts to emulate the Christian ascetics whom they admired.

The Sufi interpretation of asceticism was less extreme than that of their Christian counterparts: it was a renunciation of self rather than of the world. While orthodox Islam provides a moral code for life, Sufism aims to transcend the concerns of the world, searching for union with the source in the same way as the Christian Gnostics or the Jewish Hassidim.

Like the Buddhists, Sufis believe that the ideal state is to be "in the world, but not of it". The world, they say, is the perfect expression of God and we must view it as its creator would view it – with love. And yet, from the outset, Sufis have been in conflict with orthodox Islam, initially by declaring that praise and prayer should not be limited to *Salat*, the appointed hours of daily worship, and later by insisting that music and dance were an integral part of worship. A further cause of tension was the affinity certain Sufi sects in Eastern Persia shared with the Hindus, in particular the belief that *all* positive

Sufi mystics claimed ecstatic experiences as profound as those of Mohammed.

The Whirling Dervishes of Kurdistan seek the ecstasy of surrender.

religions – and not just their own – are paths to Reality.

Sufi mystics who claimed to have attained union with God were revered by their followers over and above the prophet Mohammed which further exasperated orthodox believers. Matters came to a head with the crucifixion of the Sufi mystic, Al-Hallaj, for blasphemy in 922 CE.

Taking Jesus as his model, Al-Hallaj had declared himself to be "Real",

meaning that the divine spirit had entered him and fused with his spirit just as it had done with the other great prophets: Moses, Jesus and Mohammed.

Ibn Arabi (1165-1240 CE), the Spanish Muslim mystic, whose descriptions of Mohammed's ascent to heaven inspired Dante, did much to reconcile the more moderate Sufi sects with Islamic orthodoxy. By re-phrasing the Sufi doctrine to make it more accessible, he helped to popularize a creed which had otherwise largely found expression through poetry, dance and music.

What differentiates Sufism from many other mystic traditions is its followers' reluctance to analyze and interpret their beliefs. For them, it is enough to experience the ecstasy of surrender.

MEVLANA JULALUDDIN RUMI

"My poetry is like Egyptian bread. Night passes and you cannot eat it. Eat it, eat it while it is fresh, before the dust settles."

Over 700 years after his death, the writings of Persia's most celebrated poet and mystic, Mevlana Julaluddin Rumi (1207-73 CE), are being rediscovered and proclaimed as a source of inspiration for our troubled times. A prolific poet, Rumi is the sublime inner voice of Islam, noted for his ability to distill the ecstatic spiritual experience of Sufism into verse:
"Though you are the talisman

protecting the world's treasure, within yourself you are the mine. Open your hidden eyes and come, return to the root of the root of your own self."
Rumi likened men to reeds cut from the river waters and fashioned into flutes. Like a reed, a man's life is hollow and empty when far from its source, and the pain pierces holes in his heart. As the wind of time blows through him, the pain of separation from the source becomes music, the yearning music of life:
"There is a sea that is not far from us.

It is unseen but it is not hidden. It is forbidden to talk about, Yet, at the same time, It is a sin and sign of ungratefulness Not to."
The simple truths he so eloquently expressed suggest that, while we have certainly progressed in a material and scientific sense, we have stagnated spiritually. It is this denial of our true nature that is the root-cause of our current crisis.

In reading Rumi and the other mystical poets, his admirers say, we can rediscover our divine origin which is being stifled by contemporary culture.

THE MODERN AGE

The dawning of the Age of Aquarius, at the beginning of the 20th century, proved to be a false dawn. It had long been prophesied as an age of earthly peace, but the first half of this century witnessed warfare and destruction on a scale previously unimaginable. Communist and fascist dictatorships threatened to drag the civilized world into a new Dark Age and, even after the Second World War, the free world was paralyzed by the Cold War with communism and the fear of nuclear annihilation.

But in the years preceding the outbreak of the First World War, there was an effort to prise open the door to the Mysteries and establish contact with the "Hidden Masters" who are said to have been entrusted with the Wisdom of the world.

Flamboyant figures such as Madame Blavatsky, MacGregor Mathers and Dion Fortune claimed to have established telepathic contact with these spiritual sages and to have "channelled" their secret doctrines for the illumination of the West.

While Freud and Pavlov were formulating their theories on the workings of the mind, Blavatsky and the occultists were making the first serious forays into parapsychology and the super-conscious. Their writings attempted to assimilate the "Ageless Wisdom" of the East into the Western Mystery tradition and, in so doing, they inspired a proliferation of secret societies which attracted some of the most brilliant minds of their time as well as, inevitably, many of the most notorious.

In the confusion, the first rays of the new age were diffused as if through a prism, with each sect or society fascinated and dazzled by the reflection but with few searching for the source.

THE WISDOM OF THE NATIVE AMERICANS

" ... our essential message to the world is a basic call to consciousness. The destruction of the Native cultures and people is the same process which has destroyed and is destroying life on this planet ... That process is Western Civilization ... If there is to be a future for all beings on this planet, we must begin to seek the avenues of change."

(THE HAU DE NO SAU NEE ADDRESS TO THE WESTERN WORLD, 1978)

The Medicine Men were shamans, skilled in healing, divination and magic.

According to the Native American tradition, the world is nearing the end of an age whose trials and tribulations were foretold long ago. We now have the opportunity to set the pattern for the coming age, to choose between a peaceful co-existence or full-scale destruction.

Despite over a hundred years of persecution and prejudice, the Native Americans are now seen as having mastered the secret of how to live in harmony with nature. For them nature was the stage where the world of spirit manifested in the world of matter and where the human, animal, spirit and celestial worlds all came together.

By adopting a particular animal as its symbol, a Native American tribe would identify itself with the characteristics of that creature, thus reinforcing their bond with the natural and supernatural worlds. Similarly, using eagle feathers in a head-dress was thought to lend a warrior all the supernatural and physical qualities associated with the bird.

This way of thinking survives today. According to Thomas Yellowtail, a contemporary Crow medicine man, "a man's attitude towards the Nature around him and the animals in Nature is of special importance, because as we respect our created world, so also do we show respect for the real world that we cannot see."

The power of the spirit world was known to the tribes by various names – to the Iroquois it was *Orenda*; to the Algonquin it was called *Manitou* – but its significance was the same for each. The spirits could be called upon for guidance or for healing, manifesting themselves in ritual objects or in the shamanistic practices of the medicine men. Sacred sites were marked by stones in the images of men or animals. Many of these have now been shown to be aligned to equinoxes and solstices – they were used for quiet contemplation and the practice known as "vision seeking".

Before guidance or help was sought from the spirit world in this way, permission was needed from a holy man. If he consented, offerings were given, not to appease the spirit but out of respect and thankfulness. The seeker would then retire to a consecrated place, often with a spiritual guide or teacher who would protect him from psychic forces eager to enter the world of matter and also be on hand to interpret the dream vision or signs. Some tribes prescribed the use of hallucinogenic mushrooms, or peyote, to stimulate the psychic faculties or "spirit vision". The holy man, too, would often seek guidance in this way, sitting against a rock or tree to draw upon the spirit of the earth and of the sky. A Sioux holy man, Lame Deer, confirmed that in silence the secret voices of plants and animals can be heard. "What you see with your eyes shut is what counts," he said.

Without written texts, Native American tribes gave vent to their spirituality by participating in ceremonies. Central to the ceremonial and to community life was the symbol of the medicine wheel, a sacred circle of stones, representing the seasons and the cycle of birth, death and rebirth. The wheel reminded the tribe that life is movement and change. To remain in one place was to cease to grow.

Life was transitory, a test of character in preparation for the next world. For the warriors, a noble death in battle was to be valued more highly than a life of self-preservation and inactivity. A young brave eager to prove himself would ride into battle armed only with a "coup stick" with which to strike an opponent. Killing was reserved for self-defence, or when the life of the tribe was threatened.

Stoicism and self-discipline, though often taken to extremes of cruelty, were intended to call forth noble conduct (even under torture) as well as a belief in the afterlife – in much the same way as religious martyrs calmly accepted torture and execution, braves could face

Buffalo were hunted for food and for the magical properties of their horns and hide.

death with equanimity. This belief that life was a test of character was naturally reflected in Native Americans' sense of values. Their word was their bond, a code which they were dismayed to discover was not shared by many of the white settlers.

It was the white man who introduced the idea of land as personal property. The tribes had always shared the land as a community, believing that, if they honoured the land and the animals, the tribe would prosper: central to this was the idea that the destiny of mankind would be determined by the respect it paid to nature. "Each man will pass from this earth in his own time. Some of the prophecies talk only about the end of time; others speak about the break-up of the modern world ... and a return to the traditional ways of our ancestors ... each one of us must choose at this present moment which path to follow." (Thomas Yellowtail)

BLACK ELK'S VISION

Black Elk, holy man of the Oglala Sioux, was only nine years old when he had a vision that was so awe-inspiring that he was afraid to speak of it to anyone for the next six years. During a prolonged period of illness, he lay in a trance-like state for 12 days, during which he saw celestial horses and animals of every kind. Then he saw the suffering that was to come to his people. But the impression that remained with him was one of harmony between humans and all the elements of nature.

"I saw more than I can tell and I understood more than I saw; for I was seeing in a sacred manner the shapes of all things in the spirit and the shape of all things as they must live together in one being. It was the pictures I remembered and the words that went with them; for nothing I have ever seen with my eyes was so clear and bright as what my vision showed me; and no words that I have ever heard with my ears were like the words I heard. I did not have to remember these things; they have remembered themselves all these years. It was as I grew older that the meanings came clearer and clearer out of the pictures and the words; and even now I know that more was shown to me than I can tell."

ELIPHAS LEVI - A TRUE AND FALSE SCIENCE

"There is a tremendous secret which has already turned the world upside down ... "

(ELIPHAS LEVI)

Levi, a prolific writer on the occult, practised magic only once in his life.

Eliphas Levi (1810-75), the son of a Parisian shoemaker, became one of the most celebrated occultists of his time and the figurehead of the modern magical revival. His flamboyant theories concerning "another reality" were an inspiration for the Surrealist movement and a prime (if unacknowledged) source for much of Madame Blavatsky's writings. They continue to hold a fascination for modern occultists and magicians to this day.

Born Alphonse Louis Constant, Levi entered the Roman Catholic church as a young boy under the sponsorship of his local parish priest who considered him highly intelligent and was concerned for his education. After taking minor orders, he went on to study at the seminary of Saint Sulpice at Issy, where he was introduced to magic by the Abbé.

Levi considered magic to be "the traditional science of the secrets of nature ... (through which) the adept is invested with a sort of relative omnipotence and can act in a superhuman fashion ... Magic combines in a single source that which is most certain in philosophy with that which is eternal and infallible in religion."

He qualified his remarks by acknowledging that there is a "true and false science, divine magic and devilish, or dark magic; we are to reveal one and unmask the other. We must distinguish between the magician and the sorcerer, between the adept and the charlatan. The magician is the high priest of nature, the sorcerer is nature's profaner."

Despite his heretical beliefs, Levi continued in the church and was ordained a deacon before being expelled in 1836, after falling in love with one of his pupils. After his departure, he fell in with the leaders of a revolutionary

Levi's theories of "another reality" influenced Surrealist artists such as Dali.

French Socialist movement and a literary circle including Balzac and Alphonse Esquiros. Balzac's occult novel *Louis Lambert* and Esquiros' book *The Mage* fired Levi's enthusiasm for the occult.

Nevertheless, he returned briefly to the church in 1839, entering the Abbey of Solesmes where he took the opportunity to study the writings of the Gnostics and various mystics, including works by the then unknown Madame de Guyon.

Returning to Paris in 1840, Levi became actively involved with Republican revolutionaries and was sent to prison for 11 months, during which time he discovered the works of Swedenborg. On his release, he turned his back on the priesthood and formulated his own occult philosophy.

"Occult philosophy seems to have been the nurse or Grandmother of all religions," Levi later wrote, "the secret lever of all intellectual forces, the key to all divine obscurity and the absolute

queen of society throughout the ages when it was the exclusive preserve of kings and priests."

After being introduced to the Kabbalah, he adopted the name Eliphas Levi and published a number of books, including *The Doctrine Of Transcendental Magic* (1855) and *The Key Of The Grand Mysteries* (1861) – he even became known as an authority on practical magic despite the fact that he only ever attempted one conjuration in his life!

His books are a useful summary of magical practice and theory, but they must be read with some scepticism since they reflect the richly romantic and imaginative character of their author.

"Behind the veil of all the hieratic and mystical allegories of ancient doctrines, behind the darkness and strange ordeals of all initiations, under the seal of all sacred writings ... in the cryptic emblems of our old books on alchemy, in the ceremonies practised at reception by all secret societies, there are found indications of a doctrine which is everywhere the same and everywhere carefully concealed."

INVOKING APOLLONIUS

Apollonius of Tyana, whose spirit Levi is said to have invoked.

Levi's only experience of practical magic came in 1854 during a visit to London. He returned to his hotel one day to find a calling card marked with the Seal of Solomon and a pencilled note which read "Tomorrow at three o'clock, in front of Westminster Abbey, the second half of this card will be given to you."

Levi kept the appointment and was met by a veiled Lady who beckoned him into her waiting carriage. She offered to place a complete magical cabinet, robes, rare books and instruments at his disposal, if he cared to put his theories to the test. He agreed and after 21 days of preparations, including meditation, a strict vegetarian diet and seven days of fasting, he attempted to summon the spirit of the Greek philosopher and magician Apollonius of Tyana.

In the turret room, where the

ceremony was to take place, Levi stood before the altar and began the conjurations.

"I seemed to feel a quaking of the earth," he later wrote, "my ears tingled, my heart beat quickly ... I beheld before the altar the figure of a man of more than normal size, which dissolved and vanished away."

Still shaken, Levi stepped inside the magic circle, whereupon a huge man appeared wrapped in a shroud. Raising his sword, Levi began the banishing ritual, but felt his sword arm become numb from an intense cold. It remained numb for several days. Before the apparition vanished, he received answers to two questions telepathically, which correctly prophesied death. Levi promptly ended his magical career, later writing, "I regard the practice as destructive and dangerous."

MADAME BLAVATSKY'S THEOSOPHY

"To the mentally lazy or obtuse, Theosophy must remain a riddle; for in the World Mental as in the World Spiritual each man must progress by his own efforts."

(MADAME BLAVATSKY)

Madame Blavatsky claimed her books were the master keys to the Mysteries.

Helena Petrovna Blavatsky (1831-91) co-founder of the Theosophical Society, was one of the most extraordinary women of her time. A Russian aristocrat credited with psychic powers and an insatiable passion for travel and adventure, her life story reads like a plot for a Gilbert & Sullivan operetta.

A rather excitable type, given to profanity and soothing her nerves with marijuana, she married the 40-year-old Nikifor Blavatsky, vice-governor of the province of Erivan, when she was just 16 to spite her governess who had insisted that no man would be fool enough to marry her. Having proved her point, Blavatsky fled to Constantinople and became a bareback rider in a circus. It was here she met and later ran off with a Hungarian singer, Agardi Metrovitch, whom she married despite the fact that she had yet to divorce her first husband.

During subsequent travels, Blavatsky claimed to have witnessed voodoo ceremonies in New Orleans and to have come under the influence of an anonymous Indian adept, who helped her to develop her latent psychic abilities and encouraged her to travel to Tibet to study the Eastern Esoteric Tradition under the lamas. From them, she learned much that she was to elaborate upon in her books, *Isis Unveiled* and *The Secret Doctrine*.

On returning alone to Russia in 1858, Blavatsky captivated the nobility with her mediumistic displays, cultivating a reputation for summoning spirits, materializing letters from her "Secret

A Theosophical Society convention in Adyar, India, 1927.

Masters" and producing a whole catalogue of psychic phenomena. Then Metrovitch returned and persuaded her to follow him to Cairo. Tragically, when their ship exploded, the Hungarian singer drowned, leaving Helena to settle alone in America where she soon found herself in the spiritualist firmament.

There she met Colonel H S Olcott, a rather serious-minded man, who had fought in the Civil War and was now researching psychic phenomena. Together, they founded the Theosophical Society in New York in 1875, deriving the name from the Greek words for God (*theo*) and wisdom (*sophia*).

The Society's ideals were condensed in their motto, "There is no religion higher than Truth". The declared aims of the Society were: the expression of the brotherhood of man, regardless of race, creed, colour or social position; the study of comparative religion to establish a universal ethic; and the development of

Captain Olcott witnessed Blavatsky's psychically inspired writings.

the latent powers of the human soul.

Encouraged by her new-found fame and the rapidly growing membership of the society, HPB, as she was known, decided to commit to paper her interpretation of the arcane knowledge of the East together with her own thoughts and theories.

According to Colonel Olcott, her first two-volume work, *Isis Unveiled* (1877), was written in a fever of intuition and psychic inspiration, her pen "flying over the page ... she would suddenly stop, look into space with the vacant eye of the clairvoyant seer, shorten her vision so as to look at something held invisibly in the air before her, and begin copying on the paper what she saw. The quotation finished, her eyes would resume their natural expression."

The book claimed to be the "master-key to the mysteries of ancient and modern science and theology", but was largely a confusion of Buddhist mysticism, Hindu mythology, Tibetan magic and a fanciful vision of world history

tracing the evolution of man back to the mythological races who inhabited the "lost" lands of Atlantis and Lemuria.

Now that we have easier access to the wisdom literature of the world's religions, Blavatsky's writings appear as a rather naïve muddle characterized by an uncritical enthusiasm for phenomena. But to her Victorian public it was all a revelation. *Isis Unveiled* became a massive overnight success and the first edition sold out within 10 days.

After a spell in India, Blavatsky and Olcott returned to Europe in 1884, where the Society for Psychical Research was eager to investigate her "marvellous phenomena", but they swiftly withdrew their support when allegations of fraud were issued against her by an embittered ex-employee. The scandal was sensationalized by the world's press and demolished her reputation. But HPB was not to be deterred. Although suffering from Bright's Disease, she settled down to write *The Secret Doctrine*, the culmination of her life's work.

RENE GUENON

According to the French traditionalist writer René Guénon (1886-1951), the Theosophical Society founded by Madame Blavatsky and Colonel Olcott had "absolutely no connection" with real theosophy. The latter was a spiritual undercurrent of Christianity, Judaism and Islam that had been explored by independently minded mystics within their own faith for centuries. True theosophists, Guénon argued, were those who sought the esoteric meaning in sacred texts, the Sufis, the Jewish Kabbalists, Jakob Boehme – and Guénon himself!

The French writer Faivre wrote that the theosophist "seeks to gain the ultimate vision of the principle of the world's reality. His work begins where rational philosophy ends, and finishes where theology begins, but the theosophist is more free and more creative than the theologian."

Guénon was as severely critical of what he saw as pseudo-spiritualist movements as he was of materialism. He maintained that the West was bent upon self-destruction because it had rejected tradition in favour of "progress". He wrote, "Not only have they limited their intellectual aims ... to the invention and construction of machines, but they have ended up becoming machines themselves."

Guénon saw his mission as transmitting the one true tradition common to all religious doctrines. Though a convert to Islam himself, he subscribed to the Hindu belief that the modern world corresponds to the Dark Age of Kali Yuga and must be destroyed in order to be reborn.

"Modern civilization, like all things, has its reason for being, and if it is really the end of a cycle, all we can say is that it must be, in its right time and in its right place."

MADAME BLAVATSKY –

THE SECRET DOCTRINE

"The truths of today are the falsehoods and errors of yesterday and vice versa. It is only in the 20th century that portions, if not the whole, of the present work will be vindicated."

(MADAME BLAVATSKY)

With only a few years of the 20th century remaining, it now seems unlikely that many of Madame Blavatsky's theories contained in *The Secret Doctrine* will be "vindicated" in the way she had hoped. Her insistence that the "lost continents" of Atlantis and Lemuria did in fact exist, and were the spiritual home of all the Mysteries, has seriously undermined her credibility now that the myth of Atlantis has been exposed.

In its original three-volume form, *The Secret Doctrine* purported to be a detailed Cosmogenesis and Anthropogenesis – the occult version of the evolution of the cosmos and humankind. In examining the forces which formed the Universe – as well as the five Races which are said to have preceded our own – Blavatsky claimed to be revealing "the universally diffused religion of the ancient and prehistoric world," adding that "proofs of its diffusion, authentic records of its history, a complete chain of documents, showing its character and presence in every land, together with the teaching of all its great adepts, exist to

Blavatsky predicted that the final cataclysm would be preceded by volcanic eruptions and tidal waves similar to those that claimed Atlantis.

this day in the secret crypts of libraries belonging to the Occult Fraternity."

Much of *The Secret Doctrine* is given over to lengthy descriptions of the origins and fate of the Seven Races of man, "five of which have nearly completed their earthly career." According to Blavatsky and her "Hidden Masters", evolution proceeds in cycles and we can expect the birth of the next Race within our lifetimes.

"Occult philosophy teaches that even now, under our very eyes, the new Race and Races are preparing to be formed, and that it is in America that the transformation will take place, and has already silently commenced."

Apparently, Americans have become a "primary race" and are destined to be the "germs of the Sixth sub-race". In "some few hundred years", this sixth sub-race is prophesied to succeed the Europeans. 25,000 years on from this point, they themselves will launch into preparations for the seventh sub-race; "until, in consequence of cataclysms, the first series of those which must one day destroy Europe, and still later the whole Aryan race (and thus affect both Americas), as also most of the lands directly connected with the confines of our continent and isles – the Sixth Root-Race will have appeared ... "

According to its author, this evolution will be so slow and subtle that its "pioneers" will be "regarded as abnormal oddities physically and mentally". But by the time they are in the majority, she predicts the dramatic appearance of a sixth continent rising out of the sea, where the new Sixth Race will make its home ensuring survival from the worldwide cataclysm. When this "general disaster" is to be, Blavatsky admitted,

she did not know, nor was it for her to be privileged to such knowledge, but she did prophesy that "the final cataclysm will be preceded by many smaller submersions and destructions both by wave and volcanic fires ... "

There could even be a point when mankind transcends the body and exists in the spirit as the Cathars predicted. Despite the cataclysms, this new era will herald in a golden age, for a "grander and far more glorious Race than any of those we know of at present".

Her theories concerning the superiority of this, Aryan, race and the symbol she chose to represent them – the swastika – were later adopted by the Nazis. Blavatsky's "Hidden Masters" told her to remind her followers that, if they lead the life necessary for the acquisition of knowledge and power, "wisdom will come ... naturally", but warned those in search of such knowledge not to be too free with what they find.

"When you have studied thoroughly 'the music of the spheres', then only will you become quite free to share your knowledge with those with whom it is safe to do so. Meanwhile, be prudent. Do not give out the great Truths that are the inheritance of the future Races, to our present generation."

Despite her fanciful theories, Blavatsky understood that wisdom comes when we are ready, that mankind evolves spiritually and mentally as well as physically and that only when we are "mature" do we receive the next infusion of secret wisdom from those who guide humanity.

THE THEOSOPHICAL SOCIETY

The Theosophical Society is currently active in 60 countries around the world. Although its central philosophy is still based on The Divine Wisdom "channelled" through Madame Blavatsky, it has assimilated the teachings of other wisdom traditions to become what it calls, "A spiritual Science For Today".

The Society's doctrine is now based on the following fundamental ideas:- "That matter is not limited to the perception of the five senses; That consciousness can exist independently of the physical body; That there is no proof that consciousness ends at death ... and much evidence that it continues;

That life is a continuing process; That all human beings have the potential to create for themselves and for humanity a future whose splendour has no limit."

The International President of the Theosophical Society (which is based in Madras, India), Radha Burnier, sees the members' task as helping people to understand themselves and their purpose in life: "Millions of people lost in the urban mechanisms of the world's cities ... have adopted a way of life which is out of tune with the rhythms of real life.

"Crystallizations of the mind must be broken up in order to create a new human society ..."

THE ARCANE SCHOOL

Alice Bailey believed that she was the channel for the tele-pathic teachings of a Master who wished to introduce the Ageless Wisdom to the people of the West.

In the first half of the 20th century, prior to the emergence of the current New Age movement, there existed a similar, less well-publicized movement known to initiates as the Aquarian New Age.

Comprising mystics, theosophists and European enthusiasts of all things Eastern, this nebulous collective centred around a group known as the Arcane School, founded by the author Alice Bailey.

Bailey (1880-1949) believed herself to be in telepathic contact with a brother-hood of benign spirits referred to as "The Great White Brotherhood", or "Occult Hierarchy", and entrusted with guiding mankind according to the "Great Plan", which was part of a greater purpose (the Will of God).

Bailey claimed that one of these guiding lights was Blavatsky's "Hidden Master", Koot-Hoomi, and another, known to her as "The Tibetan", is said to have "dictated" 19 volumes of his teach-ings to her over a period of 30 years.

These teachings, supplemented by the writings of Madame Blavatsky, her successor Annie Besant and Manly P Hall (founder of the Philosophical Research Society of California) among others, were collectively referred to by followers as the Ageless or Arcane Wisdom.

This Ageless Wisdom is said to be held in indestructible archives in the higher realms of existence by the benign broth-erhood who "channel" it through chosen individuals when they consider that mankind is ready for such knowledge.

According to Bailey's "Hidden Master", "The Tibetan" – later identified as the Master Djwhal Kul – the Brotherhood meet during the last quarter of each century to "energize" humanity. Plans are then laid for devel-opments on earth during the first quarter of the next century.

Some credence was lent to this claim by the intensification of interest in esoterica and the occult at the beginning of the 20th century, which was also stimulated by the great loss of life in the First World War.

And now, in the last quarter of the century, there is renewed interest in the esoteric, but this is of a more mature, spir-itual nature than was shown by the sensa-tionalist spiritualism of the earlier period. Esoteric thought, it seems, is not immune to a renewed surge of energy and looks like being stimulated into a re-evaluation of its beliefs, just at a time when the rest of humanity will have to question theirs.

Through Alice Bailey, "The Tibetan" predicted that in the first quarter of the 21st century there will be a restoration of the Ancient Mysteries, which have been debased by Black Magic. These will now be expressed at a higher level. This is part of the "Great Plan" and will pave the way for an event described as "Externalization of the Hierarchy",

This fanciful image of telepathy may one day become a reality.

when those on earth who are spiritually advanced will work consciously with the brotherhood to help humanity.

The effect of this surge in our spiritual evolution is predicted to be dramatic, especially for those who are unprepared. Such people will resist the changes, clinging all the more desperately to their materialistic values.

"The Mysteries will be restored in other ways also, for they contain much besides that which the Masonic rites can reveal or that religious rituals and ceremonies can disclose ... The Mysteries will restore colour and music as they essentially are to the world ... in such a manner that the creative art of today will be to this new creative art what a child's building of wooden blocks is to a great cathe-

Alice Bailey channelled the teachings of the "Tibetan".

dral such as Durham or Milan. The Mysteries, when restored, will make real – in a sense incomprehensible to you at present – the nature of religion, the purpose of science and the goal of education. These are not what you think today ..."

Beyond these sensational claims of a world-wide re-awakening to the Ageless Wisdom is the fundamental belief shared by many of the esoteric and religious traditions: that man must first demonstrate the will to develop, before the benign forces – whether we imagine them to be "Hidden Masters", our own Higher Self or a Messiah – are allowed to intervene to help us.

SCIENCE AND SUPERHUMANS

As a result of the "awakening" in the next century, "The Tibetan" predicted a range of new scientific discoveries which will contribute to mankind's progress and well-being.

A new form of electricity will "put man in touch with extra-systemic phenomena". A further development will come from exploration into the power and properties of sound. This, claimed "The Tibetan", "will put into man's hands a tremendous instrument in the world of creation," adding that "the release of energy, in the atom

is linked to this coming science of sound." Furthermore, Madame Blavatsky's assertion that matter is simply spirit at its lowest vibrational rate, and that consequently "all is energy", will be proven to be fact, preparing the way for the marriage of esoteric and material science. In the light of this, Alice Bailey confidently predicted: "The next step ahead for science is the discovery of the Soul, a discovery which will revolutionize, though not negate, the majority of their [scientists'] theories."

Parallel to scientific progress,

man's physical characteristics will alter too as we develop latent powers that up to now have been regarded as paranormal.

Telepathy, extra-sensory perception and other siddhis (paranormal powers) of the yogis are prophesied to become standard human abilities.

She also claimed that a new awareness of the importance of breath control will result in a refinement of the human voice which, when combined with higher consciousness, will produce remarkable, though unspecified effects!

THE HIDDEN MASTERS

"Have you so little belief in the survival of bodily death that you cannot conceive of the existence of the Masters?

(ANONYMOUS MASTER SPEAKING THROUGH DION FORTUNE)

For thousands of years highly evolved beings, whose spirits transcend time and space, are said to have guided our evolution by "channelling" the Ageless Wisdom through sensitized individuals, who literally became the "mediums" for their message.

Implausible though it might at first appear, a Brotherhood of Secret or Hidden Masters has long been a part of both the Eastern and the Western Esoteric Tradition. During the Renaissance, a pamphlet entitled "Fama Fraternitatis" was in circulation which made mention of a secret "Rosicrucian Brotherhood" made up of adepts who were said to be influencing events in Europe by psychic means.

In the 19th century, S L MacGregor Mathers, one of the founders of the Hermetic Order of the Golden Dawn, made it known that he received his instructions from a mysterious group he called the Secret Chiefs, two of whom he claimed to have met on a train! Former Golden Dawn member, Dion Fortune, said that she had been inspired by the same "Hidden Masters" who had guided Mathers and Blavatsky, although she referred to them as "Inner Plane Adepti". These *Adepti* apparently encouraged her to form her own group, the Society of the Inner Light, which is still in existence today.

Koot-Hoomi, whose teachings were apparently channelled through Madame Blavatsky.

"The Masters as you picture them are all 'imagination'," she wrote. "Note well that I did not say the Masters *were* imagination ... [they are contacted] through your imagination, and although your mental picture is not real or actual, the *results* of it are real and actual."

Even essentially Christian texts, such as the recently published million-seller *A Course In Miracles* or the teachings of the spirit guide White Eagle have allegedly been "channelled" through people claiming no previous interest or knowledge in the Mysteries. Through these "mediators", the Masters have claimed that the Ageless Wisdom has been distorted by orthodox religions, who have taken it upon themselves to be sole custodians of teachings which were meant for the whole of humanity.

The proliferation of "channelled teachings" published in the 20th century has been an attempt to redress the balance – more are promised after the Millennium.

It is believed there are hundreds of aspiring Masters now in our midst, spiritually advanced human beings subtly influencing the coming change in consciousness. But at present only nine immortal Masters are known by name. They are Maitreya, Koot-Hoomi (Madame Blavatsky's teacher), Jwul-Khul ("The Tibetan"), Hilarion, Morya, Serapis, Rakoczi, Maha Chohan and Jesus. Each is responsible for a different aspect of evolution (religion, science, philosophy, the arts *et al*) and for each specific group entrusted with carrying out the task of education. Through these various avenues of human endeavour and experience, they aim to make man aware of the unity of all creation. And, much as a conductor might train a group of musicians to play as one, they aim to encourage science, art and religion to converge one day for a single purpose.

In an effort to reconcile religious differences, it is believed one of the "Hidden Masters" instigated the Agnostic movement as a counterweight to religious extremism in the 19th century. When the Agnostics grew too strong, he inspired the birth of the Spiritualist movement, the Theosophical Society and the Christian Science Movement to restore the balance. If

true, the current upsurge of interest in spirituality and esoteric movements can be explained as having been instigated by the Masters to counter the rise in fundamentalism.

Maitreya, the World Teacher, is regarded by those who believe in the Masters as the "Father" of whom Jesus spoke, the true Christ who worked through Jesus. Many Theosophists believed that their "guru" Krishnamurti was destined to receive the spirit of Maitreya, but he began teaching before he was ready, and so Maitreya spoke through Sai Baba instead. This would certainly give new meaning to Jesus's claim that, "It is not I who do the work. It is the father in me who brings forth the great accomplishment."

After Krishnamurti declined his

destined role, Maitreya is said to have communicated his disappointment through the usual channels saying: *"What eventually may rise from the present wreckage of beliefs and traditions is a new-found determination on the part of individuals to school themselves, to acquire those faculties which will enable them to obtain by their own efforts a unique and personal contact with the Masters and with God. Henceforth I will come not through groups with recognized officials or organizations which render often what is no more than lip service in their assumptions of brotherhood. I will come to each and all who love me, no matter of what race, class or creed. The greatness of their need, the strength of their desire shall be the measure of their power to see me."*

Maitreya statuette, 4th century CE.

THE MASTERS AND THE NEW AGE

In the 1930s, the Master Koot-Hoomi made the following prediction regarding the coming change in consciousness, or what is popularly known as the "New Age".

"Any great initiate who comes in the near future will need to be a very powerful person indeed if he is to contend with the spiritual vacuum which is making itself everywhere perceptible. Only the bravest of souls dare attempt what will become a struggle to keep the lamp of Truth alight until the fresh flowering of faith at the end of the century. We who watch the struggles of humanity with compassion realize the suffering with which the present is fraught, and yet we *would not end it, even if it lay in our power. Where you see merely the wastage of frustrated effort, uncertainty, chaos, petty jealousies and bewilderments, the broken fragments of an uncompleted pattern we see that pattern a little more in perspective ... We know the suffering may be likened to a spiritual 'growing pain' ... This time the great influx of power to be poured forth at the end of the century must not, will not, fail in its object. It will be a mighty tide bearing mankind forward towards a greater comprehension, a greater enlightenment, towards the ineffable blessings of that peace which passes all understanding."*

THE HERMETIC ORDER

OF THE GOLDEN DAWN

"When I came in touch with this organization ... I immediately recognized power of a degree and kind I had never met before, and had not the slightest doubt but that I was on the trail of the genuine tradition."

(DION FORTUNE)

Between its formation in 1888 and its traumatic public disintegration in 1900, the Hermetic Order of the Golden Dawn laid the foundations for the transmission of the Mysteries throughout Europe for the greater part of the 20th century.

The Order's prevailing image as a group of "grey-bearded ancients", as occultist Dion Fortune called them, dabbling in magic and archaic rituals has overshadowed its considerable contribution to esoteric thought in the modern age. Its founders were largely responsible for compiling a coherent occult system based on their reinterpretation of the Kabbalah, the Tarot, astrology and ritual magic which continues to influence the work of Western esoteric groups to this day.

The veil of secrecy and notoriety which surrounded the Order has made it almost impossible to distinguish facts

from fiction, but it appears it was founded after Dr William Wynn Wescott, a high-ranking Rosicrucian and Freemason, chanced upon a number of coded manuscripts in an antiquarian bookstall.

Rosicrucian symbol of the Golden Dawn.

Wescott knew at a glance that he had made a most remarkable discovery and immediately set about decoding the manuscripts with the help of a fellow Freemason, S L MacGregor Mathers, an occult scholar who had made a name for himself translating several important medieval grimoires such as the *Key Of Solomon* and *The Book Of The Sacred Magic Of Abra-Melin The Mage.*

To their amazement and delight, the pair discovered the manuscript described a system of practical magic complete with the name and address of the author, an adept living in Nuremberg, Germany, by the name of Anna Sprengler. Wescott lost no time in writing to her and a regular correspondence was established in which Fräulein Sprengler elaborated on the secrets contained in the manuscript. A year later, she gave her consent for Wescott and Mathers to form their own magical lodge in England.

Initially, it was a secret society with a strong Masonic membership which met in a small set of rooms in a grubby back street in London. But it soon attracted an impressive roster of writers, artists and "free-thinkers", including the poet W B Yeats, the writers Algernon Blackwood, Bram Stoker, Arthur Machen and Sax Rohmer, and also a future president of the Royal Academy of Arts.

What attracted these men was the Order's emphasis on the power of the imagination as a key to unlocking the magical talents of the mind.

Members were not interested in magic as such, but were searching for a way to engage their intellect and imagination, which would hopefully lead to profound mystical experiences and an expansion of consciousness. One-time member Evelyn Underhill viewed magic merely as a necessary stage on the path to self-realization.

"Magic, in its uncorrupted form, claims to be a practical, intellectual, highly individualistic science; working towards the declared end of enlarging the sphere on which the human will can work, and obtaining experimental knowledge of planes of being usually regarded as transcendental ..."

The Order saw itself as continuing a tradition of arcane knowledge which they could trace from the Masons and Rosicrucians all the way back to the

Bram Stoker, author of Dracula, *was an enthusiastic member of the Order.*

Mysteries of Egypt. Many of its rituals derived from papyri purporting to be of Graeco-Egyptian origin, while Egyptian symbolism adorned the walls of its "temples", or branches, which also took their names from Egyptian deities.

Mathers, who has been described by Yeats as "half lunatic, half knave", took it upon himself to compile the teachings and reinterpret the rituals, adapting a Graeco-Egyptian invocation to enable members to contact their "Divine Genius", or higher self. Using this, Mathers maintained, one could dominate all the forces in the Universe.

The Order's most theatrical ritual was a re-enactment of the crucifixion in a room said to be a replica of Christian Rosenkreutz's funeral vault. The initiate was apparently tied to a cross and swore an oath of loyalty which began: "I will, from this day forward, apply myself to the Great Work – which is, to purify and exalt my Spiritual Nature so that with the Divine Aid I may at length attain to be more than human, and thus gradually raise and unite myself to my higher and Divine Genius, and that in this event I will not abuse the great power entrusted to me."

The atmosphere of secrecy and exclusivity was maintained by the establishment of a hierarchy within the Order, whose *adepti* remained privy to secret knowledge. The grades were modelled on those of the Rosicrucians, but were supplemented by a 10th grade of the Order's own invention, that of Ipsissimus ("most himself"), to correspond to the ten *sefirot* of the Kabbalah. Like Blavatsky before them, members of the Order claimed to be guided and inspired by "Hidden Masters", "Secret and unknown magi" possessing "terrible

The poet W B Yeats professed a lifelong fascination with magic and the occult.

superhuman powers". By 1896, there were 315 members, of whom 119 were women, including Constance Wilde, the wife of Oscar Wilde, and Florence Fary, the mistress of George Bernard Shaw, all dedicated to the "Great Work" in lodges as far apart as Edinburgh, Paris and Chicago. By the end of the decade the Order had disintegrated amidst violent and public quarrel. Mathers and his wife Moina (sister of the philosopher Henri Bergson) had moved to Paris, pursued by the notorious Aleister Crowley, who demanded Mathers initiate him into the grades he believed himself entitled to. He had joined a few years earlier and claimed he was being denied his certificates of initiation by Yeats, who apparently despised him. The ensuing legal wrangle resulted in the society's secrets being printed in the newspapers and precipitated the break-up of the Order in 1900.

ALEISTER CROWLEY –

THE BEAST HIMSELF

"Man is ignorant of the nature of his own being and powers ... Man is capable of being, and using, anything which he perceives, for everything that he perceives is in a certain sense part of his being."

Aleister Crowley (1875-1947), the notorious magician whom the popular press dubbed "the wickedest man in the world", squandered his considerable talents indulging in drugs and sexual "magick", but nonetheless succeeded in dragging practical magic out of the Middle Ages, reinventing it as a means of discovering one's true self.

An able mountaineer, expert chess player and prolific writer of pretentious, often obscene, poetry, Crowley railed against a society that he considered complacent, hypocritical and responsible for repressing the potential of the individual. His oft-quoted dictum, "Do what thou wilt shall be the whole of the law" (borrowed from William Blake), has been wilfully misinterpreted by those who wish to perpetuate the myth of "the Great Beast", the dark guru of an

alternative society dedicated to the overthrow of Christianity and the establishment of its own pagan-style religion.

What Crowley advocated was not that a man should do what he liked regardless of

Crowley saw himself as the High Priest of a new religion.

the consequences, but that he must be true to himself to realize his own greatness and not be limited or inhibited by the conventions of society. Of course, Crowley took this idea too far (as he did with most things), shocking society for the perverse pleasure it gave him.

By all accounts, he was a repulsive character, a conceited, self-centred, affectionless man, of whom it was said "he was a nasty little boy who never grew up".

Born Edward Alexander Crowley at Leamington, Warwickshire, in 1875, young Crowley rebelled against his strict puritanical upbringing from an early age, delighting in his mother's assertion that he was the Great Beast 666 of the Book of Revelation. A precociously gifted scholar, he graduated from Cambridge in 1898 and immediately joined the Order of the Golden Dawn, ingratiating himself with MacGregor Mathers before whom he played the part of devoted pupil. But the pair soon fell out, culminating in a "magical battle" on the astral plane, which allegedly resulted in the death of Mathers and the dissolution of the Order.

Crowley later said of his fellow members: "They were not protagonists in the spiritual warfare against restriction, against the oppressors of the human soul, the blasphemers who denied the supremacy of the will of man."

Above all, Crowley viewed organized religion as the repressor of mankind, but he offered nothing constructive to replace it.

Under the influence of an old friend and former member of the Golden Dawn, Allan Bennett, Crowley temporarily

Crowley conducting the magical rite of Abra-Melin.

A WARNING TO THE CURIOUS

The cult which grew up around Crowley in the Sixties, and which has been fostered by the obsessive tendencies of rock musicians such as Jimmy Page of Led Zeppelin, has obscured the fact that "the Beast" himself detested anyone who slavishly followed him. He despised the weak, unstable women who became his disciples and once condemned one of his American imitators by saying, "I get fairly frantic when I contemplate the idiocy of these louts".

Would-be followers might do well to heed the comments of celebrated occultist and fellow Golden Dawn member, Dion Fortune, who wrote:

"The formulae ... on which he works, would be considered averse and evil by occultists accustomed to the Qabalistic tradition ... No hint is given of this in the text, and it is an ugly trap for the unwary student.

"Crowley ... gives the North as the holy point towards which the operator turns to invoke, instead of the East, 'whence light arises', as is the classical practice. Now the North is called 'the place of greatest symbolic darkness', and is only the holy point of one sect, the Yezidees, or devil worshippers ... an invocation to the North, is not going to contact what most people would consider to be desirable forces."

---

gave up magic and turned instead to Eastern mysticism and Yoga for an answer to his spiritual quest. With characteristic arrogance, he claimed to have mastered the art in no time at all, dismissing Yoga practices as "dodges to help one to acquire the knack of slowing down the current of thoughts, and ultimately stopping it altogether". It seemed he lacked the self-discipline necessary for real spiritual development, or the self-knowledge, or perhaps he just could not face what he found.

Retreating to Cairo in 1904, Crowley made contact with his own "higher Genius", a spirit named Aiwass who "channelled" the text of what became *The Book of the Law* through Crowley's clairvoyant wife, Rose. In pseudo-biblical rhetoric, Aiwass, or was it Crowley, exhorted everyone to indulge themselves as they saw fit – not a doctrine that endeared the writer to prim and prudish Edwardian England. " ... dress ye all in fine apparel; eat rich foods and drink sweet wines and wines that foam! Also, take your fill and will of love as ye will, when, where and with whom ye will ..." Crowley's moral code is crass, childish and transparently anti-puritan, but he was convinced his "wisdom" would form the foundation of a new religion for the Age of Horus. But even Nietzsche would have blanched at his assertions that "we should not protect the weak and vicious from the results of their own inferiority", or that "to pity another man is to insult him". Crowley certainly had little pity for his wife, whom he had married expressly to frustrate her other admirers. Before long, she had become a dipsomaniac and he had taken to hanging her upside down by her heels inside a wardrobe!

By 1910, Crowley was addicted to Mescaline and indulging in what he called "sexmagick" in a Satanic Temple in the Fulham Road, London, with a horde of aristocratic female admirers. Tiring of this, he took his entourage off to Cefalu in Sicily, where he founded the first and only Abbey of Thelema (the name is borrowed from Rabelais) in a run-down villa with two of his perpetually feuding mistresses. After three years of debauchery and drug abuse, the "Beast" and his cronies were expelled by the Italian government following the mysterious death of a disciple who had allegedly died after drinking a cup of cat's blood during a sacrificial rite.

Returning to England, Crowley became increasingly dependent on drugs and died sick, penniless and frightened of the dark in a seedy boarding house in Hastings. His last words were, "I am perplexed ..."

DION FORTUNE AND THE FRATERNITY OF THE INNER LIGHT

"Nature is God made manifest and we blaspheme Her at our peril."

(DION FORTUNE)

Through her books *The Cosmic Doctrine* and *The Mystical Qabbalah*, British occultist Dion Fortune (1890-1946) redefined the Western esoteric tradition for the modern age. She developed an eclectic system of practice and observance based partly on the Kabbalah, partly on Christian mythology and Egyptian archetypes.

As a self-proclaimed priestess of Isis, Fortune continued the tradition of Madame Blavatsky, proclaiming that "Isis is the All-Woman and all women are Isis", a concept which has had a profound effect upon those women seeking to realize their full potential through working with the archetype of the goddess on the occult path.

Born Violet Mary Firth on December 6, 1890 at Bryn-y-Bia in Llandudno in Wales, Fortune was a shy, nervous girl who suffered a number of minor breakdowns prior to the one she claimed she endured at the age of 23, which spurred her to study psychology and occultism as a means of "psychic self-defence". Shortly before the First World War, she enrolled at the University of London. Here she studied the hidden power of the mind and in particular the theories of Francis Aveling which he expounded in his books, *Personality And Will* and

Dion Fortune and her husband Henry Penry-Evans (left) with Mr Loveday, Dion Fortune's amanuensis and close collaborator.

Directing Mental Energy. In her search for the source of this latent force, Fortune developed practical techniques to harness and direct it. She later evolved a theory which linked the *chakras* (energy centres of the "etheric" body) with the hormone-secreting endocrine glands.

While working as a lay psychoanalyst at the Tavistock Clinic in London, she attended meetings of the Theosophical Society and there absorbed the theories of Madame Blavatsky which she hoped would one day be accepted in all branches of science and modern life.

About this time, Fortune also came into contact with the enigmatic Theodore Moriarty, whose lectures formed the basis of her book, *The Cosmic Doctrine*, central to which was the concept of a transcendent, abstract creative power whose attributes are comparable with the *sefirot* on the kabbalistic Tree of Life.

In 1919, she joined one of the two "daughter lodges" of the Amun-Ra-Temple of the Hermetic Order of the

The Fraternity's London headquarters became a school of occult initiation.

Golden Dawn, adopting the magical name Deus Non Fortuna which she later abbreviated to Dion Fortune.

Despite, or perhaps because of, her rapid progress, she became frustrated with the stale atmosphere of the lodge

and, in 1922, formed an "outer court", The Fraternity of the Inner Light. Her aim was to establish a school of initiation with a sound basis in psychology, scholarly tradition and practical occultism.

With a core of her fellow ex-members from the Christian Mystic Lodge of the Theosophical Society, she established headquarters at 3 Queensborough Terrace in London, and also at her home at Chalice Orchard, Glastonbury, in the west of England – because of the area's association with the Grail legend and the cult of the Mother Goddess.

Fortune viewed herself and her followers as servants of evolution, working with nature and the cosmic forces and not, as magicians would have it, to dominate them by force of will.

"The coming of the Cosmic Christ in the Aquarian age," she once wrote, "the return of the redeemed 'Merlin', 'Arthur' and the Arthurian Figures in the Racial spheres refer to the time when man himself will take on the remains of his karma not dealt with by the last Great Redeemer [Christ] ..."

THE WAY OF FULFILMENT

As an occultist, Dion Fortune viewed the Kabbalah as a practical framework for travelling the realms of the sefirot *"in the spirit vision" or by astral projection. Whereas the mystic has to transcend normal consciousness to worship God in essence, she believed that it was equally legitimate to work with the psychic forces, the Christian archetypes of the Grail legend and the goddess*

Isis to experience at first hand the nature of Divine essence and absorb it into one's being.

This, Fortune maintained, was not deviation from the path of human destiny, but instead led to a concentration and sublimation of that destiny – a Way of Fulfilment to obtain mastery over life just as a virtuoso masters his instrument. She sought what she described as an alternative path to Divine

Union, "the path of the mastery of manifested existence and the apotheosis of self".

By subscribing to esoteric doctrines, Fortune believed that a person would see himself "as part of the great whole" and learn to appreciate his relationship with nature and the cosmos. He would thus be in alignment with the ultimate destiny of mankind – union with its source.

DION FORTUNE – THE COSMIC DOCTRINE

"The object of these teachings is to induce a deeper understanding of Cosmic Law, and to expand consciousness that it may lift thoughts to the source from which they issued."

(DION FORTUNE)

The channelled teachings which Dion Fortune compiled for publication under the title *The Cosmic Doctrine* were, she claimed, received from an anonymous adept on "the inner planes", who in a previous incarnation had been a world famous philosopher and teacher. Under his guidance Fortune formulated an occult philosophy concerning the origins and nature of the universe and man's purpose in it. She believed this would one day be verified by science.

God, or the Logos, plays no active part in the Cosmic drama: all existence, all phenomena, are the results of the interplay of Cosmic Forces and friction in space. "The Unmanifest," she wrote, "is pure existence ... the only Unity. Manifestation begins when duality occurs."

By duality, Fortune was referring to the opposing forces which she called the "Ring of Cosmos" and the "Ring of Chaos". Good and Evil are merely the opposing polarities of these two forces, no more benign or malevolent than the negative and positive poles of a magnet.

The universe is the playground of cosmic forces.

"Evil is simply that which is moving in the opposite direction to evolution ... a force which tends to non-existence."

Our universe is the result of "swarms" of atoms caught in vortices of energy. "Movement is the basis of all things. Abstract movements, which are opposed,

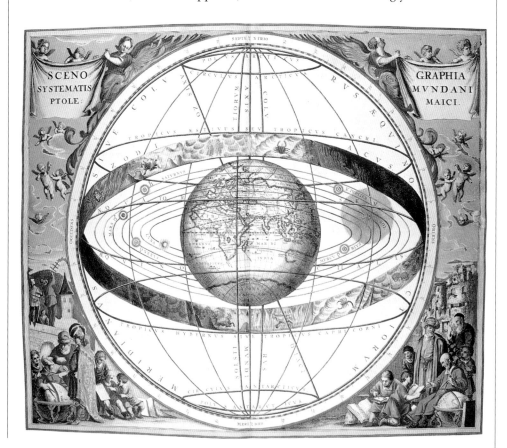

lock up force and render it static, fixed. It is these locked-up forces which become 'form'. A form is simply force which is not free to move."

Life comes into being because the Logos is conscious only of itself and needs to develop objective consciousness. It projects Its concept of Itself and this manifests as existence. Life as a reflection of the Logos is initially conscious only of Itself, but in time develops objective consciousness to understand Its true nature and that of Its creator. This is a concept Fortune had obviously taken from the Kabbalah, where the Absolute All instigated the unfolding of existence, so that it would come to know Itself through the experience of Its creation.

At the completion of each phase of evolution, the Logos assimilates the results of that cycle and modifies its own consciousness accordingly. This is then impregnated into each succeeding "swarm" of atoms, or Divine Sparks, and carried down into the universe to stimulate the next stage of evolution, in much the same way as Man carries physical data in his genes and psychic memories into each incarnation.

The forces of the Cosmos tend towards equilibrium, but there are critical periods in evolution when the friction caused by these forces produces a crisis on Earth in the form of an upsurge of evil or a crisis of conscience. Dramatic changes are impossible to predict and are likely to distort the prophecies of the ancient seers, such as Nostradamus, whose visions have previously proven to be uncannily accurate.

" ... the astrology of the ancients, though fundamentally true, is not strictly accurate at the present day. The developments caused by evolution must be allowed for. Therefore, those aspects which in primitive times might be interpreted as war and bloodshed, at the present time might be interpreted as a conflict of ideas."

According to Fortune, when the

According to Fortune the cause of our suffering is that we are sense-centred.

current evolutionary cycle is completed, the experience and matter of the Earth will be "garnered up and will pass on to other evolutions in other planets". However, some of its life-forces will one day return in another form to this world.

A MATTER OF LIFE AND DEATH

"So long as consciousness dwells in the senses," wrote Dion Fortune, "it will view things from the standpoint of the senses, of 'pain' and 'pleasure', 'beginning' and 'ending'. But when it is raised to the relation of Cosmic things, it will see all things in relation to evolution ..."

According to the great masters and mystics throughout the centuries, the significance of life and death has been distorted as a result of our fears and false values. Fortune repeatedly stated that incarnation is,

in effect, the living death of the spirit, while death is the release of spirit from the limitations of the body and the unjustified anxieties of the ego.

"Birth is death and death is birth ... learn, therefore, to look down upon your dead bodies to galvanize them with your life, but do not make the mistake of living in them."

Life, she argued, is an opportunity for learning; death, on the other hand, is a period for "meditating" on the knowledge accrued while

on the physical plane.

"The essence of evolution," she wrote, "is unification, and the manifestation of the unificatory principle upon the planes of manifestation is Love. Whether that love be intellectual sympathy on the plane of the concrete mind, or physical unity on the plane of matter, Love in all its aspects is the symbol of the Logos as One ... Whosoever expresses Love, brings spirit, which is One, into manifestation. To be separate is to be dead."

W. E. BUTLER

"The path is not a path for those who are wanting something; it is a path for those who are going to be something."

Walter Ernest Butler (1898-1978) was an impish, avuncular figure, whose innate modesty would have prevented him from accepting the honorary title of "Father of New Age occultism" had anyone been rash enough to suggest such a thing.

According to a close friend, he was often to be found dozing before the fire with a cup of tea in one hand and a cat curled up on his lap, the very antithesis of the popular image of an occultist.

An initiate of both the Eastern and Western Mysteries, Butler adhered rigorously to a principle he had learnt in the Freemasons: "I desire to know in order to serve." This doctrine he passed on to his pupils in the two mystery schools which he founded after leaving Dion Fortune's Society of the Inner Light.

In the last year of his life, Butler gave a series of lectures to his inner circle, which were posthumously published in America under the title *Lords Of Light*. In these talks he brought together disparate ideas from East and West, magic and mysticism, religion and occultism distilled into a practical philosophy which he seems to have formulated especially for the New Age.

Butler used to remind his pupils that

Butler regarded occultism as true a science as chemistry or electricity.

they were all "Followers of the Way", the title taken by the first followers of Jesus before they called themselves Christians.

The Way, Butler believed, is the way of wisdom not knowledge for, as he rightly said, "You can have someone that is all knowledge, so full that it shakes out of their ears every time they move, and

yet they may not have enough sense to come in out of the rain."

Wisdom he maintained comes with personal experience and through contact with our own Inner Teacher, intuition, which Butler calls "the only true teacher". From this Eternal "comes the gnosis, the knowledge that is above knowledge". He once recalled that not until his first conscious out-of-body experience did he lose his fear of death. He had of course been told the "mechanics" of astral projection, but knowing about them was not enough.

Butler had a very different picture of occultism to that of the general public. He saw it as merely another aspect of science and psychology, "as true a science as chemistry or electricity".

The aim of occultism, he believed, was not to master archaic lore, but to cultivate a new way of thinking. "We have to create our own universe, but it has to be built upon the true lines. Just as David received the pattern of the Temple on the Mountain and passed it on to Solomon, his son, who actually built the temple, we have to go into the mountain of exalted consciousness – we have to reach up within to gain the plan, the blueprint by which we can construct our universe here in the world ... We're going to be universe builders in company with God ... That is what occultism is to me. That is what I have been taught over the years."

Though he did not speak of the New Age as such, Butler was eager to awaken humanity to a new awareness of the earth as a living organism. "This planet of ours is not dead by any means. It is a vital living thing. Mother Earth is literally a living, conscious being, a great living organism. Life doesn't only extend to animals and vegetables, but right down to the mineral kingdom and far below that. The mystery teachings declare that in the inner depths of the planet there is a centre where all the work of the planet is done, where force and form work constantly to keep the planet working harmoniously and to allow what consciousness it has to manifest. You could call it the Heart of the World."

Butler liked to remind his pupils that we are all "children of earth, and we draw from the Earth Mother and from the racial past those things which belong to the earth. But we are also from the starry heavens ... our job is to unite the two."

Through his studies with Dion Fortune, Annie Besant and various Hindu masters in India, Butler came to the conclusion that there was little tangible difference between the wisdom traditions of East and West. "To a great extent the Eastern and Western Traditions are exchangeable, but the psychology of individuals is different ... Some of the Eastern lines are effete ... they've become effete because they're too inbred ... they haven't allowed other traditions to influence them ... the West has suffered in the opposite way. It's been a kaleidoscope of different influences coming in and out, and there's no real steady school on which you can put your finger and say,

Butler believed that we each have to build the Temple of Solomon within.

'That is the "Western Tradition".' ... The doctrine of reincarnation has been the greatest curse of the East, leaving people to take what comes, 'Oh, it's my karma', they say and lie down under it and let themselves be submitted to oppression and starvation ... The mystic East is still the light from the East, but the West has its own light and the two together can illuminate the world."

WALKING THROUGH WALLS

Although too modest a man to be tempted to prophecy, Butler did state that if mankind learnt to govern the automatic process whereby the life force is absorbed in our bodies and perhaps one day even harness **kundalini** *(the "serpent power" within), we should be able to alter our molecular structure. " ... then, if we want to walk through a wall, we resolve the physical body into pre-matter and we walk through the wall without obstruction. It is what the theologians call, 'the resurrection body', the body which walks out from the tomb."*

When we have transformed ourselves into spiritual beings the physical universe will no longer appear as form, *"but will pass into a state known in the East as pralaya – a state of no matter. Then the next phase of creation will begin when the plastic substance of the universe again comes into manifestation."*

But first we must conquer our fear of change and let go of those attitudes which have given us a false sense of security. Ultimately, the "new child", as Butler called it, must be born and occultism will provide the training for its life in eternity. "As we develop under the will and wisdom of the Eternal Spirit, we shall still persist as spiritual beings going forth into new universes. That is the goal, the end product of occultism."

THE RELUCTANT MYSTIC

" ... it is a pity so few remember what they do at night; if they did, they would be much less troubled about the state called death – and the wicked rumours circulated concerning hell and eternal damnation would have no more effect on them than the fear of the ogre in the children's fairy book affects the adult reader."

(ACHARYA)

If wisdom comes from experience, then the extraordinary experiences of Peter Richelieu must have been truly enlightening.

In July 1941, Richelieu, a nominally observant Catholic living in South Africa, was brooding over the recent death of his brother Charles, a fighter pilot who had been killed in action over England. Unable to reconcile his belief in a beneficent Creator with the cruel, apparently indiscriminate murder of his brother, Richelieu's grief gave way to despair. It was then that a mysterious Indian adept named Acharya appeared as if in answer to a prayer.

Unlike other "Hidden Masters" who have been sent with a message for humanity, Acharya did not communicate telepathically with his mediator but instead knocked at the front door, calmly announcing to a servant that he had a personal message for the master of the house!

In his detailed account of the encounter, *A Soul's Journey*, Richelieu described Acharya as being singularly unremarkable. He appeared to be about 45 years old, tall, of thin build with a beard and a benevolent expression "which seemed to contain the wisdom of the ages". He was dressed in traditional Indian costume complete with a turban and on his feet he wore simple sandals.

Acharya claimed that Richelieu had sent for him through his unconscious and that he had come to answer the questions of life and death which had plagued Richelieu since the loss of his brother. Over the next few days, Acharya taught Richelieu how to leave his physical body and travel on the astral planes. But before he took his awe-struck pupil on his first astral flight, he explained the nature of the three vehicles of consciousness within the human body. He listed these as "the mental or mind body, the astral or emotional body and the physical body".

The ego wears each of these bodies like a layer of clothes and, in death, each one falls away as we leave the denser worlds of matter behind – assuming that we can detach ourselves from the physical world. If our emotional attachments or desires are too strong, or if we cannot accept death, we may linger on the astral plane appearing to the living as ghosts. The mental and astral bodies are of finite matter which, when drawn about us, take on the impression of the physical body which is the reason ghosts are recognizable when seen by the living.

Acharya went on to describe another layer of the physical body – its spirit "twin" – the

Fear of death can imprison us in the physical world.

"etheric" double, which surrounds our nerve system and acts as a conductor of the nerve currents.

Although Acharya didn't allude to it, this is the "sympathetic" network of nerves in the "etheric" double on which spiritual healers and acupuncturists effect their cures. Gossamer in texture and elastic in substance, the "etheric" double acts as a link between the physical and astral bodies during sleep and can be "seen" as a glistening silver cord connecting the two.

"The young soul, or unevolved ego, certainly gets out of his body during sleep," explained Acharya, " – he cannot help doing so – but his intelligence (mental or mind body) is not sufficiently developed ... Therefore he usually hangs about near his sleep body, waiting for the call to re-enter it."

On a subsequent visit, Acharya described what happens at the moment of death. The "etheric" double knows that death of the physical body means death for itself too, and so clings to the astral body sustaining itself on the life force. Through an effort of will, the dying person must detach himself from this last connection with the physical world, or else he will find himself suspended between the two worlds. "Men who die fearing death often refuse to make the necessary effort of will ... in the hope of continuing their physical existence, the physical life being the only one they know." Richelieu's anxieties were dispelled as Acharya explained how our thoughts and actions in life determine our experiences after death. "There is no reward, no punishment, but there is result, there is cause and effect, and the law acts just as much in higher worlds as it acts down here on the physical plane.

Betty Shine, the world-famous healer, gained wisdom from a heavenly teacher.

As we live now and as we are now, so shall we be on the other side of death. And our life there will be conditioned by the thoughts with which we have surrounded ourselves down here. As the astral world is a world of illusion ... everything ... is produced by thought."

THE DIVINE TEACHER

Betty Shine (born in 1929), the world famous healer, who has helped to popularize the latent healing powers of the mind through her books and television appearances, has regularly enjoyed what might be considered the ultimate astral journey – to heaven itself.

Since childhood, Shine has had the ability to project herself into what she describes as another dimension, a garden of vivid colour and exotic plants incredibly similar to places described by many people who have undergone a near-death experience.

But for Betty Shine the purpose

of the sojourn in paradise appears to have been the telepathic imparting of wisdom and the recharging of spiritual batteries.

Every time she entered the garden, she found herself walking down a narrow path between a tall hedge, seemingly placed there to prevent her from seeing what lay on the other side. Beyond it, she passed a rectangular pool around which were seated robed figures, who she sensed were in telepathic communication with each other. Others, it appeared, were being "baptized" in the water.

Impelled by a feeling that she

had an "appointment" with someone, she entered a small hexagonal building which was infused with an atmosphere of peace. There she sat and awaited her "teacher".

Although she never turned around to look at the man who came to sit down behind her, she envisaged him as having a thin face, kindly eyes and long brown hair. They never spoke and, after only a few moments, Betty Shine always left, returning to consciousness in the "real" world with an understanding of spiritual laws no one here could have taught her.

YOGANANDA – THE MAKING OF A YOGI

Paramahansa helped to introduce Yoga to the West.

"The grim march of world political events points inexorably to the truth that without spiritual vision the people perish. Science, if not religion, has awakened in humanity a dim sense of the insecurity and even insubstantiality of all material things. Where indeed may man go now, if not to his Source and Origin, the spirit within him."

Paramahansa Yogananda (1893-1952) was one of the first great masters of Yoga to bring the wisdom of India to the West. Through the Self-Realization Fellowship, which he founded in America in 1920, he introduced tens of thousands of students to the science of Yoga. His *Autobiography of a Yogi* is widely regarded today as a spiritual classic.

Born Mukunda Lal Ghosh in Gorakhpur, north-eastern India, Yogananda was the fourth of eight children. Prompted by memories of a previous incarnation as a yogi in the Himalayas, he went in search of his "destined guru" while still only of school age.

During his travels, Yogananda encountered a number of saints and *sadhus*, wandering holy men who were eager to impart their wisdom. The first of these engaged him in conversation as he stood in deep

thought before a figure of Kali in the Kalighat temple in Calcutta.

"God is simple. Everything else is complex," said the sage, as if in answer to the young man's thoughts. "Do not seek absolute values in the relative world of nature. I have long exercised an honest introspection, the exquisitely painful approach to wisdom. Self-scrutiny, relentless observance of one's thoughts, is a stark and shattering experience. It pulverizes the stoutest ego."

After prophesying that Yogananda would have an unusual experience before the day was out, the stranger departed. His prediction proved to be correct. That afternoon, Yogananda was invited to meet a yogi known as the "Perfume Saint", who was able to materialize fruit and the scent of flowers by manipulating the atoms of

Catherine of Siena is said to have attained a Yogic state.

noted that the great masters of India knew that, "until there is a better assimilation in all nations of the distinctive Eastern and Western virtues, world affairs cannot improve".

Yogananda also pointed out that the sole purpose of man's life on earth is to solve the mystery of life and death. Each of our lives is an opportunity for learning. We should not waste it.

Spiritual maturity and the wisdom that comes with it is not handed out indiscriminately as we pass through the pearly gates into paradise:

"It is indeed unlikely that God has exhausted His ingenuity in organizing this world, or that, in the next world He will offer nothing more challenging to our interest than the strumming of harps ... Death is not a blotting out of existence, a final escape from life; nor is death the door to immortality. He who has fled his self in earthly joys will not recapture it amid the gossamer charms of an astral world."

Paramahansa Yogananda entered *mahasamadhi* (a yogi's final exit from the body) on March 7, 1952 in Los Angeles.

In a final demonstration of mind over matter his body did not deteriorate during the three weeks it lay on display – much to the astonishment of the Mortuary Director who declared the phenomenon to be "unique" in his experience.

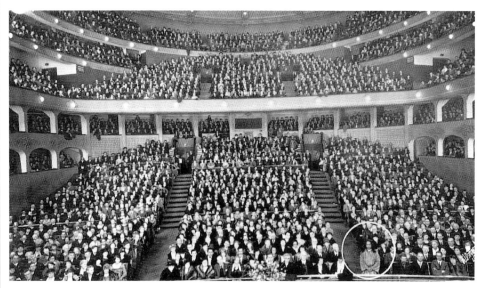

Yogananda (ringed) sits with his audience before giving a lecture in Los Angeles, 1925.

THE GOLDEN MIDDLE PATH BETWEEN EAST AND WEST

Yogananda's mission to the West was prophesied by the legendary yogi Babaji, who was believed to be an incarnation of the Divine.

Unlike Christ or Krishna, who incarnated for a specific purpose, Babaji is said to have retained his physical body for hundreds of years, so that he could assist in the slow evolutionary progress of Humanity over centuries.

Yogananda described Babaji as being in continual communion with Christ. Together, Yogananda wrote, the two have planned "the spiritual technique of salvation for this age. The work of these two

fully illumined masters – one with a body and one without a body – is to inspire the nations to forsake wars, race, hatreds, religious sectarianism and the boomerang evils of materialism."

Yogananda's guru, Sri Yukteswar, met Babaji in Allahabad, northern India, in January 1894 and was told of the importance of introducing yogic teachings to the West.

"East and West must establish a golden middle path of activity and spirituality combined," declared Babaji. "India has much to learn from the West in material develop-

ment; in return, India can teach the universal methods by which the West will be able to base its religious beliefs on the unshakeable foundations of yogic science ... The vibrations there of many spiritually seeking souls come floodlike to me. I perceive potential saints in America and Europe, waiting to be awakened."

Babaji then predicted that Sri Yukteswar would one day play an important role in this exchange and that he, Babaji, would send a disciple to Sri Yukteswar for that purpose. That pupil was Yogananda.

THE INITIATE

"An adept or High Initiate is so different in respect of greatness to the ordinary great man ... that to know him in the spirit and flesh is really the only way to know him at all."

Haig's quiet wisdom illuminated the dark drawing rooms of London's high society.

While wisdom is not of course the exclusive preserve of Eastern mystics and Western philosophers, history tends to record their miraculous deeds and sagacious sayings and yet passes over many equally remarkable adepts who choose to work quietly in the world, unnoticed by all except those whose lives they touch.

One such individual was Justin Moreward Haig, whose real identity is likely never to be known, for this was the pseudonym given to him by his friend and biographer Charles Broadbent (real name Cyril Scott). Broadbent's reticence in revealing his friend's identity was unfortunate but understandable, considering the prevailing attitudes towards mysticism and the occult at the time.

During the 1920s and 1930s the English regarded occultists as being either neurotic cranks or unscrupulous charlatans. Haig was neither. He was an adept, an enlightened being who chose to use his insight to alleviate the mental and karmic sufferings of others.

Haig's quiet wisdom illuminated the dark drawing-rooms of London's high society between the wars and was faithfully recorded by his friend, who soon found himself witness to many extraordinary demonstrations of paranormal powers and super-consciousness.

"Inside the body are certain latent forces," Haig once confided to his friend, "wake these up through purely physiological processes known to yogis, and you alter your entire consciousness; begin to see things, hear things and perceive things that are around you, but of which you were hitherto quite unaware ... Around us all are wonderful planes of happiness, perceptible to those

Haig dispensed the Ageless Wisdom in the spiritual "slums" of high society.

who open the windows of the mind ... We of the Brotherhood merely utilize laws of nature which most people are not acquainted with; that is all."

Broadbent declined to describe his friend and teacher, other than to say that he looked no older than 35, but was known to be 55, that his face was serenely happy and that he presented the appearance of perfect health. He regarded him as "a man who had reached a degree of human evolution greatly in advance of his fellow-creatures."

In public, Haig masked his true nature by professing to be presenting nothing more than an unconventional point of view. "A certain point of view," he stated, "is a prophylactic against all sorrow ... mental pain is the result of a certain sort of childishness."

Anxiety, doubt, jealousy, fear and regret, he said, are illusions "and it is a characteristic of children to like illusions." By "childishness", he seemed to be suggesting that these are symptoms of spiritual immaturity.

Haig considered it his "mission" to bring the ageless wisdom to a class of people who had everything, but enjoyed nothing: people who were too proud or prejudiced to seek spiritual teachings and only paid lip service to their religions.

"There are plenty of people who selflessly go into the slums and dispense monetary charity," he told his friend on one occasion, "but who, as it were, goes into the slums of society and dispenses comfort to deserted wives and love-sick girls and jilted lovers and bereaved husbands, and the multitude of unhappy mortals with which society abounds."

Resolving the romantic entanglements of sheltered young socialites might seem trivial, but Haig saw them as symptoms of something more serious. By reading the aura of his unsuspecting "patients" and obtaining psychic insight into their past lives, he was able to see the spiritual significance of their troubles.

" ... the poets, artists, philosophers have mentalities so receptive that they do not need our personal contact," he would explain, "but the man in the street is entirely different: only by the more clumsy method of conversing with him can something be achieved."

THE ARCHDEACON'S CONVERSION

Haig did not preach or prophesy but subtly altered the perceptions of those he had come to help by quietly encouraging them to question their own values.

"To be born in a certain belief is good," he would say, " – to die in it is unfortunate. Beliefs are the crutches by which some people hobble towards Truth – when one arrives there, one throws the crutches away."

One man whose perception he altered was Archdeacon Wilton, a portly and outwardly pious cleric, whose charity did not, however, extend to his own daughter. He discouraged her friendships and forbade her to have any male admirers. He did not love her, Haig observed, but loved himself through her.

Haig quietly convinced the Archdeacon that, if he had understood the real meaning of the Christian teachings, he would have put her happiness above his own. Haig then opened the Archdeacon to the mystic's vision of the afterlife, where peace is the reward of those who loved in life.

"Death does not change a person's character ... the inner man may be clothed with a grand physical body, but when the body is discarded all his poverty of character is laid bare."

On his deathbed, the Archdeacon sent for Haig rather than for a priest, the speculations of the clergy being no substitute for the knowledge of the occultist.

KRISHNAMURTI (1895-1985), TRUTH INCARNATE

" ... one is actually, psychologically, the world and the world is oneself."

Jiddu Krishnamurti was 15 years old when Annie Besant and C W Leadbeater, the new leaders of the Theosophical Society, discovered him and declared him to be the reincarnation of Krishna and Jesus Christ. Leadbeater, a clergyman, later claimed he had been drawn by the strength of the boy's *aura* (the "etheric" field of energy surrounding the body, visible to those with psychic sight) and had little trouble convincing his companion that they should adopt the boy. Back in England, the pair groomed the young Krishnamurti to be the next Lord Maitreya, the new World Teacher, and helped him to form his own organization, the Order Of The Star Of The East, which swiftly attracted a membership of several thousand.

What distinguishes Krishnamurti from the myriad of other gurus and self-styled modern messiahs is that he vehemently rejected the leadership role, renouncing all forms of organized religion. In 1929, he dissolved the order saying, "You can form other organizations and expect someone else. With that I am not concerned, nor with creating new cages ... My only concern is to set men absolutely, unconditionally free."

Krishnamurti went on to teach the idea that true wisdom comes from self-awareness and that all ideologies prevent the individual from achieving this. Although they may have been founded on fine principles, all religions inevitably become "obstacles preventing spiritual self-fulfilment. The Truth can only be found within oneself, not in dogma." The world, he said, will change only when we have changed ourselves and – most significantly – abandoned our resistance to change.

For Krishnamurti, man's remarkable technical and material progress has been at the expense of spiritual progress and this, he said, is the root of our problems. The only hope for the planet lies in the possibility that we as individuals will take responsibility for our world.

Krishnamurti's method was to urge his followers to assume the attitude of a researcher seeking self-knowledge. He himself rejected the idea of a formal course of instruction or spiritual practice, believ-

C W Leadbeater, a former Anglican cleric and psychic, and Annie Besant, President of the Theosophical Society, believed Krishnamurti to be the new Messiah.

Krishnamurti would reject the mantle of new World Teacher thrust upon him by his supporters.

ing that we already know all the answers but refuse to relinquish our values, because they give us a sense of security.

He further argued that, since everything is impermanent, there is no security to be found either in relationships or in ideologies. Insecurity prevents us from realizing our true selves and our full potential and only a certain quality of intelligence or wisdom offers real security. "When one sees that all our divisive endeavours, which come about when there are beliefs, dogmas, rituals, which are the whole substance of religion, when one sees all that very clearly, not as an idea, but as a fact, then that very fact reveals the extraordinary quality of intelligence in which there is complete, whole security."

Krishnamurti put forward the notion that mankind lives amidst chaos and misery, because our minds are fragmented by the conditioning which divides the human family into separate nationalities, races, religions and ideologies. A pragmatic philosopher, he had no time for theories of

consciousness, but he was concerned with the condition of the psyche.

Of man in general he said: "He is conditioned in a particular way; he may be a Catholic, a Protestant, or he may be conditioned by thousands of years of certain kinds of beliefs, superstitions, ideas and gods, as in India, but below that conditioning, in the depth of his mind, when alone, he is facing the same life of sorrow, pain, grief and anxiety. When one sees this as an actual, irrevocable fact ... one is not alone, one is the entire history of mankind – if one knows how to read that history which is enshrined in one."

According to Krishnamurti, we are preoccupied with our own thoughts, which are habitually narrowed and restricted by our concepts of time and space. Clarity comes with quietude and meditation, but not with the form of meditation that is practised as mere habit.

This desired state of mind "doesn't come to you because you lead a systemized life or follow a particular routine or

morality. It comes only when your heart is really open. Not opened by the key of thought, not made safe by the intellect, but when it is as open as the skies without a cloud; then it comes without your knowing, without your invitation ... " Ultimately we must accept "what is" and not try to force ourselves to conform to an ideal. "If you set out to be good, goodness will never flower. If you cultivate humility, it ceases to be ... One is so concerned with oneself, with one's little guru, with one's little beliefs; but when one realizes this extraordinary fact, then it gives one tremendous strength and a great urgency to investigate and transform oneself, because one is mankind. When there is such transformation, one affects the whole consciousness of man ... "

"How to become a Mahatma", 1891. The ideas of Annie Besant and her fellow Theosophists provided fuel for satirists.

TOWARDS THE
MILLENNIUM

*T*he year 2000 marks not only the beginning of a new century, but, according to those whose words are recorded in the following pages, it heralds the dawning of a New Age, an age which will witness an evolutionary leap in consciousness, culminating in a spiritual Renaissance for humanity.

Such change will not come for the asking. We may be forced to re-evaluate our attitude to organized religion, our obligation to humanity and certainly our perception of reality. There will have to be a revolutionary revision of our perception of the Universe and our purpose in it, a revolution which has apparently already begun.

The presence of two major avatars, Sai Baba and Mother Meera, suggests that the most significant changes will come about within the lifetime of most of us, but there are conflicting views as to how the change will transpire.

Some say it will be forced upon us through the catharsis of crisis and conflict in the manner of a biblical apocalypse. Others prophesy a gradual awakening of consciousness resulting from a crisis of conscience, with the conflict being waged between our self-interest and the "divine discontent" felt by our Higher Selves.

At the end of a century in which we set our sights on outer space, we may find that our future depends on our success in exploring the infinity of inner space.

THE DOORS OF PERCEPTION

"If the doors of perception were cleansed, everything would appear to man as it is, infinite."

(WILLIAM BLAKE, POET AND VISIONARY)

Aldous Huxley (1894-1963), author of *Brave New World*, was one of the major intellectual figures of the 20th century. An erudite and impassioned prophet of social and scientific change, he foresaw the dangers of genetic engineering and, as early as 1948, he described the effects of deforestation, global pollution and general ecological "imbecility", which have now become an unnerving reality.

In the early Fifties, Huxley risked his reputation to promote the mind-expanding properties of the hallucinogenic drugs Mescaline and LSD, believing that, if they were taken by individuals with a sound constitution and an open mind, they could induce a heightened state of consciousness and "a sense of solidarity with the world and its spiritual principle".

Huxley's interest in Eastern philosophy and mysticism began after he settled in California with his wife Maria in 1937. There he embarked on a spiritual odyssey which resulted in an anthology of mystical writings from around the world, *The Perennial Philosophy*, published in 1945. His aim in compiling it was to find the "Highest Common Factor" linking the writings of mystics and theologians throughout the ages in an effort to prove the existence of a common Divine Reality.

"If one is not oneself a sage or saint," Huxley wrote in the introduction, "the best thing one can do, in the field of metaphysics, is to study the works of those who were ... "

By the early Fifties, Huxley had exhausted the intellectual approach and was eager for direct experience of "The Ultimate Reality".

For some time he had considered experimenting with Mescaline, a drug derived from the active principle of Peyote, a natural hallucinogenic that had been used by Native Americans for centuries. An unexpected visit by a psychological researcher, who was looking for a suitable "guinea pig", offered the ideal opportunity. And so, on a bright May morning in 1953, Huxley ingested a minute dosage of the drug in a drink of water and sat back in expectation.

"I had expected to lie with my eyes shut, looking at visions of many-coloured geometries, of animated architectures, rich with gems and fabulously lovely, of landscapes with heroic figures, of symbolic dramas trembling perpetually on the verge of the ultimate revelation. But I had not reckoned, it was evident, with the idiosyncrasies of my mental make-up, the facts of my temperament, training and habits."

To Huxley's consternation, it was not the inner world which was illuminated,

Huxley experimented with Mescalin in his search for the "ultimate reality".

but the outer. Instead of the mystical visions of which he had read, the walls of his self-centred world crumbled before him revealing an intensity of existence he could never have imagined. Everything, from a vase of flowers to the creases in his trousers, became wonders of infinite complexity.

"A bunch of flowers shining with their own inner light ... Those folds – what a labyrinth of endlessly significant complexity! ... I was seeing what Adam had seen on the morning of his own creation – the miracle, moment by moment, of naked existence."

Huxley's experience led him to conclude that our senses are deliberately dulled, or rather that our perception of "reality" is the result of information being filtered by our brains, in order that we can function as higher animals in the physical world. Otherwise, our senses would be overwhelmed.

As he observed, "The mind was primarily concerned, not with measures and locations, but with being and meaning ... In the intervals between his revelations the mescaline taker is apt to feel that, though in one way everything is supremely as it should be, in another there is something wrong."

What Huxley considered "wrong" was the sense of separateness which Mescaline induced. Only through raising our consciousness naturally, and not artificially with drugs, can we attain the sense of unity experienced by mystics and philosophers. If we can do that, he argued, then we will have truly opened the doors of perception. "When all things are perceived as infinite and holy, what motive can we have for covetousness or self-assertion, for the pursuit of power or the drearier forms of pleasure."

The Beatles' sojourns in India popularized Eastern mysticism.

"TURN ON, TUNE IN, DROP OUT"

As an upper middle-class English intellectual, Huxley became the unlikeliest of youth gurus when the account of his drug experiments, **The Doors Of Perception,** *was adopted as a set text for the psychedelic Sixties.*

Between 1966 and 1968 a whole generation of Western youth was swept up in a seemingly spontaneous wave of idealism and attempted to go back to nature. It was the Age of Aquarius, of "Flower Power", Free Love, Free Festivals and freely available drugs. Prompted by the Beatles' sojourns in India under the spell of the Maharishi Mahesh Yogi, there was unprecedented enthusiasm for Eastern mysticism and culture.

There was also a genuine desire to "Make Love Not War" and to establish a new sense of community in the West. Many made the pilgrimage to the East, but turned back disillusioned when they failed to find instant enlightenment.

Unfortunately, in their rush to "Turn On, Tune In, Drop Out" (the slogan of LSD messiah Dr Timothy Leary), the 'hippies' did not heed Huxley's warning that a society addicted to self-indulgent drug experimentation without any spiritual insight or discipline would fall apart. However the spirit of the Sixties encouraged a greater awareness of Eastern ideas, popularized the practice of Yoga, meditation and vegetarianism, encouraged the growth of ecological movements and thus laid the foundation for today's New Age movement.

FINDHORN

"We believe that the future will be largely concerned with rediscovering and building our connectedness to each other, to nature and to the unseen spiritual realms, so that we become whole as individuals, as a species, even as a planet."

(ALEX WALKER, FORMER TRUSTEE, FINDHORN FOUNDATION)

The Findhorn Foundation, one of the first New Age communities in Europe, attracted world-wide interest in the late 1960s through a series of sensationalistic press reports, which described how the founders were growing monster-sized vegetables in conditions which appeared to defy nature. Since then, the Foundation has become a centre for spiritual and holistic education; practising, teaching and demonstrating how humanity can work in harmony with all other forms of life.

After 32 years, the Foundation's principle beliefs remain the same, namely that the source of all life is accessible to each of us at all times and that there is an active intelligence in nature and in the planet itself.

This "intelligence" was first contacted in 1962 by one of the community's three founders, Eileen Caddy who, together with her husband Peter and their friend Dorothy Maclean, was attempting to link up with an international spiritual group known as the "Network of Light".

After being guided by Eileen's "still small voice within" to a derelict caravan site in a bleak and remote region of north-eastern Scotland, the group received a telepathic message through Eileen (which she believed came from God) encouraging them to create a fruitful garden in windy Findhorn, the most unlikely and inhospitable of sites.

The inner voice assured Eileen that the group would be aided by nature spirits and further predicted that "in the new world to come these realms will be open to humans". Later, as the garden began to take shape among the sand dunes, her inner guide confided, " ... you are a life force moving among other life forces. As you recognize this and open up to them, you draw near to them and become one with them, and work with them in my purposes."

In the light of their subsequent success, it appears that the group were grounding part of the energy which is bringing the New Age, or new consciousness, into being.

On Christmas Eve 1967, Eileen had a series of dramatic visions after which her inner voice announced that the New Age had begun. "The day many have been waiting for is over," it told her. "The cosmic power released at that appointed moment, felt by you and many others, has begun to reverberate around the universe. Nothing will stop it. It will gather momentum and power and it will be sensed by many as time goes on ...

The Findhorn Community became a family of "spiritual seekers".

This is the beginning of the universal happenings all over the world ... Your feeling of uplifted consciousness is the start of great changes that will be felt by each individual everywhere."

Since then, the Foundation's spiritual education programme has been based on the belief that humanity is on the verge of a major evolutionary step. A consequence of this awakening will be the development of an acute awareness of the inner worlds of the spirit both in nature and within ourselves.

The Foundation has now become a planetary centre for spiritual renewal and initiation rather than a "mystery school" or retreat. In building an ecological village where the caravans once stood, the

Findhorn is a centre for spiritual renewal, a model for the New Age.

community hopes that it will become a model for the new world which must be founded on the ideal of common identity and the divinity of all life.

What makes Findhorn so important as a centre for this transformation is not so much its ecological experiments, or its staging of international conferences on all things esoteric, or even its miraculous collaboration with the nature spirits. Its real significance lies in the evidence it provides of the first flowering of a new consciousness.

As David Spangler, former Foundation member and prolific writer on the New Age, wrote: "It is an exciting place, but a challenging one ... not a spiritual retreat, a place for quiet meditation. It is a place for strong, dedicated, joyously creative souls who are willing to work ... to unfold and demonstrate a practical vision for a new world. In so doing, they find that the new world has been within themselves all the time."

THE ELEMENTAL FORCES AT WORK

In August 1970, David Spangler channelled a message from a being identifying itself as an emissary of the elemental kingdoms. This spirit described its role in creation and the necessity of working in harmony with humanity.

"We represent the beings who make possible the growth and development of the forms of nature before a planet can come into existence ... we draw freely upon the powers of cosmic creativity ... As we enter the etheric world, we may take on various forms which are provided by the imaginations of human beings ... At one time, we were the sole masters of earth, we made it possible for humanity to

develop upon this world."

The being then described humanity as a manifestation of this same force. "In a way you reflect within yourselves aspects of the elemental and angelic kingdoms, but you are blessed with the power of creative imagination ... You are evolving to perform a role upon the Earth that is related to ours but different as well, involving different capabilities. We have the task of assisting you in your role ... "

The spirit explained that when humanity was created it was the elemental beings' task to teach and protect us until we were able to discover our unique identity and purpose.

Once we humans awaken the angelic aspects of our natures, we will be able to communicate and co-operate with these forces of nature which at present are the sole province of the elementals.

"You must learn that you are part of the nature kingdom as well; though you have a certain dominion over it, you cannot destroy it without destroying yourselves ... You have reached a crisis point. As you continue to exert unthinking authority and domination over the world simply because you seem to have the power to do so, you will destroy the ecological pattern of this planet and yourselves in the process."

SIR GEORGE TREVELYAN

"We are in the second Renaissance. In the first, our ancestors explored the seas and discovered new continents .... in this, our present age, we are setting out to explore the cosmos and reality."

(SIR GEORGE TREVELYAN)

Sir George Trevelyan, one of the founding fathers of the New Age movement.

In 1969, Sir George Trevelyan (born in 1906), a pioneer of the New Age movement and spiritual education in Britain, set up the Wrekin Trust at Ross-on-Wye in Herefordshire to offer courses in "New Age consciousness".

Since then, in the belief that only a change in personal consciousness can bring about social renewal, he has dedicated himself to promoting a greater awareness

Student unrest in the Sixties challenged anti-quated attitudes.

of spiritual knowledge, esoteric psychology and the Ageless Wisdom.

Trevelyan sees the violent changes that are occurring at the present time as the result of a crisis at psychic, material and spiritual levels of existence. "Armageddon is indeed being fought out within human hearts", he has written, "outward events merely mirror the condition of the soul."

Taking a particularly Eastern viewpoint, he suggests that our current sufferings are intended to teach us to overcome our desires so that we can be receptive to the influence of our higher selves.

" ... the sick soul of planetary man is drawing to itself a sort of cosmic cleansing to clear out debris accumulated through centuries of egoism, selfishness and greed."

We may be witnessing the breakdown of civilization, but these are symptoms of a crucial spiritual awakening. We are currently emerging from an epoch in which we had the luxury of being mere observers, into an age where we will be forced to take an active role if we truly wish to bring about transformation. This transformation is likely to manifest itself in both dramatic and subtle ways.

One of these manifestations is a growing awareness that man and the earth are each dependent upon the other. Our planet is not an inanimate lump of rock which we can plunder at will, but a living organism which we are slowly poisoning. "Ecologists are becoming aware of how delicately poised the living organism is, and that our reckless exploitation of the earth's resources may well lead to retribution."

Since the earth is sentient, it follows that its rejuvenation can only come about by the infusion of the life force, something man has all but suffocated under a blanket of pollution. "We must cultivate techniques of cleansing and catharsis, thus preparing ourselves to receive the 'ordeal by fire'."

If we succeed, Trevelyan believes this "divine dispensation" will then be able to enter "the very heart of matter to transmute and cleanse polluted earth, air and water by molecular change."

Trevelyan repeatedly urges Humanity to awaken to the creative spirit and the Higher Intelligences in the Universe which will bring the new world into being, saying that never before in our history "has man been so strongly supported by such high power ... waiting to sweep through human consciousness". But he acknowledges that the forces of darkness are abroad in the form of ignorance, fear, crime and violence. "But the worse things appear to be," he reassures us, "the more we must fervently embrace the hope of the light which will follow .... We may be certain that, as outward conditions worsen, our invisible guides will draw closer and show themselves the more ready, even eager, to help ... seers and adepts foretell a great spiritual crisis or turning point for mankind by the end of the 20th century ... "

How this manifests itself, Trevelyan says, will depend on whether we act as receptive channels to "ground" the energy or "block the flow" through our fear of change and love of materialism. The New Age energies are apparently all around us, but they will only begin to flow if we "open ourselves and invoke them". Individually and collectively, we retain the free will to either bring about this new consciousness, or smother it at birth.

Trevelyan believes that what he calls "the barriers between the worlds" are being broken down, so that we will soon be able to appreciate the interdependency of all things. "We are truly involved with a second coming," he states. "The only real anxiety is that we may not be awake and aware when our moment comes."

Ecological groups protest against the "reckless exploitation" of the earth's resources.

YOUTH AND THE NEW AGE

Trevelyan takes a radical view of the part youth is playing in our current spiritual crisis. He views their disillusion as part of the solution, not the problem.

His theory is that the evolution of society reflects the cycle of nature. Growth involves the breakdown "of matter into formlessness, or chaos, as in the seed". The "revolt" of youth in the late Sixties and early Seventies should therefore be seen as the seed of our evolution, a necessary breaking

down of antiquated attitudes before new growth can take place. However, he goes further, believing that the youth of the 1960s had consciously chosen to incarnate after the Second World War so that they would be in readiness for the "coming spiritual crisis".

Trevelyan believes that "many are no doubt advanced and mature souls who chose the task of leading the new society into social forms consonant with the spirit". This may well account for the spirit of

the Sixties generation, many of whom are now at the forefront of the New Age movement, but not the current younger generation who appear more despairing, disillusioned and alienated than previously. Modern Kabbalists would argue that, aside from the economic and social factors that have contributed to this attitude, these are among the last souls to incarnate from the "House of Souls" and that they are merely reacting to "trial by existence".

RAMALA – GROUNDING THE NEW AGE ENERGY

"Though you may possess all the knowledge in the World, without the Wisdom to use it, it is as nothing."

(THE RAMALA SOURCE)

In the mid-1970s, a small group of seekers living in Glastonbury, England claimed to have made telepathic contact with spiritual teachers from a higher plane of existence through "channelled" meditation.

These beings were apparently eager to impart their knowledge to humanity which they believed was ill-prepared for the fast-approaching New Age.

Initially, the teachings were circulated in privately printed pamphlets, but such was the interest they aroused that eventually two remarkable books were published, *The Revelation Of Ramala* and *The Wisdom Of Ramala*.

Through their contact with the Ramala Teachers (as they became known), the group learnt that a great planetary upheaval is imminent and that, with the millennium almost upon us, now is the time for Humanity to build a new ark, an ark of consciousness, to escape the deluge of negative forces that threatens to drag us down.

In his introduction to the second book, the anonymous author and leader of the Glastonbury group states: "This is our supreme moment of choice – either to recognize or to deny our spiritual birthright ... The purpose of the Ramala teachings is to help humanity to prepare

for this great moment of transformation and transmutation so that we may be ready for the Golden Age that is to come."

Although 10 different beings were contacted, the bulk of the revelations came from three Teachers.

At the Ramala Sanctuary at Chalice Hill House, known to its members as the Sanctuary of the Holy Grail, the group built up an energy field to which the Teachers were drawn. Members would then speak through the leader of the group who was fully conscious of what was being said – he later likened the experience "to standing behind someone who is giving a talk yet being able to hear the words before they are actually spoken".

During one of these talks, the group learned that the current Aquarian cycle is destined to be "the greatest cycle in Humanity's evolutionary path", more important even than the last Piscean Age which saw "the grounding of the Christ energy".

The Teacher explained that, although the "cosmic energy pattern" for the New Age is already present, it still requires individual human effort to ground the energy and usher in the new cycle, "in just the same way as the Nazarene grounded the Christ Energy 2,000 years ago".

During the question and answer sessions which followed each of these meditations, the group's personal guide, known to them as Zen Tao, would elaborate on what the Teachers had told them.

The Ramala Teachers prophesy a Golden Age of transformation.

The revelations of Ramala were "channelled" from higher beings.

In response to a plea to be more specific about the New Age, ZT said "it will see a new race of Humanity on the earth", adding that the events which mark the age are reflected in the life of the master, or masters, who initiate it. "That, of course, is why people talk of a violent ending to the Piscean Age," explained ZT, "why they compare the crucifixion of that Master with the crucifixion of Humanity that is to take place ... There are souls of great evolution incarnating on the earth at this time ... It is therefore imperative that an environment be created where these great souls can manifest their true wisdom and potential ..."

Unlike the "Hidden Masters" the Ramala Teachers remain nameless. They are the teachers for the New Age speaking through mediators around the world, not just to the group in Glastonbury. Channelled teachings received in Australia, India and the USA echo the message that the New Age will be a world-wide awakening and not merely a fashionable alternative culture.

The Ramala teachers will be our guides in the New Age.

THE END OF THE WORLD

It is an irony of our age that we appear to have come full circle back to a point where we are willing to consider the earth as the source of a living force – the Mother Goddess, Gaia, call it what you will. But, however we perceive it, spiritually or scientifically, it seems certain that the earth must one day die just as we will.

The end might come through a natural or nuclear apocalypse, a slow poisoning by man, or a lingering death as the sun burns itself out. Whatever form it takes, the Ramala Teachers are eager to reassure us that this will not be the end of the world, but only the end of the world as we know it.

" ... the Earth, like you, is imbued with spirit. It will, therefore, never die ... " However, ... its physical form might change as it experiences periods of transformation and transmutation ... in the same way that you in your physical bodies die and are born again onto a higher plane of life so the Earth, on another level, undergoes a similar experience."

The Ramala Teachers explained that the earth had undergone this rebirth many times and will do so again.

" ... the Lord of this Earth, the Goddess, the Earth Mother whose form it is, is a great and evolved spiritual being ... Humanity is now tampering with that sacred being, Mother Nature, in order to achieve a short-term gain without considering the long-term implications."

We can therefore expect a time of famine, drought and pestilence in return. "This reaction should not be seen as a form of punishment by the Divine," we are assured, "but rather as the flowering of the seeds which Humanity itself has sown."

OSHO – GURU OF THE NEW AGE

"The new man is not a hope: you are already pregnant with it. My work is just to make you aware that the new man has already arrived. My work is to help you to recognize and respect him."

(OSHO)

Osho – the greatest spiritual teacher of the 20th century or cult guru?

Bhagwan Shree Rajneesh (1931-90), better known as Osho, has been called "the most dangerous man since Jesus Christ" and "the greatest spiritual teacher of the 20th century".

Although he professed a dislike for worship of any kind, he became the centre of a personality cult which continues to draw disciples to the high-tech commune he established in Poona, India, once described as a "spiritual Disneyland for disaffected First World yuppies".

Intellectuals in India named Osho among the 10 people who have most affected the destiny of India, for "liberating the minds of future generations from the shackles of religiosity and conformism", while the *Sunday Times* in London listed him among the 1,000 "Makers of the Twentieth Century". Yet during his life, Osho was banned from 21 countries and condemned by religious leaders and communist authorities alike for being the leader of what they considered to be an insidious cult.

Osho certainly did his reputation no favours by allegedly amassing 93 Rolls Royces and openly preaching the virtues of sex as a path to super-consciousness. However, for those who were prepared to listen, he would explain that when we repress our basic nature, sex takes root in the unconscious, leading to an unnatural obsession. "Sex is man's most vibrant

Osho attracted criticism for his fleet of Rolls Royces.

energy," he taught, "but it should not be an end unto itself: sex should lead man to his soul."

Osho's spiritual shock-tactics may have misfired, but his reinterpretations of the ageless teachings of Jesus, Buddha, the Sufi mystics and the Zen masters (recorded in over 600 books) suggest that he possessed a truly remarkable mind. Although thousands of followers around the world continue to venerate him as the guru of the New Age, Osho preferred to think of himself as a "true existentialist".

He was born in India in 1931 and taught philosophy at the University of Jabalpur. At the age of 32, he turned his back on the academic world and began speaking to huge crowds throughout India: his vision was of a new breed of man who would throw off the chains of political and religious slavery. The New Age, he explained, was an opportunity for man to assert his individuality, to rebel against conformity and institutionalized belief.

The new man, Osho asserted, must rediscover simplicity and innocence and free himself of the misconceptions of separation, the notion of a division between creator and the created, the believer and belief. "The idea of God is an imprisonment, and only when one is free from this prison can one know what it is to live in a celebrative way."

To this end, Osho dedicated himself to reinterpreting the ageless wisdom of the great masters, mystics and philosophers for the New Age and beyond. He considered that the ageless truths had to be presented in terms the modern mind could respond to, otherwise we would, in effect, be using an old key for a new lock.

Throughout the 1970s, Osho's discourses on the teachings of Jesus, the Zen masters, the Sufi mystics and the great philosophers of the past, from Pythagoras to Nietzsche, resulted in a flood of books at the rate of one a month. Of Buddha he commented, "Buddha is one of the most important masters who has ever existed on the earth – incomparable, unique. And if you can have a taste of his being you will be infinitely benefited, blessed ... Buddha's message is the greatest that has ever been delivered to man ... "

Osho described Taoism as a "no-method, simple spontaneity – living life according to nature with no fight". The Sufis he credited with being "great storytellers, and their stories are very pregnant with the significance of the ultimate. The Sufi story is a persuasion, a seduction. It reveals its mysteries to you

Osho's commune at Poona has been dismissed as a spiritual Disneyland.

when you are enjoying it."

He considered the Hindu Upanishads "the essence of all religion" and Zen as "the one true religion". a religion of paradox for a paradoxical age. "Life, in every dimension, is paradoxical. So religion has to be paradoxical. If religion is not paradoxical then it is just poor philosophy. Then it is just man-made, mind-created, just a theology – not religion."

A RELIGION FOR THE NEW AGE

Osho considered Zen to be the one "true" religion, which, if reinterpreted to take account of the modern mind, would become the religion of the New Age.

"As far as I can see, Zen is going to be paving the path for the new man to come, and for the new humanity to emerge. That's why I'm talking so much on Zen. I want you to understand as deeply as possible."

According to Osho, the West's interpretation of Zen philosophy has amounted to little more than *intellectual appreciation.*

"Zen is a way of dissolving philosophical problems, not of solving them. It is a way of getting rid of philosophy, because philosophy is a sort of neurosis. The greatest thing that Zen has brought into the world is freedom from oneself."

In No Water, No Moon, *which he described as a Zen "guide book", Osho wrote:*

"Life is not a riddle to be solved, it is a mystery to be lived. It is a deep mystery, so trust and allow yourself to enter it."

OSHO – ZORBA THE BUDDAH

"From fish to man there has been evolution. But from man to a Buddha, from man to a Christ, from man to a Kabir, it is not evolution it is revolution."

(OSHO)

An often provocative and controversial figure, Osho saw no merit in compromising what he considered to be the Truth in order to spare the religious sensibilities of his audience.

He once dismembered Christianity before a group of Jesuit priests who were visiting his commune, having first written a number of commentaries on the gospels in which he made a distinction between Jesus the master and the religion founded in his name. "When I talk on Jesus I am trying to peel off the paint with which Christianity has tried to improve upon the original face of the master."

A year before the collapse of the Soviet Union, the presence of a Soviet camera crew prompted Osho to deliver a damning indictment of communism and a warning about the effects Gorbachev's reforms would have on the Russian people. In the same talk, he predicted the eventual downfall of the United States, illustrating his irreverent observations with the timeless wisdom of Zen anecdotes.

Osho was equally outspoken in his criticism of the United Nations whose Universal Declaration of Human Rights he condemned as a charter for "political slavery", while reserving his most fervent attacks for priests and politicians whom he accused of organizing the spiritual enslavement of mankind.

As a result of this outspokenness, Osho's world tours drew adoration and condemnation in roughly equal measures. In the Soviet Union, he was accused of being a "front" for the CIA; in Crete the Christian bishops allegedly called for him to be stoned; meanwhile in Greece, he raised the spectre of Socrates when the government deported him for "corrupting the youth".

Nor was Osho above criticizing other spiritual leaders, although his comments were always incisive and revealing. Krishnamurti, he once said, had "gone wrong", because he doubted everything until he had proven its validity to himself. Osho, on the other hand, began from a position of trust but added doubt to protect himself – the spiritual equivalent of "innocent until proven guilty" perhaps. He shared Krishnamurti's distaste for organized religion, stating that he found it too sugary sweet but that there was much truth to be had in its teachings if one savoured them with the saltiness of the intellect.

Like Krishnamurti, Osho detested personality cults, believing that anyone you worship you will later despise. In the end, he insisted, everyone has to walk the path alone. Nevertheless, he himself became the focus of adoration and its attendant in-fighting. At one

Osho claimed to detest personality cults but nevertheless became the focus of one.

Osho's mass Dynamic Meditations were intended to "shake up" the participants and release their excess energy.

"Our commune is not a religion," proclaims the glossy brochure, " ... it is just a meeting place for people who have dropped all conditionings, all religions, all ideologies ... who are no longer searching for a prophet and a saviour ... the only way is to save yourself."

Assessment of the value of Osho's teachings is for each individual to decide. Was he "the greatest incarnation after Buddha in India ... a living Buddha", as Lama Karmapa believed; or merely the "giggling guru" of the New Age?

"My message is not a doctrine, not a philosophy," Osho insisted. "My message is a certain alchemy, a science of transformation ... People ask, 'is there life after death?'. First ask, is there life before death? First live life totally."

point, there was an attempted coup by a disaffected group within his American commune after which someone allegedly tried to poison him and his doctor!

Incensed politicians and religious leaders lobbied for his deportation from the United States and, after a spell in jail, Osho was forced into "exile". The affair prompted author Tom Robbins to comment, "If crucifixion were still in vogue, of course he would have been nailed up. But since we're civilized, they had to force him into exile instead. I'm sure they would have much preferred to crucify him on the White House lawn."

Osho rejected all messianic comparisons claiming that he was instead the first manifestation of a new man he called "Zorba the Buddha" – a balance between the earthy and ebullient Zorba the Greek and the self-realized Buddha. But whether he liked it or not, messianic comparisons were made. After his death in January 1990, Osho's ashes were enshrined in the beautiful landscaped grounds of the 24-acre Poona commune, which continues to attract thousands of international visitors each year.

MEDITATION FOR MODERN MINDS

Osho considered the traditional methods of meditation which centred on quiet contemplation as unsuitable for the modern mind. Instead he taught what he called "Dynamic Meditation" to "shake up" the mind before it can contemplate "passive awareness". There is no use, he believed, in forcing today's executives or housewives to sit in silent meditation as they will only meditate on their inner conflicts and emotions. " ... energy needs acting out, it needs catharsis. You have too much energy with no action for the energy ... Let the energy flow. You melt into existence through action. And when the energy is gone and you relax, then be silent."

From this silence, he said, comes a new awareness. And from awareness comes wisdom. "Once you enter the world of meditation, your perspective immediately changes. You start feeling that you are not here by accident, that you are fulfilling a certain need of existence. Existence itself is behind you, but can be discovered only in deep silence, when your thoughts, your mind, your ego completely cease."

Osho repeatedly reminded his followers that, no matter how learned they might be, there is no substitute for meditation. He called it "the greatest miracle there is. It is the greatest gift that has been given by the awakened ones to humanity."

AMORC – UNIVERSITY OF THE NEW AGE

"As Brethren of the Rosy Cross, our personal endeavours, our minds, our laboratories, clinics and institutions are devoted to the rebuilding of the human race and the advancement of civilization."

(H. SPENCER LEWIS)

AMORC (the Ancient and Mystical Order Rosae Crucis), the worldwide fraternal organization for esoteric studies founded in 1915 by American occult philosopher H Spencer Lewis, claims to be perpetuating the true traditions of Rosicrucian movements since the time of Ancient Egypt. However, unlike its secretive, mythical predecessor, AMORC openly promotes its educational activities from its very public headquarters at the Rosicrucian Park in San Jose, California.

The Order's image as proprietors of a model university for the New Age is reinforced by the scale and splendour of the complex at Rosicrucian Park, which houses a planetarium, an Egyptian museum, an international university, a temple, a library and a huge administration block, all designed along mock-Egyptian lines.

AMORC's preoccupation with Egypt stems from its founder's fascination with the exotic and rather fanciful theories of the 19th century occultists, who saw Egypt as the source of all wisdom, rather than from the printed manifestos which launched the Rosicrucian orders of the 17th century.

Lewis believed that the mystical movement which evolved into Rosicrucianism grew directly out of the Mystery traditions of Ancient Egypt. He side-stepped the thorny issue of Christian Rosenkreutz's existence, by naming AMORC's Traditional Grand Master as none other than Pharaoh Akhenaten himself!

While the Rosicrucian brotherhoods of the 17th, 18th and 19th centuries were primarily Christian in outlook, the modern movement draws upon a wide range of esoteric traditions and techniques for developing the mind, body and spirit. These include the yogic philosophy of the East, Theosophical mythology, the Kabbalah and the pseudo-sciences.

The organization considers its highest purpose lies in assisting individual members on a "journey into self", encouraging them to develop a personal philosophy to guide their own destiny. Home study courses include lessons on the development of "personal magnetism", and learning to banish superstitions – both certainly of little value on the spiritual path. As with many organizations

AMORC's headquarters are of mock Egyptian design.

which function as centres for the New Age, AMORC gives the impression that it considers anything that can be described as "esoteric" to be of value.

Inspired by a list of illustrious Rosicrucians, which includes Sir Isaac Newton, Michael Faraday and Sir Francis Bacon, members are expected to follow a curriculum encompassing science subjects, mysticism, ancient and modern philosophy, parapsychology and metaphysics in the hope that they will develop their own psychic and spiritual awareness, and thus further the evolution of humanity as a whole. The lodges, which have a substantial proportion of female members, encourage an atmosphere of "fraternal" unity, while functioning as centres of esoteric knowledge and psychic exploration.

New members are initiated through an introductory course providing an overview of the evolution of the Ageless

H Spencer Lewis believed Rosicrucianism originated in Ancient Egypt.

Wisdom, including basic principles as interpreted by the Order. Over the next five years, they are guided through the higher degrees by a Class Master who instructs them in such matters as reading

the aura and astral projection. Rituals (carried out in the member's home before private study, as well as in the temples of the lodge) are intended to impress the lesson or experience upon the subconscious by means of symbolism.

Whether the Order's emphasis on Egyptian symbolism is seen as the door to an ancient wisdom or a hangover from 19th century occultism is something-which is open to debate.

AMORC claims that the uniqueness of the Rosicrucian teachings owes more to the system of learning, which is designed to produce gradual evolution in consciousness, than to the body of knowledge on offer. Its organizers assert that "the Light of Knowledge will always face the adversity of darkness, but with persistence and fortitude the Light will grow, elevating the minds of men, and women to higher and higher degrees of illumination".

INITIATION IN THE PYRAMIDS

Herbert Spencer Lewis, founder of AMORC, wrote extensively on the symbolic measurements of the Great Pyramids, which Madame Blavatsky and her acolytes believed were once used as initiation chambers. The theory was that the Egyptian priests placed candidates in a sarcophagus in the King's Chamber, whose symbolic structure created a unique atmosphere capable of triggering astral projection, thereby providing neophytes with first-hand experience of the nature of the spirit and proof of its survival after death.

Fanciful though the theory might appear, the ability of the Pyramid to induce astral projection appears to have been confirmed by the experience of the author and occultist Dr Paul Brunton.

In the 1930s, Brunton obtained permission to spend a night alone in the King's Chamber, one of the last men to do so. Afterwards, he claimed that during the night he heard disembodied voices just as the chamber filled with a brilliant light.

At this point, he became psychically subdued and his astral body was drawn out against his will,

" ... all my muscles became taut, after which a paralyzing lethargy began to creep over my limbs ... My entire body became heavy and numb ... All sensation in the lower limbs was numbed ... I appeared next to pass into a semi-somnolent condition ... I felt myself sinking inwards in consciousness ... I had the sensation of being caught up in a tropical whirlwind and seemed to pass upwards through a narrow hole; then there was the momentary dread of being launched into infinite space ... I had gone ghostlike out of my earthly body."

SAI BABA – THE AVATAR

OF LOVE

"I have come to restore a golden chapter in the story of humanity, wherein falsehood will fail, truth will triumph, and virtue will reign. Character will confer power then, not knowledge, or inventive skill, or wealth. Wisdom will be enthroned in the councils of nations"

Devotees of Sathya Sai Baba (born in 1926) believe him to be the second of three incarnations of the "Avatar of Love", prophesied 5,600 years ago in the Upanishads.

These ancient Hindu texts (see pages 78-79) predicted that the 19th and 20th centuries would be a Machine Age characterized by a grossly materialistic culture which was destined to produce the means by which the whole planet could be destroyed. The triple incarnation of Baba was intended to help us avert this catastrophe.

The first incarnation of the avatar is believed to have been Shirdi Sai Baba, a Muslim saint with 250 shrines to his name in modern India. Before he died in 1918, he specified the Indian state in which he would be re-born eight years later, Andhra Pradesh, and that is exactly where Sathya Sai Baba was discovered.

At six years old, Baba was reported to be performing miracles and enjoying deep philosophical discussions with devotees who had known him in his previous incar-

nation. The boy was even quoting lengthy passages from Hindu scriptures which he could not have read.

Further proof of Baba's divinity is said to be recorded in palm leaf manuscripts written 5,000 years before by the Indian sage Shuka. Shuka correctly predicted Baba's date of birth to the very day – Tuesday, November 23, 1926 – and

he even named the village in which Baba would be born, although the village did not exist during Shuka's lifetime.

Believers also draw attention to a collection of Mohammed's sayings, in which the founder of Islam listed 300 signs by which "the One to come" would be recognized. These included physical details which corresponded uncannily to those of Baba, right down to the gap in his teeth and the mole on his cheek. Mohammed added that, despite such signs, the "One to come" would not be recognized as such until nine years before his passing.

Baba himself makes no public claims to be a Messiah. "My task is the spiritual regeneration of humanity through Truth and Love," he has said. "I have come to light the lamp of love in the hearts of all humanity."

However, his biographer, Professor Kasturi, once stated during a private interview in 1980 that Baba had confided to him that he was the One whom Jesus had called the Father and that he had sent Jesus into incarnation. Kasturi added

"Man is living at the dawn of a Golden Age" (Sai Baba).

that Baba also claimed to be the Cosmic Christ, the spirit which Jesus had invoked to aid him in his mission.

The professor, who devoted the last 40 years of his life to preserving and promoting the teachings of Baba, believed him to be a major avatar, "the first descent from the Godhead since Krishna, 5500 years ago. I believe him to be the Godforce in manifest form," wrote Kasturi. "It is up to Him (and the inspiration He gives us to help Him) whether this planet lives or dies."

Baba himself says, "In this human form of Sai every Divine Entity, every Divine Principle, that is to say all the Names and Forms ascribed by man for God are manifest ... Call me by any name, Krishna, Allah, Christ ... I am the embodiment of all forms which men have imposed on Godhead ... I shall respond by whatever name you know me by ... I am God: you, too, are God. The only difference is that I know it and you do not."

Baba's followers, of which there are now over 50 million all over the world, are drawn by his simple doctrine of love and compassion. For Baba, love is the way to true wisdom. For him, unconditional love and compassion for humanity is beyond wisdom.

"Wisdom is all-knowing. Possessing it means there is no longer any doubt in the mind. Wisdom grows with the evolution of the soul, natural growth from many lives of experience. Perfect wisdom exists when man and God are one, at the same level of consciousness, completely merged. At that point man and God ARE one."

Of his mission, Sai Baba has said:

"I have not come to speak on behalf of any teaching ... Nor have I come to collect disciples for any doctrine. I have come to tell you of this universal, initiary faith ... this obligation to love ...

Baba's followers believe him to be the third incarnation of the Avatar of Love.

Cultivate this attitude of Oneness between men of all creeds, all countries and all continents. That is the message of love that I bring."

THE COMING AGE

Baba has often spoken of a Golden Age to come, an age of spiritual renewal, although his vision differs from previous prophecies in that he sees man and not God as determining when it will dawn.

"The Golden Age is the creation of man, not of God ... Man is living at the dawn of a Golden Age and he himself will determine the timing of the transition by his own acts and thoughts ... The arrival of the Golden Age will be heralded by a new coming, as well as some upheavals, sufficient to uproot the evil that is so prevalent today ..."

We can expect these upheavals to include natural as well as man-made crises. Only Baba, it is said, will be able to control the furies of nature to be unleashed at the turn of the century. But he insists that we must not be afraid of change no matter how violent a form it may take. "Life is change and change is taking place all the time."

When Baba speaks of a new age he is not predicting a pre-ordained epoch but a gradual awakening of consciousness.

" ... today there is a growing number of more evolved souls who

are beginning to see the light and there are signs of a new awakening. That awakening is in its early stages, but it will gradually spread to every corner of the globe ... Today you cannot visualize such a state because there is chaos everywhere, fighting, scheming, hatred, evil; all the negative emotions are in the ascendant. But eventually the change will come ... I assure you that very soon the dark clouds will be scattered and you will witness a happy era all over the world. Right will be restored and evil put down ..."

ANDREW HARVEY – THE

MYSTIC JOURNEY

"The Tibetans are giving the world a wisdom that is extremely important for the transformation that is happening, and I became one of the vehicles for the transmission of that wisdom to the West."

Andrew Harvey, writer, prolific poet and western intellectual, does not fit the dictionary definition of a mystic. Yet in his writings, which include *The Hidden Journey*, the book which introduced the avatar Mother Meera to the West, he has conveyed the mystical experience more eloquently than most. His story is that of Everyman's journey to Enlightenment.

A solitary, sensitive child of mixed-race parents, Harvey grew up in India until, at the age of six, he was sent to boarding school in England. While he was away, his Mother, to whom he was devoted, gave birth to another child. He later described these two events as "a series of devastating mutilations", which caused him to retreat into a private inner world that was the beginning of both his artistic and spiritual search.

A brilliant academic and precocious talent he became, at the age of 21, the youngest fellow of All Souls College, Oxford, were as he later confessed he felt he was "starving in a gilded cage". As a result of his spiritual deprivation, he turned to Buddhism, reading voraciously and visiting the Ashmolean Museum three or four times a week, where he would gaze fixedly upon a small broken Khmer head of a Buddha, contemplating its transcendent serenity.

Harvey finally turned his back on Oxford in 1976 and returned to India to study Buddhism "in all its forms" remarking: "I am a man searching to understand myself before it is too late." His search led him to the remote village of Ladakh in Kashmir, where one of the last Tibetan Buddhist communities

Andrew Harvey's story is that of Everyman's journey to Enlightenment.

survives. There he was granted the first of many audiences with Thucksey Rinpoche, Ladakh's elderly spiritual leader, a serene and compassionate holy man bubbling with good humour. During their many discussions, the Rinpoche told Harvey, "The man who really helps (others) is the man who is in the world, but not of it."

Harvey also learned that man is now living in the age of destruction (*kali Yuga*) and that "this world is illusion. But within this world and within man there are great powers – powers of love, of healing, of clarity, that can lead man to liberation".

In questioning its values, the Buddhist monks believed that the West is coming of age, searching for a wisdom that is without "false hope or consolation". Nevertheless, many deny their potential because then it is easier for them to live with their own imperfection.

Andrew Harvey's experiences in Ladakh proved to be only one in a series of increasingly incredible awakenings, which began in 1978, when he met Mother Meera who was then 18. Mother Meera is believed by many, Easterners and Westerners alike, to be an avatar, an incarnation of one aspect of the Divine. Though Harvey was convinced of her Divinity at their first meeting, he admits that again and again he fought the insight she offered – he was simply afraid to give up his indulgent, sensualist lifestyle and face the ultimate reality for which he had searched so long.

Harvey concluded from this experience that, whenever one makes an advance in the spiritual life, this is inevitably followed by an ordeal as the new-found belief is put to the test. The spiritual journey, it seems, is never-ending.

Harvey's journey to the remote region of Ladakh was not a search for secret knowledge, such as Madame Blavatsky had undertaken, but for self-knowledge.

OUT-OF-BODY EXPERIENCES

*In Ladakh Harvey had what he describes as one of the strangest experiences of his life while being entertained by musicians from a local village. He saw everything and everybody in the room as both real and illusory, solid and doll-like at the same time. He realized that what may have been for him a fleeting glimpse into **Sunyata** or "Emptiness" had, through practised meditation, become a continual state of being for the Rinpoche. "I knew, as I have never known before or since, that anything but that feeling of joy and spaciousness was unworthy of myself, of everyone and everything that lives ... "*

A few years later, Harvey had a series of increasingly incredible revelations in the presence of Mother Meera which culminated with another out-of-body experience. "One night my mind split open. I left my body and entered a deep calm ... and I saw for the first time the Divine light, the diamond white light of the Divine soaking everything and streaming from everything. I was exalted, and petrified."

THE DIVINE MOTHER

Mother Meera – her presence is significant for the whole of humanity.

"The consciousness of mankind is being prepared for great leaps and discoveries – in a gentle way wherever possible ... God is giving man a great chance ... Now man must choose."

(MOTHER MEERA)

The Divine Mother has been worshipped in many forms throughout the ages. The Hindus envisaged her as Kali, the Christian mystics as the Virgin Mary, while the Egyptians mythologized her as the goddess Isis. In the Hindu tradition, she is usually depicted with a third eye between the eyebrows to denote Divine Wisdom.

In our own time, we are told, there are several incarnations of the Divine Mother moving among us. The most widely known and revered is Mother Meera, a young Indian woman currently living in a small village in central Germany.

Born in 1960 in southern India, she first came to public prominence through the writings of Andrew Harvey, the English poet and mystic. These days, her quiet wisdom and illuminating presence attract thousands of devotees from all over the world for *darshan*, the silent bestowing of the Divine Light and the awakening of heightened consciousness. But her presence in the world is significant for the whole of humanity.

Avatars choose to incarnate at moments of supreme crisis not only to help us avoid the disaster we bring upon ourselves but also to aid us on the next evolutionary step. Avatars are the embodiment of an aspect of the Divine, incarnated as fully realized beings without the psychic burden we carry from our past lives.

"The possibility for mankind to evolve and change is always there whether or not an avatar comes," explains Mother Meera. "People naturally believe in a greater reality. However, when an avatar comes, people feel the possibility more and aspire more strongly."

Each avatar is said to have an individual task to fulfil. Mother Meera's unique "mission" is the bringing down of the Paramatman Light (the Light of the Divine) to heal the world's wounds and bring about our spiritual transformation.

"Many divine persons are here," she

The Hindus envisaged the Divine Mother as the goddess Kali.

says. "We are showing man a way out; we are offering him the divine Light, the divine Knowledge. We are bringing down into the consciousness of the Earth that divine consciousness ..."

Mother Meera's presence on earth is said to be a sign that man has finally reached a stage in evolution where he is in a position to collaborate with the Divine in re-making the world. The transformation will take place more swiftly if people are open to it, but the pressure and power of the Light is so great that no one will be able to resist its influence.

Mother Meera has described the Light as being like electricity: it is everywhere, it pervades everything – but it has never actually been *used* before and she has come to activate it.

The coming transformation will involve the breakdown of certain beliefs

The presence of an avatar encourages man to search for his spirituality.

and institutions, so that the foundations of the new world will be firm, true and long-lasting. But such a change will not be given to man for the asking.

"Man has to do a great labour," she maintains. "God will not do everything. When people become conscious of the presence of the Light, the transformation can go faster. It is working anyway but few people are conscious. More will become conscious soon, many more, and then the work can be done with greater efficiency ... The transformation will come in its own time." However, transformation is only part of the process. "Transcendence, union with the Divine, is the primary aim of the human being. The goal of the Divine Personality, or avatar, is to help the human being to be in the Divine. Transformation is not the final aim – but it enables all people to attain union with God more easily ... I have not come only to be a refuge; I have also come to give the joy and strength necessary for change."

THE CRISIS TO COME

We are living on the threshold of a change in consciousness, a change that will come not as a blessing bestowed upon us from Heaven, but out of a crisis here on earth. The catalyst which will bring about this change is an upsurge of evil – the actions and attitudes which result from the lack of Divine Light.

Evil exists to force us to face the consequences of our own free will, to instill in us a divine discontent with the ways of the world, prompting us to search for our true natures.

Evil may appear to have the upper hand, but Mother Meera assures us that the Divine is the supreme force. It is in control and knows how to use evil to bring about its will on earth.

We must cease to be afraid of negative forces, she says, but instead root ourselves in the Light.

By transforming ourselves we can transform the world. The evil of this century, she says, has been necessary to awaken humanity to the danger of living without God-consciousness. Once we accept this, we can prepare for the next stage in our spiritual evolution. "This leap is certain ... it will happen: It is happening now". When asked if the Old World will resist the change, she promises: "It will lose".

THE NEAR-DEATH

EXPERIENCE

"I DO believe – but not just on the basis of my own or other's data regarding near-death experiences – that we continue to have a conscious existence after our physical death and that the core experience does represent its beginning, a glimpse of things to come."

(KENNETH RING, PROFESSOR OF PSYCHOLOGY, CONNECTICUT UNIVERSITY)

The number of recorded cases of what has come to be called the Near-Death Experience has increased dramatically since the Sixties, when advances in medical technology made it possible to revive people who had been declared clinically dead.

Such experiences first came to public attention in 1975 with the publication of Dr Raymond Moody's collection of case studies, *Life After Life*. Moody, a former teacher of philosophy, was criticized by sections of the medical establishment for his unscientific approach, but he argued that the 150 accounts he had recorded spoke for themselves. His findings were subsequently confirmed by the scientific surveys of Professor Ring and others.

A common element of near-death experience is the descent through a long, dark tunnel.

Moody began to collect first-hand reports of Near-Death Experiences (a term which he coined to distinguish them from standard Out-of-the-body experiences) out of idle curiosity. He soon became overwhelmed by the number of previously unreported cases and was struck by their similarity as well as the profound effect they had had on ordinary, seemingly well-balanced people.

Some of his subjects had come close to death through severe illness or accident. All had been clinically dead during the time they recalled being outside their physical bodies, but were either successfully resuscitated, or said they had been "sent back" from the other side to continue their lives.

Moody identified a number of key common elements in what he called the "core experience", although these did not always occur in the same sequence, nor were all of them present in any single case.

Even in instances of violent accidents, often the first sensation the dying person experienced was a feeling of extreme peace, stillness and serenity. A man who had received a severe head injury recalled: "At the point of injury there was a momentary flash of pain, but then all the pain vanished. I had the feeling of floating in a dark space. The day was bitterly cold, yet while I was in that blackness all I felt was warmth and the most extreme comfort I have ever experienced."

Sometimes, unusual sounds were

heard, occasionally inner voices or even celestial music. A common experience was for the "dead" person to hear doctors or onlookers pronounce them dead while, unable to communicate, they vainly protested that they were completely conscious. In every case, the person floated effortlessly out of their body and looked down with complete emotional detachment at their own empty shell.

Once out of their bodies, they found themselves entering a long, dark tunnel at the end of which was a brilliant, irresistible white light which drew them onward and enveloped them in an all consuming wave of Love.

Even those with no religious convictions or belief in an afterlife had a similar experience and described the light as emanating from a loving being. Some recalled being met at the end of the tunnel by loved ones who had previously passed over, while others were met by spiritual beings or the religious figures they had worshipped in life.

At this point (apparently the threshold between life and death), the

Once out of the body the subject views the shell with complete detachment.

"deceased" glimpse a pastoral paradise, but before they can enter they are asked telepathically (or perhaps it is their own conscience or Higher Self which asks them), what they have done with their lives.

None of the people Moody interviewed felt that the question was asked in a judgmental tone but that it was

simply to prompt them to review their lives. Many later recalled watching their past flash before them as if replayed on a stage or screen, though one woman remembered actually walking through scenes from her past. Some were calmly asked if they wanted to die or were told that they must go back, that their purpose on earth had not been completed. All who came this far felt such peace that they did not want to return. One woman described it as "coming home".

There have been attempts by medical experts to dismiss these experiences as the hallucinations of a dying brain, but this does not explain how these people – some of them young children – were able to clearly recall details of the resuscitation techniques or describe the people who were present while they were supposedly unconscious.

All subjects viewed life in a new light after their recovery, attaching less importance to transient things, becoming generally more compassionate and tolerant and having lost not only their fear of death but also their fear of life!

THE LOST KNOWLEDGE

One of the most illuminating, and apparently not uncommon, experiences recorded by Dr Moody was that described as a "vision of knowledge".

His anonymous subject recalled, "for a second I knew all the secrets of all the ages, all the meaning of the universe." But in that same instant unseen spiritual beings explained to him, as if by telepa-

thy, that such knowledge was not for man to know while he remained incarnate. The subject was told that, on returning to his body, he would suffer a series of illnesses which was partly to erase what he had learned.

The question raised by such experiences is why we struggle to learn in life what appears to be ours for the asking once we pass

from this world. Moody's subject admitted he was still driven by the desire to learn after his recovery even though, incredibly, he had concluded that the answers to the most important questions are not to be found in this world. "I sort of felt that it was part of our purpose," he confided, "but that it wasn't just for one person, but that it was to be used for all mankind."

AFTERWORD

"Know Thyself."

(INSCRIPTION OVER THE ENTRANCE OF THE TEMPLE OF APOLLO AT DELPHI)

The New Age, we are told, will be characterized by an awakening consciousness, a new spirituality and an increased awareness of the unity of all Life.

This does not mean that science and religion will become redundant, nor that we will laze in a Utopian paradise on earth allowing our civilization to crumble away as the Eloi race did in HG Wells' novel *The Time Machine*. It is more likely that we will continue to strive as we have always done. For history shows that humanity requires the challenge and crisis of life to raise its greatest monuments. This is the triumph of spirit over matter and mortality.

Alex Walker, a member of the Findhorn Community, has written that this new epoch is likely to witness a rejection of the past: " ... where differences have been emphasized; not only distinctions between groups within the human family but also separation between humanity and nature, body and soul, and masculine and feminine ... We believe that the future will be largely concerned with rediscovering and rebuilding our conncectedness to each other, to nature and to the unseen spiritual realms, so that we may become whole as individuals, as a species, even as a planet".

But if science and religion are to partake of the infusion of cosmic energy, which we are told will kick-start this new stage of evolution, then they will have to assimilate the idea that man is no longer the centre of creation but an active, responsible participant in its development.

Mind, or consciousness, is the eternal part of man and it may well be that the Divine is pure Mind Energy. Our evolution, our future and the future of this planet may therefore depend on our willingness to bring into manifestation the very future we wish for ourselves.

The scientists who shared Einstein's mystical sense of wonder never lost sight of this idea. The English physicist and astronomer Sir James Jeans (1877-1946) once stated, "The stream of human knowledge is impartially heading towards a non-mechanical reality. The universe begins to look more like a great thought than a great machine. Mind no longer appears to be an accidental intruder into the realm of matter. We are beginning to suspect that we ought rather to hail it as the creator and governor of this realm."

If organized religion is to survive into the New Age, it cannot fossilize its teachings but must accept the idea that no single tradition has the monopoly on the truth.

The New Age philosopher Alan Watts once wrote, "Irrevocable commitment to any religion is not only intellectual suicide; it is positive un-faith because it closes the mind to any new vision of the world."

An old story tells of the devil, who was walking with a friend when he saw a man pick something up from the ground, some distance away. "I wonder what he has found," said the friend. "A piece of the truth," answered the devil. "That's

The Temple of Apollo at Delphi enshrines the philosophy of a New Age.

bad for you," observed the friend. "Not at all," replied the devil, I'm going to help him organize it."

The Benedictine monk and mystic Bede Griffiths considered a reappraisal of orthodox religion essential if we are to survive the coming crisis.

"Western Europe rejected the perennial philosophy at the Renaissance and has been led step by step to the materialistic philosophy which rejects fundamental human values and exposes humankind to the contrary forces at work in the universe. The only way of recovery is to rediscover the perennial philosophy, the traditional wisdom, which is found in all ancient religions and especially in the great religions of the world. But those religions have in turn become fossilised and have each to be renewed … so that a cosmic, universal religion can emerge … This is a task for the coming centuries as the present world order breaks down and a new world order emerges from the ashes of the old."

The credo of this new religion will be Unity. Not the bland unity of "One World" envisaged in the popular imagination, but an echo of the Unity of the universe, Unity in diversity. Unity is the underlying theme of the Ageless Wisdom.

"Between heaven and earth, there is a unity reflected, on the one hand in the real or supposed influence of the sun, stars and planets on the life of plants, animals and men and on the medicines

The waters of the Ageless Wisdom flow on through the centuries.

derived from them, and, on the other hand, in the repetition of the structures from which sprang the notions of macrocosm and microcosm." (Paracelsus)

We speak blithely of "harmony" as the global ideal and see life on planet earth as chaos and disharmony. But disharmony in existence, as in music, science or art, is simply a harmony that we have not yet attuned to, a symmetry or perspective that we do not appreciate. That primordial state of harmonic perfection, which many foresee as the Elysian fields of the New Age, only existed in the Divine prior to existence. The perfection of the Absolute was a static state. To know itself it had to mani-

fest in existence, not in innumerable models of Itself, but in every aspect of existence, in diversity.

Although from our perspective all is chaos, everything is apparently as it should be. All the various parts of the machinery of the universe are working according to plan. Our part is to understand the interplay, the actions and reactions of the myriad parts and to refine, or perfect, ourselves so that it all runs smoothly.

The greatest threat to this vision of our development in the next century is our fear, our fear of change, fear of discovering a greater reality in which we would no longer be the centre of creation. As T S Eliot once remarked, "Human kind cannot bear very much reality."

But, as this book records, change brings growth. If we fear change, we stunt our own spiritual growth and with it our evolution. We have been denying our own spirituality for far too long and that is more dangerous and self-defeating than denying any other aspect of our true nature.

Attempts have been made to dam, divert and cloud the clear, sustaining waters of the Ageless Wisdom but the true stream has flowed on, unbroken through the centuries, each culture unknowingly refreshing itself from the same source.

"Happy is he who passed through the mysteries: he knows the origin and the end of life." (Pindor)

Page numbers in **bold** type refer to main entries.

Abelard, Peter 47
Abulafia, Abraham 39
Acharya 122-3
Adam Kadmon 28, 31, 35, 36-7
Agnostics 111
Agrippa Von Nettesheim, Cornelius 60, 61
Ahura Mazda 22, 23
Akhenaten 9, 16-17
Al-Hallaj 97
alchemy 59, 60, 62-3, **64-5**, 66, 71
Alexander the Great 18
Alexandrian school of philosophy 28, 52
alphabet, Hebrew 39
America *see* Native American traditions
AMORC **146-7**
Analects of Confucius 95
Antichrist 62
Anubis 11
Aperel, tomb of 17
Apollonius of Tyana 13, 18, 103
Aquarius, Age of 99, 135
Arab scholarship 65
Arcane School **108-9**
Aristotle 27
Arthurian legend 54-5, 117
Aryans 107
Asiyah (Kabbalah) 34, 35
Asmodeus 20
astrology 42, 43
Aten (god) 16
Atlantis **26-7**, 106
Augustine, Saint 28
Authie, Jacques 57
avatars 133, 148, 149, 152
Aveling, Francis 116
Azilut (Kabbalah) 33, 34

Baba, Sathya Sai 133, **148-9**
Babaji 127
Babylonians 21, 27, 59
Bacon, Roger (Friar Bacon) **62-3**
Bailey, Alice 27, **108-9**
Bala, Giri 125
Balzac, Honoré de 103
Bardo Thodol (Tibetan Book of the Dead) **86-7**
Beatles 135
Bennett, Allan 114
Berdiaev, Nicholas 73
Bergier, Jacques 65

Beriah (Kabbalah)) 33, 34-5
Besant, Annie 108, 130, 131
Bible 12, 16, 17, 20, 36, 38, 52
 and Gnosticism 53
 and Kabbalists 33, 34-5, 40
 see also Christianity; Jesus Christ
Black Elk (Sioux) 101
Blackwood, Algernon 112
Blake, William 72
Blavatsky, Helena Petrovna 27, 99, 102, **104-7**, 108
Boehme, Jakob 60, 65, **72-3**, 105
Book of the Dead, Egyptian 11, 16
Bors, Sir 54
Brahminism 87
Branchus (god of prophecy) 42
Broadbent, Charles 128
Brunton, Paul 147
Buddhism 27, 45, 77, **84-5**, 87, 91, 143
 Andrew Harvey and 150-1
 Zen 88-9, 93
Burnier, Radha 107
Butler, W E **120-1**

Caddy, Eileen 136
Cathars 47, **56-7**
Catherine of Siena, St 124, 125
Cayce, Edgar 27
Centuries (Nostradamus) 42
chakras 37, 81, [B]82-3[b], 91, 116
Champollion, Jean-François 69
Cheops, Pharaoh 69
Chinese traditions 82, 88-9, 92-5
Christianity 47, 68, 91
 Boehme and Berdiaev **72-3**
 and Cathars **56-7**
 Christian Kabbalists **40-1**
 Christian Science 111
 Gnosticism **52-3**
 and Neoplatonism 28, 29
 and Osho 142, 144
 see also Bible; Jesus Christ
Chuang Tzu 94
Clement IV, Pope 62
Columbus, Christopher 63
communism 144
Confucius 93, 94, 95
Corpus Hermeticum see Hermetica
Cosmic Doctrine (Fortune) 117, 118-19
Creation, Book of (Sefer ha Yetzirah) 39
Crete 27
Crowley, Aleister 58, 113, **114-15**
"cups of knowledge" 54

Dali, Salvador 102
Dante 97
de Guyon, Madame 103
Dead Sea scrolls 44-5, 49, 53
Dervishes 96, 97
Devananda, Swami Vishnu 81, 90, 91
Dionysian cult 24
Divine Mother 152-3
Donnelly, Ignatius 27
drugs, hallucinogenic 134-5
Dyhana school of Buddhism 88
"Dynamic Meditation" (Osho) 145

Earth Goddess (Passive Principle) 15
Ecclesiastes, Book of 20
ecological concerns 138-9
Egypt, Ancient 9, **10-15**, 21, 59, 64
 influences 113, 146, 147
 and Kircher's Ark 68, 69
 and Moses 16-17, 33
Eightfold Path (Buddhism) 85
Eleazar, Rabbi 38-9
Enneads, The (Plotinus) 28
Epicuros 25
Esquiros, Alphonse 103
Essenes **44-5**, 48-9, 53
Euclid 25
Exodus from Egypt 33
Ezekiel 35

Fary, Florence 113
Findhorn Foundation **136-7**, 156
fire worship 22
Flegetanis 54-5
Fortune, Dion 58, 90, 99, 115, **116-19**
Four Noble Truths (Buddhism) 84-5
Four Worlds, The (Kabbalah) 33, 34-7
Fraternity of the Inner Light 117
Freemasonry 21, 59, 74-5
Freud, Sigmund 16
Fulcanelli (Jean-Julien Champagne) 65

Galahad, Sir 54
Garden of Eden 27, 35
Gathas (Zoroastrianism) 23
Genesis, Book of 34-5
Glastonbury Group (Ramala) **140-1**
Gnosticism 20, 47, 52-3, 56
Golden Age(s) 27, 140, 149
Golden Dawn, Order of the 112-13, 114, 115, 117
Gopi Krishna 83
Grail *see* Holy Grail
Graves, Robert, and Nostradamus 43
Great Fire of London 41

Greek traditions 9, 19, 24-7
Griffiths, Bede 157
Guenon, Rene 105
Guirdham, Arthur 57

Haig, Justin Moreward **128-9**
Hall, Manly P. 108
Ham (son of Noah) 69
Harvey, Andrew **150-1**, 152
Hebrew prophets 16-17, 33
Hegel, Georg 73
Hermes Trismegistos 13, **18-19**, 69
Hermetica 18-19, 28, 66
Herod, King 49
Hidden Masters, Brotherhood of **110-11**
hieroglyphs 59, 69
Hilarion 110
Hindu traditions 27, 78-9, 87, 125, 152
Hiram Abiff 21
Holy Grail **54-5**, 57
homeopathy 67
Horus 14
House of Life 12-13
Human Rights, Declaration of 144
Huxley, Aldous **134-5**

Iamblichus 28, 29, 42
Ibn Arabi 97
India, traditions of 27, 78-9, 82-3, 87, 124, 125, 148, 152
 see also Osho
Innocent III, Pope 56
Inquisition 56
Iran 23
Isis 12, **14-15**, 27, 116, 152
Isis Unveiled (Blavatsky) 104, 105
Islam 23, 96-7

Jacob 34
Jainism 87
James, First Apocalypse of 53
Japanese traditions 89
Japhet (son of Noah) 69
Jeans, Sir James 156
Jerusalem, temple at 21
Jesus Christ 21, 44, 45, **48-9**, 50-1, 59, 87, 97
 and Maitreya 111
 and Sai Baba 148-9
 see also Bible; Christianity
John, Gospel of St 52
John the Baptist 45
Joseph in Egypt 33
Judaic traditions 20-1, 27, 35, 82, 87

and Essenes 44-5, 48-9, 53
see also Kabbalistic Mysteries
Jung, Carl Gustav 65, 71
Jupiter 64
Jwul-Khul *see* "Tibetan, The"

Kabbalistic Mysteries 28, 31, 32-41,
    42, 64, 105
    and Dion Fortune 117, 118
    and magic 58
    see also Judaic traditions
Kali 152
karma 87, 121
Kasturi, Professor 148-9
Kircher, Athanasius **68-9**
Koot-Hoomi 108, 110, 111
Koran 17
Krishna 27
Krishnamurti, Jiddu 111, **130-1**, 144
Kundalini 83, 121
Kyot 54-5

Lamaistic Buddhism 27
Lame Deer (Sioux) 101
Lao Tzu 48, 92, 93, 94
le Plongeon, Augustus 27
Leadbeater, C W 130
Lemegeton of King Solomon 61
Lemuria 106
Leo X, Pope 41
Levi, Eliphas **102-3**
Lewis, H Spencer 146, 147
Lieh Tzu 94-5
Luke, Gospel of St 51
Luther, Martin 41
Luxor temple, Egypt 11

Machen, Arthur 112
Maclean, Dorothy 136
magic 17, 58-61, 102-3
Maha Chohan 110
Maharisi Mahish Yogi 135
Maitreya 110, 111
Mandaism, Gathic 23
mantras 82
Mars 64
Mathers, S L McGregor 112, 113,
    114
Matthew, Gospel of St 51
Maximillian I, Emperor 41
Medicine Men 100
meditation, techniques of **90-1**, 145
Meera, Mother 133, 151, *152-3*
Mehitousklet, the Lady 15
Mercury 19, 64
Metrovitch, Agardi 104
miracles, Christ's 48-9
Mirandola, Giovanni Pico della 40
Miriam, Joshua ben 45
Mithras 48
Mohammed, Prophet 97, 148
monotheism 16, 17, 23

Moody, Raymond 154-5
Moon 9, 64
Moriarty, Theodore 116
Morya 110
Moses **16-17**, 32, 33, 44, 69
mummification 27
Muslim traditions 20
Mystery of the Cathedrals, The 65

Nag Hammadi codices 53
Native American traditions **100-1**,
    134
Nazis and Nostradamus 43
Near-Death Experiences 86, **154-5**
necromancy 59
Neoplatonism 28-9
New Age 99, 133, 136-41, 142, 143,
    156-7
Noah's Ark 68, 69
Nostradamus, Michael **42-3**
number:
    Pythagorean 24
    in sefirotic system 39

Olcott, Colonel H S 104, 105
Old Testament *see* Bible
Oracle, Didyma 42
Orion (star) 15
Orphic Mysteries 24
Osho (Bhagwan Shree Rajneesh)
    142-5
see also India, traditions of
Osiris 11, 12, 14
Osman, Ahmed 17

Page, Jimmy 115
Pahlavi literature (Persia) 22
Paracelsus 60, **66-7**, 157
Parzival 54
Path Working 54
Paul, St 47
Pentagram 59
Perceval, Sir 54
Persian traditions 22-3
Peter, St. 52
Philo of Alexandria 52
Philosopher's Stone 64, 66
Pillars of the Tree of Life 31, **32-3**, 37
Plato 25, 26, 27
Plotinus 28, 29
Porphyry 28-9
Proclus 28, 29
pyramids, Egyptian 10, 11, 15, 21,
    147
Pythagoras 9, **24-5**, 41, 48

'Q', gospel according to 51
Raja Yoga 80-1
Rakoczi 110
Ramala Teachers **140-1**
Randall Stevens, H C 27
reincarnation 87

Reuchlin, Johann 40-1
Richelieu, Peter **122-3**
Ring, Kenneth 154
Rinzai (Zen Buddhism) 88
Rohmer, Sax 112
Rosenkreutz, Christian 70, 71, 113
Rosetta Stone 69
Rosicrucians 59, **70-1**, 112, 113,
    146-7
Rumi, Mevlana Julaluddin 96, 97

Sankara 78
Saturn 64
Saul of Tarsus 47
Secret Doctrine, The (Blavatsky) 104,
    105, 106-7
Seer of Salon *see* Nostradamus
Sefer ha Zohar *38-9*
sefirotic Tree *see* Tree of Life
    (Kabbalistic)
Serapis 110
Seth 14
seven angels:
    Essene 45
    of Trithemius 41
seven *chakras* **82-3**
Seven Liberal Arts 24
Seven Races (Blavatsky) 107
Seven Rishis (Hindu) 27
Seven Sages (Babylon) 27
seventeen Gathas (Zoroastrianism) 23
Shambhala, City of 27
Shem (son of Noah) 69
Shine, Betty 123
Shuka 148
Siddharta Gautama *see* Buddhism
Sivananda, Swami 81
Sixtus V, Pope 43
Socrates 25
Solomon: **20-1**, 38
    Lemegeton of 61
    Little Key of 59
    Seal of 58, 59
Solon 26
Soto Zen 88
Spalding, Baird T. 49
Spangler, David 137
Sphinx, The 10, 27
Spiritualist movement 111
Sprengler, Anna 112
Sri Yukteswar Giri 125, 126
Stoker, Bram 112, 113
Sufism 77, 82, 91, **96-7**, 105, 143
Sun 9, 64, 68
Suzuki, D.T. 77, 89

Tantric tradition 82
Taoism 82, **92-5**, 143
Tarot 38, 39
telepathy 108, 109
temples:
    Egyptian 10-11, 156

Temple of Solomon 21, 69
Ten Commandments 16, 17, 44
10 Kabbalistic sefirot, the 32-3, 34
Ten Paths of Yoga 81
Tetragram 59
Theosophy 27, **104-7**, 111, 130
Thiering, Barbara 48-9
Thomas, Gospel of 50-1
Thoth **12-13**, 18
three stages of death (Tibetan) 86-7
Thucksey Rinpoche 151
"Tibetan, The" 108-9, 110
Tibetan traditions 86-7
Tiye, Queen 17
Torah, the 31, 38
Tracing Board, Masonic 75
Tree of Life:
    Essene 45
    Kabbalistic 21, 31, 32-3,
    40, 82
Trevelyan, Sir George **138-9**
Triangle 59
Trithemius, John 40, 41

Underhill, Evelyn 113
Upanishads 77, **78-9**, 80, 143, 148

Vaisesika philosophers 125
Valentinus 52
Vaughan, Thomas 60
Vedata, The 81
Venus 64
Virgin Mary 152
von Andrea, Johann Valentin 71
von Eschenbach, Wolfram 54-5

Wagner, Richard 54
Walker, Alex 156
Watts, Alan 156
Westcott, William Wynn 112
"Whirling Dervishes" 96, 97
Wilde, Constance 113
Wilton, Archdeacon 129
Wisdom Texts, The 13
Work of the Chariot (Jewish) 35, 39
Wrekin Trust 138

Yeats, W B 112, 113
Yellowtail, Thomas 100, 101
Yetzirah (Kabbalah) 33, 34, 35, 38, 39
Yin and Yang 92, 93
Yoga 79, **80-1**, 91, 115, 124
Yogananda, Paramahansa **124-7**
Yokhai, Rabbi Simon bar 38
Yuya (vizier) 17

Zen Buddhism 77, **88-9**, 93, 143
Zen Tao (Ramala) 140, 141
Zohar (Book of Splendour) **38-9**
Zoroastrianism 9, **22-3**, 68

CREDITS

AUTHOR ACKNOWLEDGEMENTS

I would like to acknowledge the following publications as sources of material and to thank those who gave their permission to reprint brief extracts: *Answers* by Mother Meera; *The Cosmic Doctrine* by Dion Fortune; *The Doors of Perception* by Aldous Huxley; *Hidden Journey* and *Journey to Ladakh* by Andrew Harvey; *The Initiate* by Cyril Scott; *The Kingdom Within* (Findhorn Press); *Lords of the Light* by W E Butler; Osho – various titles (Osho International); *Paramahansa Yogananda – Autobiography of a Yogi*; *Sai Messages*, vol 2, by Lukas Ralli; *A Soul's Journey* by Peter Richelieu; *A Vision of the Aquarian Age* by Sir George Trevelyan (Gateway Books, Bath, Avon); *The Wholeness of Life* by Krishnamurti; *The Wisdom of Ramala* (The Ramala Centre, Glastonbury, Somerset).

My thanks go also to Estella Machen of the Ibis Fraternity, St Austell, Cornwall; Peggy Mason of the Kent and Sussex Sai Baba Centre, Tunbridge Wells, Kent; Karen Lanza of the Self-Realization Fellowship, Los Angeles, California; Theosophical Society, London; and AMORC, Crowborough, East Sussex.

My love and appreciation to Sylvia Provins, Margaret Withersby, Gerry Foster and Rosemary Dent for their inspiration and encouragement.

My sincere gratitude for their encouragement and invaluable help to Claudia Jaeger and to my project editor Tessa Rose, without whom this book would not have been possible.